Longman Pocket Companion Series

KV-637-759

Pocket Companion

True Characters

Real People in Fiction

Alan Bold and Robert Giddings

Longman

FOREWORD

This dictionary has been designed to reveal the facts of life that lurk behind the business of fiction. Some of the most celebrated characters and incidents in literature are modelled on actual originals and events and an awareness of these has an intrinsic interest as well as providing a key to the house of fiction.

E. M. Forster said 'We all like to pretend we don't use real people, but one does actually'. The real people might be friends transformed dramatically in the literary process; ordinary people writ enormously large by the author. Or they might be so spectacularly larger than life that they demand artistic attention. Examples of these and other categories abound in this book.

Having compiled it we are convinced that the identification of the originals in no way detracts from the authority of the author and that the genesis of literary characters is a matter of some complexity. In moving from the original to the finished fictional product the writer does not aim for photographic accuracy so much as for a piece of inspired portraiture whose emotional impact transcends simple observation.

This book has been an enjoyable one to write and research – being, we hope, an entertaining combination of scholarship and sleuthing.

Our work will have been worthwhile if the raw material of fiction rises from the following pages and provides the reader with some illuminating insights into the background of many tantalizing texts.

Alan Bold
Robert Giddings

Dedicated to
Louis Robinson and Trevor Royle

ALICE

Lewis Carroll, *Alice's Adventures in Wonderland* (1865),
Through the Looking Glass (1872)

Alice Liddell (1852–1934)

On Friday 4 July 1862, a 'golden afternoon', the Revd Charles
Dodgson and his friend the Revd Robinson Duckworth took
three young sisters – Lorina, Alice and Edith – on a three-mile
rowing trip from Folly Bridge, near Oxford, up the Thames
to Godstow. Dodgson amused the children by telling them
stories and Alice later remembered that 'Nearly all of *Alice's
Adventures Underground* was told on that blazing summer
afternoon with the heat haze shimmering over the meadows
where the party landed to shelter for a while in the shadow
cast by the haycocks near Godstow.' Afterwards Alice implored Dodgson to 'write out Alice's adventures for me'; he
obliged and spent almost the whole night writing out what he
could recall of the tale. At the end of 1864 Alice received, as a
'Christmas present to a Dear Child in memory of a Summer's
day', a handwritten copy of *Alice's Adventures Underground*
complete with Dodgson's own illustrations.

Dodgson was a lecturer in mathematics at Christ Church,
Oxford, and the Dean of the college was Henry George Liddell,
a lexicographer. Fascinated by photography, Dodgson especially delighted in taking pictures of the Dean's daughter, Alice
Liddell. She was a precocious child and, as fitted the daughter
of a lexicographer, was enchanted by words – an interest
Dodgson encouraged. Naturally she was greatly flattered by
Dodgson's gift and, when the manuscript was shown around
Oxford, pressure was put on the author to have his book
published with professional illustrations. On 4 July 1865, the
third anniversary of Wonderland Day, Alice was given the
first copy of *Alice's Adventures in Wonderland*, as the story was
retitled, at Dean Liddell's suggestion. Dodgson was a painfully
shy man and used the pseudonym Lewis Carroll to protect his
privacy.

SQUIRE ALLWORTHY
Henry Fielding, *The History of Tom Jones* (1749)

Ralph Allen (1694–1764)

Squire Allworthy is a noble character who more or less adopts Tom Jones, a foundling, not realizing that Tom is the son of his own sister. Allworthy is goodness and generosity personified: '[he] might well be called the favourite of both nature and fortune; both of these seem to have contended which should bless and enrich him most. In this contention, nature may seem to some to have come off victorious, as she bestowed on him many gifts, while fortune had only one gift in her power; but in pouring forth this, she was so very profuse, that others may think perhaps this single endowment to have been more than equivalent to all the various blessings which he enjoyed from nature. From the former of these he derived an agreeable person, a sound constitution, a solid understanding, and a benevolent heart; by the latter, he was decreed to the inheritance of one of the largest estates in the country.' He lives in the county of Somerset, and his generous hospitality is well known: 'Neither Mr Allworthy's house, nor his heart, was shut against any part of mankind, but they were both more particularly open to men of merit. To say the truth, this was the only house in the kingdom where you were sure to gain a dinner by deserving it. Above all others, men of genius and learning shared the principal place in his favour.'

This is a portrait of Fielding's friend, Ralph Allen, known as the 'Man of Bath'. His philanthropy was a byword. He was employed in the post office in Bath and earned the patronage of General Wade by his discovery of a Jacobite plot; he raised and equipped a troop of volunteers in 1745. He became Deputy Postmaster at Bath and evolved a system of cross posts for England and Wales which earned him a vast fortune. He built the magnificent mansion at Prior Park and there entertained celebrities including Pope and the Earl of Chatham. Fielding was of course a frequent visitor.

ALVAN
George Meredith, *The Tragic Comedians* (1880)

Ferdinand Lassalle (1825–64)

The Tragic Comedians deals with the dramatic love affair
between Clothilde and Alvan. She is the daughter of a noble
family who disapprove of him. They hope to marry, but
Alvan insists that they should not defy her family. On his
advice, she returns to her family in the hope of gaining their
approval of their marriage. But she is coerced into marrying a
suitor from her own class of whom they approve – Marko.
Alvan is deeply distressed by the course of events, and writes
an insulting letter to Clothilde's father. Alvan and Marko fight
a duel and Alvan is killed.

This is based on the real life tragedy of Helene von Dönniges
and her love affair with Ferdinand Lassalle, the German socialist. Marko is based on Count Racowitza of Wallachia. Lassalle
was the son of a Jewish banker, and was a disciple of Hegel. He
met Heine in Paris. He defended the Countess Sophie Hatzfeld
in litigation against her husband, a case which lasted eight
years, and took part in the revolution of 1848. He founded the
German Working Men's Association, which was pledged to
universal suffrage and agitated in the Rhineland and Berlin. In
1864 he met Helene von Dönniges. In spite of considerable
opposition from her family, they resolved to marry. Her
parents exerted tremendous influence upon her and in the end
she gave up Ferdinand Lassalle and intended to marry Count
Racowitza. Lassalle responded to this news with a challenging
letter both to Helene's father and to the Count. Count Racowitza and Lassalle fought their duel in Geneva, and Lassalle was
mortally wounded, dying two days later. He was an idealist
socialist who predicted the ultimate democracy of labour, the
triumph of social democracy. He was greatly helped by Karl
Marx, some of whose ideas he adopted and modified. Helene
von Dönniges married Racowitza, the man who had killed her
lover. She committed suicide in 1911.

DR ANGELUS
James Bridie, *Dr Angelus* (1947)

Dr E. W. Pritchard (1825–65)

James Bridie's drama *Dr Angelus*, set in the Glasgow of 1920, presents a protagonist who is convinced that his own greatness justifies any action against those he regards as his intellectual and spiritual inferiors. Dr Cyril Angelus (whose name suggests the fallen angel rather than a conventional melodramatic villain) poisons his mother-in-law and his wife, but feels smugly self-righteous about these crimes since they enable him to continue to exercise his ego and indulge his appetites. Before he is arrested at the end of the play he produces his credo: 'I regard religion, philosophy and science not as ends in themselves but as means to an end. This realisation of oneself is the aim and object of existence. . . . Suppose [such a man as myself] to be subjected to the incessant attempts of two ignorant and narrow-minded women to mould him to their miserable conception of what a right-thinking domestic animal ought to be. . . . What is he to do? . . . He must make circumstances, like Napoleon. He must break the bonds of oppression. He must be ruthless. He must hew Agag in pieces before the Lord. It is the only thing he can do consistent with his self-respect.'

Bridie took the material for his play from the trial of Edward William Pritchard, a Glasgow doctor found guilty of the murder of his mother-in-law and his wife in 1865. As Bridie discovered when he studied the trial, Dr Pritchard was regarded as a pillar of the local community and held court at home in Sauchiehall Street as a man of the strongest religious principles. Yet he was willing to murder to preserve his position and his reputation; it is likely that, some time before his trial, he had caused the death of a young girl by setting fire to the house she worked in as his maid and mistress. When he was arrested for the murder of his wife and mother-in-law he was involved with another servant-girl, Mary McLeod.

Benjamin Gunn (1888–1917)

Neil M. Gunn's novel *Highland River* concerns the search for the source of a river running through his birthplace, the village of Dunbeath. The quest is symbolic as, after a struggle with a salmon, 'the river became the river of life for Kenn'.

Kenn Sutherland who comes to maturity in the novel, is largely a self-portrait of the author who is encouraged in his adventures by his brother Angus. When Angus takes Kenn on to the moor, the 'immense distances drew Kenn's spirit out of him. He had come into the far country of legendary names. As Angus murmured them, pointing from under his nose with the heather stalk he nibbled, his excitement went out from Kenn like heat vibrations from a moor, and left him exposed to the feel of hidden watching eyes; and yet, for that very reason, his brother's companionship deeply warmed him'. Neil Gunn had six brothers. Benjamin, three years older than him, emigrated to Canada but then came home to join the army on the outbreak of the First World War, and died stranded on barbed wire in front of the trenches. In Gunn's novel Benjamin is represented as the 'good-natured and kind' Angus whose relationship with Kenn is close and crucial to the development of the central theme. Benjamin Gunn's death is recorded in the book when a Canadian soldier tells Kenn of the manner of Angus's death: 'Shrapnel in his back and legs. He was lying out in front of us. We could see him. We said to the officer we would go out for him. He said it meant death. Heavy machine-gun fire. We said we would go. He handled his revolver. He said he would shoot anyone who made a move to go. . . . We could have saved him. We should – have – saved him. . . . In the dark, I brought him in. But he had bled too much.' Angus represents Kenn's original ideal of physical courage, and the horrific facts of his death shock him into a greater understanding of his own life.

DR PESSIMIST ANTICANT

Anthony Trollope, *The Warden* (1855)

Thomas Carlyle (1795–1881)

The matters debated during the public outcry about the warden of Hiram's Hospital and the sinecure he was supposed to enjoy (see MR POPULAR SENTIMENT) are taken up and treated to analysis by a fashionable pamphleteer, Pessimist Anticant. This is a satirical portrait of Thomas Carlyle: 'Dr Pessimist Anticant was a Scotchman, who had passed a great portion of his early days in Germany . . . and had learned to look with German subtlety into the root of things, and to examine for himself their intrinsic worth and worthlessness. . . . Returning from Germany, he had astonished the reading public by the vigour of his thoughts, put forth in the quaintest language. He cannot write English, said the critics. No matter, said the public; we can read what he does write, and that without yawning. And so Dr Pessimist Anticant became popular. Popularity spoilt him for all further real use. . . . While . . . he confined his objurations to the occasional follies of mankind . . . we were glad to be told our faults and to look forward to the coming millenium, when all men, having sufficiently studied the works of Dr Anticant, would become truthful and energetic. But the doctor mistook the signs of the times . . . instituted himself censor of things in general, and began the great task of reprobating everything and everybody, without further promise of any millenium at all. This was not so well. . . .'

The philosopher, historian and pamphleteer, Thomas Carlyle, was greatly influenced by German literature and used a Germanic syntax, as well as Scottish pulpit rhetoric and a somewhat biblical tone. One of his earliest essays was 'Signs of the Times' (1829) and Trollope is accurately characterizing his ranting and denunciatory tendencies.

Elisa Schlesinger (1810–88)

Sentimental Education is a novel which deals with the personal development and relationships of a group of characters in France between 1840 and the 1860s – the period of the July monarchy, the Second Republic and the Second Empire. The political background deals with the rising opposition to Louis Philippe, who abdicated in 1848, with the moderate republican government which followed it and the complex events which resulted in the *coup d'état* of Louis Napoleon in 1852.

The novel explores the parallels between the personal ambitions and personal failures of the various characters, and the similar failures and frustrations of hope to be found in the larger political and social context. The main character, Frédéric Moreau, is eighteen years old when the book begins. He is coming back by boat from Paris to his home at Nogent on the Seine. On the boat he meets and falls in love with Marie Arnoux, who is married to an art dealer and owner of a pottery business. Frédéric is immediately enchanted with the older woman: 'She was sitting in the middle of the bench, all alone; or at least he could not see anybody else in the dazzling light which her eyes cast upon him.' He had never seen anything like her before, 'her splendid dark skin, her ravishing figure . . . her delicate, translucent fingers'. He is befriended by the Arnouxs and naturally Marie becomes aware of his infatuation, but he is incapable of making any advances to her. He also has a friend from his childhood, Deslauriers, and there is some suggestion of homosexual attraction between them. Frédéric inherits money and tries to realize himself socially but his life remains empty at the centre. Arnoux fails in business and eventually it seems likely that Marie will give herself to Frédéric, but the illness of her child prevents her from keeping the arrangement. He believes she has betrayed him and embarks on an affair which results in the birth of a child who dies. Much later Marie visits him and offers herself, but he now cannot accept her affection. He is shocked that her hair is now grey. He is afraid of being disgusted later. She cuts him a lock of hair and leaves him.

When he was fourteen Flaubert had seen the 26-year-old wife of a music publisher at Trouville, Elisa Schlesinger, feeding her baby. He fell in love with her and she may have become his mistress for a time. They kept in touch. Her husband's business failed and he fled to Germany. The child was not his but the child of a lieutenant from whom Schlesinger had bought Elisa.

Gustav Mahler (1860–1911)

Thomas Mann's story *Death in Venice* depicts the dying days of Gustav Aschenbach, a world-famous writer who has sacrificed his life on the altar of stylistic purity. Alone with his aesthetic ideals he comes to Venice to renew his creative energy. When Aschenbach beholds a beautiful long-haired boy of about fourteen he is captivated. He even has his own appearance retouched cosmetically in order to appear younger before the boy. While the vision of beauty appears before him Aschenbach is gradually aware of the progress of disease through the city and dies watching 'the pale and lovely Summoner' in the water.

In appearance Aschenbach has the features of Gustav Mahler: 'The nose-piece of his rimless gold spectacles cut into the base of his thick, aristocratically hooked nose.' When the artist Wolfgang Born sent him lithographs based on *Death in Venice* Mann replied: 'The conception of my story, which occurred in the early summer of 1911, was influenced by news of the death of Gustav Mahler, whose acquaintance I had been privileged to make in Munich and whose intense personality left the strongest impression upon me. I was on the island of Brioni at the time of his passing. . . . Later, these shocks fused with the impressions and ideas from which the novella sprang. So that when I conceived my hero who succumbs to lascivious dissolution, I not only gave him the great musician's Christian name, but also in describing his appearance conferred Mahler's mask upon him. I felt quite sure that given so loose and hidden a connection there could be no question of recognition by readers.'

Mahler's exquisitely orchestrated music dwells on death with some justification: in 1907, for example, his elder daughter died at the age of four and he was told he had an incurable heart disease. He died in a Vienna sanatorium on 18 May 1911.

Duff Smurthwaite (1896–1938)

The Sun Also Rises is a novel which concerns the 'lost genera-tion' of expatriate Americans living in Europe after the First World War. The earth is seen as permanent and self-renewing, whereas man is creature enduring between the twin polarities of birth and assured death. The key to the book is the text from Ecclesiastes: 'One generation passeth away, and another gen-eration cometh; but the earth abideth forever. . . . The sun also ariseth, and the sun goeth down, and hasteth to the place whence he arose.' War and death (symbolized by the bullfight) are present constantly in the background of the novel, which deals with a group of footloose and – on the face of it – fairly dissipated characters, trying to piece their lives together again somehow. They seem to be representative figures of modern man, starting the process of living all over again, attempting to rise from the ashes of the past. Jake Barnes, Bill Gorton and Pedro Romero represent various facets of Hemingway's con-cept of the heroic. The war has made Jake sexually impotent. Bill despairs of making any sense out of life. Pedro is able to come to terms with the idea of death within the ritual of the bullfight. Lady Brett has been marred by the war as she has lost the man she loved. There is something in her of the pagan deity, she is almost associated with Circe, who turned men into swine. In other respects she is like Helen of Troy. She is aware of the destruction she brings to others, and rejects Romero because she knows ultimately she would bring him destruction and ruin. 'She was damn good looking,' Hemingway writes, 'she wore a slipover jersey sweater and a tweed skirt, and her hair was brushed back like a boy's. . . . She was built with curves like the hull of a racing yacht.' Carlos Baker, in *Heming-way*, describes her as: 'Tall dark slant-eyed Englishwoman of thirty with a storied past and a notable capacity for drink and a string of admirers.' She was married to Sir Roger Twysden in 1917, and separated in 1926. Evelyn Waugh met her and considered her a monster. In Hemingway's novel, however, she emerges with more nobility, beneath the socialite exterior.

LUCY ASHTON
Sir Walter Scott, *The Bride of Lammermoor* (1819)

Janet Dalrymple

Scott's novel *The Bride of Lammermoor* and Donizetti's Scott-inspired opera *Lucia di Lammermoor* (1835) have familiarized the public with the story of the tragic Lucy Ashton who attempts to murder her husband, Bucklaw, and then dies insane. Anticipating criticism of the melodramatic nature of his book Scott wrote 'those who are read in the private family history of Scotland during the period in which the scene is laid, will readily discover, through the disguise of borrowed names and added incidents, the leading particulars of AN OWER TRUE TALE.'

Janet Dalrymple was the eldest daughter of James Dalrymple, Lord of Session, and Margaret Ross of Balniel. She promised to marry her sweetheart Archibald, Third Lord Rutherford, but Lady Dalrymple disapproved of the match since Archibald had a title but no wealth to his name. It was Lady Dalrymple's wish that Janet should marry David Dunbar, son and heir of Sir David Dunbar of Baldoon. In order to persuade Janet to break her promise to Archibald, Lady Dalrymple cited the Bible's authority that a woman can break a vow 'if her father disallow her in the day that he heareth . . . and the Lord shall forgive her, because her father disallowed her' (Numbers 30:5). Although in despair, Janet duly married David Dunbar on 12 August 1669 at the Kirk of Glenluce, two miles from her home at Carscreugh. She then went to her husband's home at Baldoon, near Wigtown, and was dead within a month of her marriage.

Local gossip elaborated on the facts and Scott drew on this when composing *The Bride of Lammermoor* in which Janet becomes Lucy Ashton and Lady Dalrymple becomes the evil-minded Lady Ashton who is described, at the close of the book, without 'the slightest symptom either of repentance or remorse'.

ASTARTE
Lord Byron, *Manfred* (1816–17)

Augusta Leigh (1783–1851)

Manfred, published in 1817, is a dramatic poem, which portrays Manfred, a kind of Faustian outcast, who is living in exile as a result of some serious crime, tortured by remorse. He conjures various universal spirits, but they cannot grant him the one solace he seeks – oblivion. He tries to throw himself from a high peak in the Alps, and after other harrowing adventures is granted a vision of his beloved, Astarte. He had exhausted the entire scope of sensational experience, including an incestuous relationship with Astarte, who is his own sister. In her guilt she has taken her own life. Her spirit now tells him that the next day he is to die, and does not answer his appeals: 'Hear me, hear me – /Astarte! my beloved! Speak to me:/I have so much endured – so much endure – /Look on me! the grave hath not changed thee more/Than I am changed for thee. Thou lovedst me/Too much, as I loved thee: we were not made/To torture thus each other, though it were/The deadliest sin to love as we have loved./Say that thou loath'st me not – that I do bear/This punishment for both.' His time comes and demons appear to take him away on the morrow. Manfred denies their power over him, and they disappear. Manfred dies. Goethe characterized this key poem of the romantic period as possessing 'the gloomy heat of an unbounded and exuberant despair'.

It is another portrayal of Byron's illicit passion for his half-sister, Augusta. His publisher, Murray, hesitated to publish *Manfred* as he was concerned that the public would perceive the obvious identification with Byron as Manfred and Astarte as Augusta Leigh. Murray's fears were correct. When the poem was reviewed in the London *Day and New Times* the writer commented on the autobiographical significance of *Manfred*. Is Manfred's guilt expiated? The end of the poem is ambiguous. The Abbot who attempted to offer him comfort ends the poem with the lines 'He's gone – his soul hath ta'en its earthless flight – /Whither? I dread to think – but he is gone.' (See also ZULEIKA.)

Sarah, Duchess of Marlborough
(1660–1744)

Atossa is portrayed in Pope's poem as a bad-tempered and unforgiving creature, with mercurial changes of mood. The main positive characteristic which comes through is Atossa's incredible energy: 'With herself, or others, from her birth/ Finds all her life one warfare upon earth:/Shines in exposing knaves, and painting fools,/Yet is whate'er she hates and ridicules.' She is as bold as a man, but as spiteful as a feline: 'Offend her, and she knows not to forgive;/Oblige her, and she'll hate you while you live.' She is married and in a position of power and influence, and spends her time and energies supporting her lord and helping her friends and quarrelling with her immediate family.

Pope takes the name from Atossa, the wife of Darius and mother of Xerxes, the Persian king who attempted in the 5th century BC to conquer the Greeks – without success – and is a leading figure in Aeschylus's tragedy, *The Persians*.

Atossa is generally taken to be Sarah, Duchess of Marlborough, whom Pope knew well. It has been claimed that Pope was paid £1,000 to suppress the character of Atossa, and indeed it is the case that Atossa and two other characters (see CHLOE) were not printed until the edition of 1751, ten years after Pope's death. Sarah Churchill was certainly a strong-willed and tempestuous character, although she and Pope were quite good friends. She married John Churchill in 1678 and became Lady Churchill four years later. She served as lady-in-waiting to Princess Anne and dominated her mind. She helped Anne receive a large parliamentary allowance and after Anne's accession in 1702 wielded considerable power to her husband's advantage, though ousted eventually by Abigail Masham (a relative) and lived abroad after 1713. When she sent in her accounts as keeper of the privy purse in 1711, she deducted £2,000 a year since 1702 as her pension.

Joseph Addison (1672–1719)

In the *Epistle to Dr Arbuthnot* there is a portrait of a critic, named 'Atticus', who wants to attack writers but has not the courage to be straight about it, but he eggs others on to attack. Other critics, Pope says, such as Dennis and Gildon, can be dealt with in an open manner, but Atticus is too crafty, his method is to: 'Damn with faint praise, assent with civil leer,/ And without sneering, teach the rest to sneer,/Alike reserved to blame or to commend,/A tim'rous foe and a suspicious friend;/Fearing e'en fools; by flatterers besieged,/And so obliging that he ne'er obliged;/Willing to wound, and yet afraid to strike.'

This is a portrait of Addison, whom Pope disliked for the manner in which he received Pope's translation of Homer. Addison preferred Thomas Tickell's version, which Pope believed Tickell only did at the instigation of Addison. John Gay relayed to Pope remarks made about him and his translation, which further inflamed Pope's feelings. Gay told him: 'I am informed that at Button's (coffee house) your character is made very free with as to morals, etc., and Mr Addison says that your translation and Tickell's are both very well done, but that the latter has more of Homer.'

Addison was educated at Charterhouse and Oxford and was a distinguished classical scholar. He had quite a career in the diplomatic service and achieved fame as poet and essayist, but in 1711, when the Whigs fell from office and he too was out of office, he turned to the stage. His *Cato* was produced with great success in 1713. He was a major contributor to the *Spectator* and the *Tatler*. When the Whigs returned to office, he was appointed chief secretary for Ireland and undertook political journalism. He was buried in Westminster Abbey. His place in literary history is assured by his contribution to the establishment of periodic journalism, and his creation of the immortal squire, Sir Roger de Coverley.

AYESHA

H. Rider Haggard, *She* (1886), *Ayesha, or the Return of She*
(1905), *She and Allan* (1921)

A rag doll

H. Rider Haggard's celebrated romance *She* portrays a female
figure who is exquisitely evil. When the narrator, Ludwig
Horace Holly, asks to see Ayesha's face he is astonished: 'I have
heard of the beauty of celestial beings, now I saw it; only this
beauty, with all its awful loveliness and purity, was *evil*.'
Ayesha, the white queen who rules over the Amahagger people
of Kôr, has been alive for two thousand years waiting for the
rebirth of Killikrates, the Egyptian priest she killed for rejecting
her offer of immortality. Holly is guardian of Killikrates's
descendant, Leo Vincey, who watches as she steps into 'the
flame of Life' and is consumed by it.

Haggard was a morbid child who was brought up by various
nurses at the family home in Bradenham Hall, Norfolk. As the
author's daughter, Lilias Rider Haggard, wrote in *The Cloak
That I Left* (1951) one of the nurses terrified him by keeping,
in a cupboard near his bed, 'a disreputable rag doll of particularly hideous aspect, with boot-button eyes, hair of black wool
and a sinister leer upon its painted face'. When the nurse left
the room she would assert her authority by opening the
cupboard door and telling the child to behave since he was
being watched by 'She-who-must-be-obeyed'. The figure
haunted Haggard's imagination and lurks beneath the skin-
deep beauty of Ayesha who, in the transformation scene in
She, becomes hideous as she increasingly assumes the features
of the figure of Haggard's childhood: 'smaller and smaller she
grew; her skin changed colour, and in place of the perfect
whiteness of its lustre it turned dirty brown and yellow, like
an old piece of withered parchment. . . . Smaller she grew, and
smaller yet, till she was no larger than a baboon.'

BABES IN THE WOOD

Anon, *The Children in the Wood* (ballad on traditional subject, earliest version dates from 1595; reprinted in Percy's *Reliques of Ancient English Poetry*, 1765)

Male and female children of the family of Wayland Hall, Norfolk

The traditional British pantomime story tells how two children, a boy and a girl, are murdered by their wicked uncle, who stands to benefit from their father's will. He hires two murderers, one of whom does not have the heart to go through with the crime. In a quarrel he is killed by his partner. The children are left in the wood where they die during the night. Birds cover them with leaves. The wicked uncle does not profit from the deed. His farm is burned down. His own sons die. His cattle perish. He becomes a highwayman and dies in prison after confessing to his crime.

The ballad version, entitled *The Norfolk Gentleman*, was published in Norwich in 1595, and was the subject of a stage play, *Two Lamentable Tragedies; the one of the murder of Maister Beech, a chandler of Thames Street; the other of a young child murdered in a wood by two ruffians, with the consent of his uncle*, by Robert Yarrington. It dates from 1601. Yarrington's version sets the story in Padua, and there is but one child murdered by a stab wound.

The original incidents are supposed to have happened in the vicinity of Wayling Wood (or Wayland Wood) between Watton and Kimberley, in Norfolk. There is the stump of the oak tree where, it is claimed, the children's bodies were discovered. The master of Wayland Hall had a son and daughter: 'The one a fine and pretty boy,/Not passing three years old;/ The other a girl more young than he,/And fram'd in beauty's mold.' When he died, he left them in the care of his wife's brother. According to his will the children were to inherit his money. But if the children were to die, it was to pass to the uncle. A year after the father's death, the wicked uncle plans their murder: 'He bargain'd with two ruffians strong,/Which were of furious mood,/That they should take these children young,/And slay them in a wood.' Thomas Percy claims the ballad to be later than the play of 1601, yet it is clearly earlier, and based on a real murder case.

David Passi (died 1589)

In Marlowe's drama, *The Jew of Malta*, the Grand Seignior of
Turkey demands that the Jews of Malta should pay him tribute.
Barabas is one of the wealthiest Jews on the island: 'Who hateth
me but for my happiness?/Or who is honoured now but for
his wealth?/Rather had I, a Jew, be hated thus,/Than pitied in
a Christian poverty,' He suffers the indignity of having his
riches impounded and his mansion turned into a nunnery, as
he attempted to resist the edict and pay the tribute. He hides a
store of riches under the floor and gets his daughter, Abigail,
to pretend Christian conversion to gain access. She regains the
gold and returns it to Barabas. He is aided in his machinations
by the Christian-hating Arabian slave, Ithamore. They arrange
the death of Abigail's lover, among others, and Abigail flees to
become a genuine convert to Christianity. Barabas's revenge
is to murder the whole convent with a gift of poisoned rice.
Before she dies, Abigail betrays her father. Malta is now
beseiged by the Turks. Barabas betrays the fortress to the
invaders and his reward is to be made governor. His next plot
is to destroy the Turkish garrison by means of a collapsible
floor, beneath which is a boiling cauldron. He perishes when
he is hurled through the floor himself.

Marlowe's sources are various, including Lonicerus's chronicles and Contarini's history of the Turkish war in the Mediterranean. The latter involved an account of the extraordinary
career of Joseph Nassi (or Miques). He was a Jew and a sworn
enemy of the Venetians. He gave himself to the service of the
Turks. His reward was to be made governor of the island of
Naxos – which was Christian. This exactly parallels the story
of *The Jew of Malta*. During the time Marlowe composed his
drama the adventures of one David Passi, an ambitious Jewish
merchant, were well-known in the circle in which Marlowe
moved, the Walsingham intelligence network. Walsingham
was chief of the secret service in London from 1569, ambassador to France 1570–73 and Secretary of State 1573–90. Walsingham's system of espionage and bribery resulted in the
convictions of William Parry in 1585 and Anthony Babington
and Mary Queen of Scots in 1586. Passi was rewarded for his
services to the Turks by being given the very highest offices at
Constantinople. Marlowe based the political and military
background on the Turkish siege of Malta in July 1551.
François de Belleforest, a writer used by Marlowe and other
dramatists as a source of material, refers to the career of David
Passi.

Revd John Gwyther (died 1873)

George Eliot's earliest writings deal with life and incident which she observed around her in her early days in Nuneaton. The three tales which make up *Scenes of Clerical Life* originally appeared in *Blackwood's Magazine*. 'The Sad Fortunes of the Rev Amos Barton' tells the story of a perfectly ordinary clergyman, who is the curate of Shepperton. He has neither deep learning, nor sophistication nor the human touch. He is devoid of humour and is not at all popular with his parishioners. But even so, this man – who in so many respects might be perceived as a mediocrity – does in fact earn in some measure the respect of his flock, through suffering and misfortune with which mankind can identify – his wife dies. He was married to a beautiful young woman, Milly Barton, and she dies from hard work and the stress and strain of her life as the wife of a poor parish priest. In deep regret, the Revd Amos Barton moves to the north of England.

His character and the major incidents of the story were based on the Revd John Gwyther, who was the curate of the parish of Chilvers Coton, where Mary Ann Evans (George Eliot) went to church. She was seventeen when Mrs Gwyther died, and, like the Revd Amos Barton, John Gwyther left his parish and went to the north of England. He went to a parish in Sheffield and moved later to Fewston, in Yorkshire. In January 1857 the first part of *Amos Barton* appeared in *Blackwood's* and the Revd Gwyther's eldest daughter, Emma, exclaimed 'Who in the world could have written this? Is it you, papa?' Emma appears as Patty in the story. Gwyther wrote to congratulate the unknown author 'now the pain I felt at the first publication is past off . . . yet I fully forgive for old acquaintance sake'.

MISS HETTY BATES

Jane Austen, *Emma* (1816)

Miss Molly Milles

Jane Austen's *Emma* contains one of her finest comic creations
in the person of the tiresomely nice Miss Bates who lives with
her mother Mrs Bates at Highbury. The self-indulgent altru-
ism of Miss Bates provides Jane Austen with an amusing
quality to contrast with the selfish magnanimity of her heroine
Emma Woodhouse. 'Mrs Bates,' writes Austen, 'the widow of
a former vicar of Highbury, was a very old lady, almost past
everything but tea and quadrille. She lived with her single
daughter in a very small way, and was considered with all the
regard and respect which a harmless old lady, under such
untoward circumstances, can excite. Her daughter enjoyed a
most uncommon degree of popularity for a woman neither
young, handsome, rich, nor married. . . . Her youth had passed
without distinction and her middle life was devoted to the care
of a failing mother, and the endeavour to make a small income
go as far as possible. And yet she was a happy woman, and a
woman whom no one named without good-will.'

When Jane Austen visited her brother Edward, at Godersham
Park, Kent, in 1813 she had dinner with a Mrs and Miss Milles
and agreed to call on them at Canterbury: 'I like the
mother . . . because she is cheerful and grateful for what she is
at the age of ninety and upwards [whereas] Miss Milles was
queer as usual, and provided us with plenty to laugh at. She
undertook in *three words* to give us the history of Mrs Scuda-
more's reconciliation, and then talked on about it for half-an-
hour, using such odd expressions and so foolishly minute, that
I could hardly keep my countenance.' In recreating Mrs and
Molly Milles as Mrs and Hetty Bates, Jane Austen made good
use of Molly's garrulous nature, for her dramatic monologues
are among the finest moments of *Emma*.

BAZAROV
Ivan Turgenev, *Fathers and Sons* (1862)

V. G. Belinsky (1811–48)

Turgenev dedicated *Fathers and Sons* to the memory of V. G. Belinsky and gave his hero, Bazarov, characteristics in common with the great Russian critic. Bazarov is the son of a poor army doctor, as was Belinsky; moreover Bazarov's argumentative intensity is derived from Belinsky, a man Turgenev regarded with admiration and awe. Turgenev lived near Belinsky in St Petersburg, in 1843, and the aspiring novelist became part of the critic's literary circle. Though he could not accept all Belinsky's arguments Turgenev watched closely as his friend moved from a reactionary artistic and political position to an urgent advocacy of literary naturalism and socialism. A member of Belinsky's circle recorded the radical impact of Belinsky on Turgenev: 'Belinsky was the first of us to notice [his affections] and sometimes laughed at them mercilessly. . . . Turgenev very much respected Belinsky and submitted to his moral authority without question. . . . He was even a little afraid of him.' Belinsky died of consumption at the age of thirty-seven, and Turgenev speculated on how he might have developed, given his volatile temperament.

Bazarov, who also dies prematurely and pointlessly, is a nihilist, one of the 'sons' who treats with contempt the romanticism of the older generation of 'fathers'. His mission in life is the destruction of antiquated attitudes and he is sweeping in his statements on human nature: 'It is enough to have one single human specimen in order to judge all the others. People are like trees in a forest: no botanist would dream of studying each individual birch-tree.' When the novel first appeared young Russians misinterpreted the character of Bazarov, with his intolerance and love of wine and women, as an attack on the radicals N. A. Dobrolyubov and N. G. Chernyshevsky who wrote *What is to be done?* (1863) as a rejoinder to Turgenev's novel. Turgenev, however, thought of Bazarov as 'my favourite offspring' and meant the character to be sympathetic.

Rasputin (1871–1916)

Norman Douglas's novel *South Wind* hangs a whole sensuous attitude to life on a slim narrative peg. Thomas Heard, Bishop of Bampopo in Africa, breaks his journey to England by stopping off on the island of Nepenthe where he encounters the strangest creatures. Among these is the self-styled Messiah Bazhakuloff, the ex-monk from Russia, who limits his disciples to the Sacred Number 63 and calls them Little White Cows. The Russian colony on the island is resented especially after violence breaks out over one of the Messiah's Revelations: he decides that the flesh and blood of warm-blooded beasts is Abomination to Little White Cows, a decision that enables him to continue to enjoy fish. Bazhakuloff is presented as a preposterous figure: 'The voluptuous surroundings of Nepenthe, the abundant food, adoration of disciples, alcoholic and carnal debaucheries, had impaired his tough Moujik frame and blunted his wit, worked havoc with that energy and peasant craftiness which once ruled an Emperor's court. His body was obese. His mind was in a state of advanced putrefaction. Even his personal cleanliness left something to be desired. Sitting there, puffy and pasty, in a darkened room, he looked more than ever like some obscene vegetable that has grown up in the shade.'

Douglas intended Bazhakuloff as a caricature of Rasputin, the Russian prophet whose scandalous personal behaviour and influence over the Tsarina led to his assassination. Rasputin managed successfully to exploit the sectarianism that was so rampant in the Russia of his time and he managed, at first, to convey a sense of holiness that was above suspicion. He took over the mind of the Tsarina because she believed completely in his power to treat her son's haemophilia. Like Bazhakuloff in Douglas's novel, Rasputin 'fought and wormed his way into the favour of the Court. A good deal of his worldly success may well have been due, as his enemies assert, to an incredible mixture of cringing, astuteness and impudence.'

Eduard Hanslick (1825–1904)

In Wagner's comic masterpiece, *The Mastersingers*, the young knight, Walther von Stolzing, hopes to gain admittance to the Mastersingers Guild in order to compete in the coming singing festival. The prize is to be the hand in marriage of Eva, the beautiful daughter of Veit Pogner. The town clerk, Beckmesser, wants Eva for himself, and is bitterly jealous of Walther, whom – he suspects – Eva loves in any case. When Walther has to sing before the Guild before he can be considered, his song has to be assessed by the Marker. On this occasion the Marker is Beckmesser. He takes advantage of his position to mark Walther's trial song down. He finds fault with everything – obscurity, bad rhyming, poor imagery, lack of balance – the whole thing is simply far, far too outlandish and outrageous for Beckmesser's taste and judgement. Some of the mastersingers who hear it find things to admire in it, others say they could not understand a word of it. Hans Sachs, the elder statesman of the Guild, suspects that Beckmesser is motivated by personal spite. Eva and Walther both turn to Sachs for advice and consolation. Sachs explains that tradition and rules are there as an aid to inspiration, not as a means to destroy it. In the meantime, Beckmesser, is trying to write a song with which to win the competition – and Eva. Walther is inspired to compose a superb prize-song which Beckmesser attempts to purloin. Beckmesser has insufficient time properly to master it and on the day of the festival sings it, makes a fool of himself, and is laughed off the stage. Walther sings the prize-song, wins universal approbation and is united with Eva.

In the character of Beckmesser, Wagner portrays his archenemy Eduard Hanslick, the Viennese conservative music critic, who opposed the modernist tendency in his day, especially as represented by Liszt and Wagner. He found much to admire in Wagner's early operas – especially 'Tannhäuser' – but bitterly opposed the 'music of the future' which Wagner pioneered in 'Tristan' and 'Der Ring des Nibelungen'. Beckmesser was originally called Hans Lick in Wagner's opera. Hanslick complained of the restless accompaniments and excessive modulations, long-winded and declamatory style, submarine and subterranean legends, melodic poverty and cacophany : 'we sit there, helpless and bored, amid these endless dialogues, thirsting equally to articulate speech and intelligible melody'.

BELINDA

Alexander Pope, *The Rape of the Lock* (1712)

Arabella Fermor

Alexander Pope's mock-heroic *The Rape of the Lock* (enlarged 1713) was written at the request of his friend, John Caryll, who wanted a poetic peace-offering to settle the differences between two of England's most prominent Catholic families. Caryll's ward, Lord Petre, had snipped a side-curl from the hair of the celebrated beauty Arabella Fermor; as a result the Fermors seethed with indignation at the audacity of Lord Petre and his apparently unrepentant family. Pope was called in, he said, because Caryll liked both families and wanted the poet to 'laugh them together again', which he did by inflating a trivial incident into an epic event. He also produced a glowing verbal portrait of Arabella in the person of Belinda: 'Her lively looks a sprightly mind disclose,/Quick as her eyes, and as unfixed as those:/Favours to none, to all she smiles extends;/Oft she rejects, but never once offends./Bright as the sun, her eyes the gazers strike,/And, like the sun, they shine on all alike./Yet graceful ease, and sweetness void of pride,/Might hide her faults, if belles had faults to hide:/If to her share some female errors fall,/Look on her face, and you'll forget them all.' Although Arabella was flattered when she read a prepublication copy of the poem she had second thoughts when Belinda materialized in print and became public property.

On 8 November 1712 Pope told Caryll that 'the celebrated Lady herself is offended, and, which is stranger, not at herself but me'. However the two Catholic families were reconciled and Arabella learned to live with her celebrity and to enjoy it. When Arabella married Francis Perkins in 1715 she was pleased to receive the congratulations of the poet who had immortalized her. Subsequently she basked in being Belinda; when Mrs Hesther Thrale toured Europe in 1775 she met Arabella's niece, an abbess in a Parisian convent, who 'remembered that Mr Pope's praise made her aunt very troublesome and conceited'.

BIG BROTHER
George Orwell, *Nineteen Eighty-Four* (1949)

Joseph Stalin (1879–1953)

George Orwell's devastating critique of totalitarianism, *Nineteen Eighty-Four*, is dominated by the ubiquitous figure of Big Brother who permeates the story as a presence. As Winston Smith begins another day in 1984 he is immediately aware of Big Brother as he sees a coloured poster: 'It depicted simply an enormous face, more than a metre wide: the face of a man of about forty-five, with a heavy black moustache and ruggedly handsome features. . . . It was one of those pictures which are so contrived that the eyes follow you about when you move. BIG BROTHER IS WATCHING YOU, the caption beneath it ran.' After Smith's love affair with Julia, which amounts to an act of rebellion against the state, he is brainwashed back into the fold of total conformity and as the book ends he 'gazed up at the enormous face. Forty years it had taken him to learn what kind of smile was hidden beneath the dark moustache. . . . He loved Big Brother.'

Orwell's state of Oceania is structured, politically, on the Soviet model and Big Brother is obviously made in the image of Stalin whose kindly avuncular appearance contrasted with his dictatorial habits. When Orwell wrote *Nineteen Eighty-Four* in 1948 (hence the title) Stalin was an apparently indestructible figure whose authority in the Soviet Union was absolute. Orwell had already portrayed Stalin as the boar Napoleon in *Animal Farm* (1945) where the dictator triumphs over his old adversary Trotsky, personified as the pig Snowball. The Stalin-Trotsky struggle is recreated in *Nineteen Eighty-Four* when the party propaganda suggests that the icon of Big Brother is threatened by the Trotsky-like face of Emmanuel Goldstein, the Enemy of the People – 'a lean Jewish face, with a great fuzzy aureole of white hair and a small goatee beard'.

BIGGLES

W. E. Johns, *The Camels are Coming* (1932) and ninety-seven subsequent Biggles books

---

C. G. Wigglesworth (1893–1961)

Captain James Bigglesworth – the First World War flying ace known to tens of thousands of readers as Biggles – made his first appearance in April 1932 in the pages of *Popular Flying*, an aviation magazine edited by W. E. Johns. Introducing *The Camels are Coming*, the first Biggles collection, Johns described his creation as 'a fictitious character, yet he could have been found in any RFC mess during those great days of 1917 and 1918 when air combat had become the order of the day and air duelling was a fine art'. As the hero of the Royal Flying Corps, Biggles is a dashing figure possessed, however, of some sensitivity: 'His deep-set hazel eyes were never still and held a glint of yellow fire that somehow seemed out of place in a pale face upon which the strain of war, and sight of sudden death, had already graven little lines. His hands, small and delicate as a girl's, fidgeted continually with the tunic fastening at his throat. He had killed a man not six hours before. He had killed six men during the past month – or was it a year? – he had forgotten. Time had become curiously telescoped lately. What did it matter anyway? He knew he had to die some time and had long ago ceased to worry about it.'

Johns himself flew with the RFC and was able to observe the air aces closely. One of these men was Air Commodore C. G. Wigglesworth who served with the Royal Naval Air Service and the Royal Air Force during the First World War. As Johns admitted in 1949, when hinting that the original Biggles had a similar name to his hero, he first thought of 'a shadowy figure created by my admiration for the courage and resource displayed by some of the men with whom it was my good fortune to spend several years of my life'. From Wigglesworth, Johns took the name and the nature of his flying ace and fleshed out this ideal with a projection of himself.

ANTHONY BLANCHE
Evelyn Waugh, *Brideshead Revisited* (1945)

Sir Harold Acton (born 1904)

The arrogant aestheticism of Oxford in the 1920s is observed with great accuracy in Evelyn Waugh's *Brideshead Revisited*. As the narrator Charles Ryder recalls his own days at Oxford, from the perspective of the Second World War, he thinks of Sebastian Flyte with his immature 'eccentricities of behaviour' and of the outrageously affected Anthony Blanche: 'He was tall, slim, rather swarthy, with large saucy eyes. . . . This, I did not need telling, was Anthony Blanche, the "aesthete" *par excellence*, a byword of iniquity from Cherwell Edge to Somerville.' Blanche is an enthusiast for the modernist poetry of the 1920s and disclaims T. S. Eliot's *The Waste Land* through a megaphone. Later he comes to an exhibition of Ryder's pictures and lectures him on art: 'Charm is the great English blight. . . . It kills love; it kills art; I greatly fear, my dear Charles, it has killed *you*.'

Blanche was modelled, somewhat maliciously, on Waugh's Oxford contemporary Harold Acton who combined an outlandish appearance with a determination to remake Oxford in his own aesthetic image. Some of the details of Blanche are borrowed from Acton's rival Oxford aesthete Brian Howard (1905–58), previously caricatured as Ambrose Silk in Waugh's *Put Out More Flags* (1942). Blanche's way of punctuating his speech with 'my dear' was taken from Howard as was the character's partly Jewish origin. Howard, however, was a pathetic figure in real life whose promise petered out in self-pity. Blanche, like Acton, is an intellectually alert individual who has a considerable impact on the Oxford of the 1920s. Ryder regards him with awe: 'At times we all seemed children beside him – at most times, but not always, for there was a bluster and zest in Anthony which the rest of us had shed . . . his vices flourished less in the pursuit of pleasure than in the wish to shock. . . . He was cruel, too, in the wanton, insect-maiming manner of the very young, and fearless like a little boy.'

LEOPOLD BLOOM

James Joyce, *Ulysses* (1922)

Alfred Hunter/Ettore Schmitz

Leopold Bloom, the hero of James Joyce's *Ulysses*, is at once a convincing naturalistic figure and a mythical embodiment of various archetypes – Homer's Odysseus, the Wandering Jew, the eternal Everyman. In the Ithica section of the book Joyce concentrates on Bloom as the Wandering Jew: 'Ever would he wander, selfcompelled, to the extreme limit of his cometary orbit, beyond the fixed stars and variable suns and telescopic planets, astronomical waifs and strays, to the extreme boundary of space, passing from land to land, among peoples, amid events.' Ithica, in the novel, is Eccles Street where, in 1904, Joyce was knocked down in a scuffle with the escort of a lady he had accosted. Joyce (Dedalus in the novel) was brushed down by Alfred Hunter, a Dublin Jew who came to his assistance; subsequently Joyce learned that Hunter was painfully aware of his wife's infidelity.

When Joyce left Ireland he settled, after some wandering, in Trieste where he earned a living as an English tutor. Among his pupils was Ettore Schmitz (1861–1928) who disclosed that he had once published two novels under the pseudonym Italo Svevo. Joyce read the novels, pronounced Schmitz a neglected writer and encouraged his gifted pupil to complete *Confessions of Zeno* (1923), now recognized as a comic classic. Schmitz was a lapsed Jew as well as a businessman (whose factories manufactured anti-corrosive paint) and he provided Joyce with details of his former religion. Joyce admired Schmitz and greatly appreciated his sense of humour. As he wrote *Ulysses* he used memories of Alfred Hunter and observations of Schmitz in his creation of Leopold Bloom who 'ate with relish the inner organs of beasts and fowls. He liked thick giblet soup, nutty gizzards, a stuffed roast heart, liver slices fried with crust-crumbs, fried hencod's roes.'

MOLLY BLOOM

James Joyce, *Ulysses* (1922)

Nora Barnacle (1885–1951)

According to the Homeric pattern of James Joyce's *Ulysses* the heroine, Molly Bloom, is Penelope. At the end of the book she lies in bed, dwells on life and love and thinks 'a woman wants to be embraced twenty times a day almost to make her look young no matter by who so long as to be in love or loved by somebody if the fellow you want isnt there'. Molly's affirmative monologue is regarded as one of the greatest of all literary insights into feminine psychology, a subject Joyce pursued energetically with Nora Barnacle – the woman he left Ireland with in 1904 and married, in London, in 1931.

Joyce met Nora on 10 June 1904 in Dublin and was immediately attracted to her. She worked as a servant in a hotel and had no interest in, or knowledge of, literature. However, her interest in sex was strong and when she made a sexual advance to Joyce on 16 June 1904 the day became momentous to him and was subsequently commemorated as Bloomsday, the time of the action of Joyce's masterpiece. Nora's background was harsh: her father, a baker, drank what money he made; her mother was unable to look after her. Nora was brought up by her grandmother, sent to a convent, then employed as a portress by nuns in Galway City. Joyce was fascinated by Nora and encouraged her to write sexually frank letters to him. The unpunctuated style and erotic subject of these letters contributed to the making of Molly Bloom in Nora's image. Nora's erotic letters have been lost but a note she wrote to Joyce's brother Stanislaus shows the headlong style that would characterize Molly Bloom: 'I hope you are very well I am sure you would be glad to see Georgie now he is well able to run about he is able to say a lot he has a good appetite and he has eight teeth and also sings when we ask him where is Stannie he beats his chest and says non c'e piu'.

Robert Browning, *Bishop Blougram's Apology* (1855)

Nicholas Patrick Stephen Wiseman
(1802–65)

A journalist and a bishop agree to have dinner together, to take wine afterwards, and to see the dawn come up, while fundamental beliefs are discussed. The bishop senses that the journalist despises him for accepting the position of a beneficed priest even though his beliefs do not extend to all the doctrines of the Church of Rome. It is a classic analysis of the position of the 'worldly' priest: 'The common problem . . . Is not to fancy what were fair in life/Provided it could be – but, finding first/ What may be, then find how to make it fair/Up to our means.' Blougram is not placed in a sympathetic light, and Browning's irony has a fine cutting edge.

The figure of Blougram was based on Cardinal Wiseman. He was an English Cardinal, born in Seville of Anglo-Irish parents, educated at Durham and in Rome. For twelve years he was rector of the English college in Rome, and was a brilliant scholar in his own right, who became curator of the Arabic manuscripts in the Vatican and professor of oriental languages at Rome. He came to England in the mid 1830s and preached the doctrines of the Roman Catholic faith and in 1840, now a consecrated bishop, made Oscott College, near Birmingham, the centre of English Catholicism. In 1850 he was appointed Cardinal Archbishop of Westminster, vehemently supporting Pius IX's policy of restoring the faith in England. He greatly influenced the Oxford Movement and earned a wide reputation as lecturer on social, aesthetic and literary topics. As he grew older his religious views hardened into a less liberal mould, he opposed Christian unity and forbade Catholic parents to send their sons to Oxford or Cambridge, though earlier he had managed to combine high principles in matters of faith with liberal views in ecclesiastical matters.

BLUEBEARD

Charles Perrault, *Histoires et Contes du Temps Passé* (1697)

Gilles de Rais, Marshall of France (1404–40)

This collection of tales was published in an English translation by Robert Samber in 1729. They were popular French tales from various sources, and included Little Red Riding Hood, the Sleeping Beauty, Puss in Boots, Cinderella, Hop o' my Thumb and the grisly tale of Bluebeard. This narrative is placed in an oriental setting and concerns a powerful potentate with a blue beard. He has an evil reputation as he has married several times but his wives have disappeared. He asks for the hand of the fair Fatima, the younger of two handsome daughters of a local lady of quality. Fatima agrees to the match but then Bluebeard says he has to go away on business and leaves Fatima in charge of his castle. As he gives her the keys he warns her not to use one particular key which he says opens a particular chamber. Of course she is overwhelmed by curiosity and as soon as he has gone opens the door and finds the bodies of all Bluebeard's previous wives. She is so shocked that she drops the forbidden key which is thus stained with blood. This leads to her discovery by Bluebeard, but her life is saved by her sister Anne and her brothers and Bluebeard is killed.

Although the story has many similarities with widespread folkloric tales of forbidden chambers containing dreadful secrets, there are some disturbing parallels with the life story of Gilles de Rais who was executed for abnormal sexual crimes in Brittany in October 1440, after a 15th-century *cause célèbre*, second only to the trial of Joan of Arc, with whom he is associated. A wealthy baron and landowner, patron of the arts and brilliant soldier, in 1420 he married Katherine of Thouars, a great heiress in Brittany, La Vendée and Poitou. He fought against the British and was an avid supporter of Joan of Arc at Orleans, Jargeau and Patay. Financial difficulties caused him to begin selling some properties, though his family protested. He hoped to regain his wealth by alchemy and necromancy, at the same time protecting his soul by charity and ritualistic devotion to the Church. Rumours began to circulate of his torturing and killing boys, procured for him by servants, reputed to number over 150. He was tried for heresy and murder and, terrified by excommunication, he confessed and was hanged.

JAMES BOND

Ian Fleming, *Casino Royale* (1953), *Live and Let Die* (1954), *Moonraker* (1955), *Diamonds Are Forever* (1956), *From Russia with Love* (1957), *Doctor No* (1958), *Goldfinger* (1959), *For Your Eyes Only* (1960), *Thunderball* (1961), *The Spy Who Loved Me* (1962), *On Her Majesty's Secret Service* (1963), *You Only Live Twice* (1964), *The Man With the Golden Gun* (1965), *Octopussy and the Living Daylights* (1966)

Dusko Popov

When Ian Fleming wrote his first novel, *Casino Royale*, in 1952 he wanted to find 'the simplest, dullest, plainest-sounding name' for his hero and so turned to one of his favourite books – James Bond's guidebook *Birds of the West Indies*. Written rapidly at Fleming's Jamaican home of Goldeneye, the first Bond book was – so the author insisted – produced to 'take my mind off the shock of getting married at the age of forty-three'. But if the Bond saga began as a fond farewell to bachelor life it was not all fantasy. Bond is, superficially, Fleming writ large: both smoke heavily, drink discriminately, gamble cleverly and dress elegantly.

During the Second World War Fleming worked as personal assistant to the Director of Naval Intelligence and was able to observe several agents closely. Of these the most formidable was Dusko Popov, the Yugoslavian whose work as a British agent involved infiltrating the Nazi Secret Service. He was greatly valued by Britain's XX Committee which, as the name implies, double-crossed the enemy by feeding it misleading information through its own agents. Like Bond, Popov combined a taste for expensive living with a deadly efficiency. Some of Popov's audacious adventures are described in his book *Spy/Counterspy* (1974) where there are interludes with beautiful women, ferocious bouts of fighting and displays of coolness in the face of great danger. Popov writes: 'I'm told that Ian Fleming said he based his character James Bond to some degree on me and my experiences. As for me, I rather doubt that a Bond in the flesh would have survived more than forty-eight hours as an espionage agent. Fleming and I did rub shoulders in Lisbon, and a few weeks before I took the clipper for the States he did follow me about.' On one occasion Fleming watched Popov in action in the Casino which is where the whole Bond saga begins.

JULIANA BORDEREAU
Henry James, *The Aspern Papers* (1888)

Claire Clairmont (1798–1879)

The narrator of Henry James's *The Aspern Papers* is drawn to Venice on a shady literary mission. On learning that Juliana Bordereau, inspirational mistress of lyric poet Jeffrey Aspern, is living in the city he determines to relieve her of the priceless Aspern papers. When he first sees the legendary Juliana he is astonished by her age: 'The divine Juliana as a grinning skull – the vision hung there until it passed. . . . She would die next week, she would die tomorrow – then I could seize her papers.' The narrator rents a room in the 'big, imposing house' so he can ingratiate himself with Juliana and her niece Miss Tita, 'a ridiculous, pathetic, provincial old woman'. When Juliana dies, Miss Tita offers the papers if the narrator will marry her; when he turns her down she burns them.

Such a fictional scenario was suggested to Henry James by the way Claire Clairmont was pestered in Florence by the Shelley-fanatic Captain Edward Augustus Silsbee when she was eighty-one and a recluse living at 43 Via Romana, Florence, with her niece Paula. After Claire Clairmont died, Silsbee approached Paula about the Shelley papers; she agreed to give them to him if he married her but it was too high a price for Silsbee to pay. Claire Clairmont was the stepsister of Mary Godwin. In 1814 Mary eloped with Shelley, and Claire came along too. Later Claire offered herself to Byron who took advantage of the offer. As a result, on 12 January 1817 Claire gave birth to a daughter Allegra. Hurtfully, Byron took the child from Claire and eventually put Allegra in a convent near Ravenna (where she died, of typhus, at the age of five). Byron liked to claim that Allegra was Shelley's child. There are persistent rumours that the baby, Elena, adopted by Shelley in 1818 was his child by Claire.

EMMA BOVARY
Gustave Flaubert, *Madame Bovary* (1857)

Louise Colet (1808–76) and Delphine Delamare (died 1848)

Madame Bovary is set in Normandy, near Rouen. Emma is a convent-educated young woman whose mind is stuffed with notions of romantic love uncritically absorbed from shallow literature. She marries a youthful medical practitioner, Charles Bovary, but finds him boorish and her life unfulfilled. In desperate attempts to find romance she has affairs with a local landowner and a lawyer's clerk and runs up considerable debts. Her creditors threaten to expose her to her husband and she kills herself by taking arsenic. The power of the novel lies in Flaubert's ability to create creative tension between the shoddy activities and motivations of the characters and the brilliant beauty and precision of its style.

There are several significant contradictions at the basis of Flaubert's novel. One is his assertion that his art was impersonal. 'I have put nothing of my own feelings or life [in that book]', and a further comment that 'I had no model for Madame Bovary. She is purely an invention.' This seems to be countered by his claim that 'Madame Bovary is myself'. But there is incontrovertible evidence that Flaubert was drawing on real-life characters and experiences when composing *Madame Bovary*. One source is the poetess Louise Colet, with whom Flaubert had a love affair. She was thirteen years older than he was, and separated from her husband. She was a romantic poetess who had twice won the poetry prize of the Académie Française. Their relationship lasted ten years. Flaubert found her shallow, possessive and affected and was distressed by her poor taste. She gave him a cigar case which had the same motto as that on the signet ring Emma gives her lover Rodolphe: 'Amor nel cor.'

Another, more influential, source was the story which Louis Bouilhet, the poet and friend of Flaubert, told the young writer about Delphine Delamare. She was a seventeen-year-old girl, daughter of one of the patients of Eugène Delamare near Rouen. They were married in 1839. Like Emma she was filled with romantic delusions and soon tired of her bourgeois existence and sought relief in numerous affairs. Debts mounted and rumours spread. She committed suicide with arsenic in March 1848. Emma thought at the end, 'no longer of her need for money, only of her martyred love and her humiliation'.

LAWRENCE BOYTHORN
Charles Dickens, *Bleak House* (1852)

Walter Savage Landor (1775–1864)

Boythorn is an irascible but kindly and open-hearted man, who is the friend of John Jarndyce: 'There was a sterling quality in his laugh, and in his vigorous healthy voice, and in the roundness and fulness with which he uttered every word he spoke, and in the very fury of his superlatives, which seemed to go off like blank cannons and hurt nothing. . . . He was not only a very handsome old gentleman – upright and stalwart . . . with a massive grey head, a fine composure of face when silent, a figure that might have become corpulent but for his being so continually in earnest that he gave it no rest, and a chin that might have subsided into a double chin but for the vehement emphasis in which it was constantly required to assist; but he was such a true gentleman in his manner, so chivalrously polite, his face was lighted by a smile of so much sweetness and tenderness, and it seemed so plain that he had nothing to hide, but showed himself exactly as he was.'

Landor was the basis of this portrait. He was a poet and essayist. In 1840 Dickens visited him in his house in St James's Square in Bath and here conceived the idea for the story he was to develop into *The Old Curiosity Shop*. Landor's most famous work was *Imaginary Conversations*. He had a quarrelsome nature. He bought Llanthony Abbey in Monmouthshire but quarrelled with the authorities in Llanthony in 1814, was asked to leave Como by the authorities as the result of a poem in Latin he wrote which, they considered, insulted them. Dickens named one of his sons Walter Savage Dickens after him, and when he visited Bath after Landor had died the novelist wrote: 'Landor's ghost goes along the silent streets here before me. . . . The place looks like a cemetery which the Dead have succeeded in rising and taking. Having built streets of their old gravestones, they wander about . . . trying to look alive. A dead failure.'

SALLY BOWLES

Christopher Isherwood, *Sally Bowles* (1937), *Goodbye to Berlin* (1939)

Jean Ross (1912–73)

In 1930 Christopher Isherwood found lodgings at 17 Nollendorfstrasse, Berlin, where he was befriended by his landlady Fräulein Meta Thurau. Since she called him Herr Issyvoo the author retained the name for the observer of the episodes collected in *Goodbye to Berlin* in which Fräulein Thurau becomes Fräulein Schroeder. Among Isherwood's fellow lodgers was Jean Ross. As the daughter of a cotton merchant she was accustomed to comfort but by then earned her living singing in a seedy bar. By 1936 Isherwood had conceived a story 'about an English girl who sings in a Berlin cabaret': *Sally Bowles* was first published in 1937 and then incorporated in *Goodbye to Berlin*. Sally herself is an innocent who remains unaltered by experience; even her abortion leaves her unchanged. For all her love affairs she remains vulnerable: 'Her face was long and thin, powdered dead white ... "Hiloo," she cooed, pursing her brilliant cherry lips as though she were going to kiss the mouthpiece: "Ist dass Du, mein Liebling?".'

By the time Sally Bowles materialized in print Jean Ross was a committed left-winger married to the English writer Claud Cockburn and did not identify with Isherwood's creation though she remained friendly with the author. Sally Bowles subsequently appeared in John van Druter's Isherwood-inspired play *I am a Camera* (1951) which in turn inspired the stage musical *Cabaret* (1961) – filmed by Bob Fosse in 1971 with Liza Minnelli as Sally. Isherwood recalled Jean Ross with affection in *Christopher and his Kind* (1977): 'Jean was more essentially British than Sally; she grumbled like a true Englishwoman, with her grin-and-bear-it grin. And she was tougher. She never struck Christopher as being sentimental or the least bit sorry for herself. Like Sally, she boasted continually about her lovers.'

GUDRUN BRANGWEN
D. H. Lawrence, *Women in Love* (1920)

Katherine Mansfield (1888–1923)

D. H. Lawrence's friends John Middleton Murry and Katherine Mansfield (who lived together for several years before they were able to marry in 1918) helped create the literary climate of modernism in England. They had a close and typically tense relationship with Lawrence who often enchanted them and frequently enraged them with his self-centred sexual aesthetic. Although they did not at first realize it both of them featured in Lawrence's *Women in Love*: Murry was physically enlarged as Gerald Crich; Katherine became Gudrun Brangwen whose artistic gifts are visual rather than verbal. Gerald and Gudrun share a fierce physical passion whereas a more metaphysical love seems possible between Gerald and Rupert Birkin who (representing Lawrence himself) wants 'eternal union with a man too: another kind of love'. What Gerald sees in Gudrun is an independent quality he finds irresistible: 'Gerald watched Gudrun closely. . . . There was a body of cold power in her. . . . He saw her a dangerous, hostile spirit, that could stand undiminished and unabated. It was so finished, and of such perfect gesture, moreover. . . . The bond was established between them, in [her] look, in her tone. In her tone, she made the understanding clear – they were of the same kind, he and she, a sort of diabolic freemasonry subsisted between them. Henceforward, she knew, she had her power over him. Wherever they met, they would be secretly associated. And he would be helpless in the association with her. Her soul exulted.'

Katherine Mansfield was one of the most formidable intellectuals active in England. She came from New Zealand and made an early reputation as an incisive critic, then as Murry's assistant editor on *Rhythm*, a quarterly committed to revitalizing art. Mansfield's own short stories established her as one of the most subtle writers of the century.

SUE BRIDEHEAD
Thomas Hardy, *Jude the Obscure* (1895)

Tryphena Sparks (1851–90)

Introducing the first edition of *Jude the Obscure* Thomas Hardy wrote 'The scheme was jotted down in 1890, from notes made in 1887 and onwards, some of the circumstances being suggested by the death of a woman in the former year.' The woman was Tryphena Sparks (1851–90), the model for Jude's 'darling little fool' Sue Bridehead. Jude, the stonemason who longs for learning, is enchanted by Sue as he sits watching her 'pretty shoulders' aware that 'his interest in her had shown itself to be unmistakably of a sexual kind'. Jude and Sue are 'simpletons' (Hardy's first title for the novel) whose attempt to put love before marriage ends in catastrophe and Sue's 'mental volte-face' back to convention. Hardy's fiction is an imaginative reconstruction of what might have happened had he pursued Tryphena in his youth.

In 1867 Hardy was working part-time in a Dorchester architect's office and about this time began to see his cousin Tryphena, a student-teacher at Puddletown School. On 16 January 1868 Tryphena was rebuked for 'neglect of duty' and probably dismissed; she went to Stockwell Training College, London, and was eventually appointed headmistress at Plymouth Public Free School in 1871, by which time Hardy had taken up with Emma Gifford. Hardy married Emma in 1874; three years later Tryphena married Charles Gale and had four children. When she died at the age of thirty-eight Hardy wrote a poem, 'Thoughts of Phena', in which she is described as his 'lost prize'.

In *Jude the Obscure* the Hardy-Tryphena relationship is transformed into a great tragedy but the origins of the story are still apparent: Jude and Sue are cousins as were Hardy and Tryphena; Jude uses books to better himself, as did Hardy; Sue trains as a schoolmistress, as did Tryphena. *Jude the Obscure* caused a sensation and Hardy said that 'the experience completely [cured] me of further interest in novel-writing'.

REVD MR BROCKLEHURST

Charlotte Brontë, *Jane Eyre* (1847)

Revd Carus Wilson

Jane Eyre is orphaned as a baby and looked after by her aunt, the cold-hearted Mrs Reed of Gateshead Hall. For ten years Jane is treated like a servant, while Mrs Reed's own children are totally spoilt. As a punishment on one occasion, Jane is put into the room in which the late Mr Reed had died. Jane is a very sensitive girl, and she faints and becomes ill. When she is better she is sent to Lowood School, run by the Revd Brocklehurst, who seems to Jane like a 'black pillar', with the 'grim face at the top'. His regime is a tyrannical one, and the accommodation austere in the extreme, but in some ways it seems to Jane a relief after Gateshead Hall. Jane at one stage is punished by making her stand in isolation outside in the elements which makes her ill.

Brocklehurst is a portrait of the Revd Carus Wilson, who ran a school at Cowan Bridge, on the coach-road between Leeds and Kendal, where the daughters of the clergy could be educated for £14 a year plus extras. Charlotte Brontë was a pupil here, under the puritanical Revd Wilson. Wilson regarded himself as a philanthropist, but the conditions in the school seem to have been prison-like. He wrote little magazine stories for children, which are full of death-bed scenes. In one of them a child aged less than four is asked whether he would choose life or death, and answers: 'Death for me. I am fonder of death.' The desirability of continual prayer is stressed and in one story a child who screamed and cried is struck down by God and sent to hell. Children were punished, he claimed, in order to save their souls.

Cowan Bridge was cold all the time, and come rain or shine the pupils regularly had to walk to Revd Wilson's church at Tunstall. The food was uneatable. Two of Charlotte's sisters contracted tuberculosis there. Mrs Gaskell recorded of Wilson that 'his love of authority' led to much 'unnecessary and irritating meddling with little matters'.

LEWIS BROGAN
Simone de Beauvoir, *The Mandarins* (1954)

Nelson Algren (1909–81)

After the liberation of France in 1945, Simone de Beauvoir visited the USA and was encouraged to go to Chicago to meet Nelson Algren. She was greatly impressed by the novelist who lived (as she said in her autobiography) 'in a hovel, without a bathroom or refrigerator, alongside an alley full of steaming trash cans and flapping newspapers'. Algren and de Beauvoir were deeply attracted to one another and when she returned to Chicago she lived with him for six weeks. Algren asked her to move in with him permanently but she was drawn back to France and her deep friendship with Jean-Paul Sartre. For several years Algren and de Beauvoir met regularly for holidays but he realized she could never be separated from Sartre for long and decided to end the affair.

This relationship was recreated by de Beauvoir as the romantic aspect of the otherwise rigorously intellectual *The Mandarins* which is dedicated to Nelson Algren. On a visit to the USA, Anne – wife of prominent French thinker Robert Dubreuilh – goes to meet the writer Lewis Brogan. She is overwhelmed by his personality: 'He was twenty when the great depression struck and for several years he lived the life of a hobo, crossing America hidden in freight cars, in turn peddlar, dishwasher, waiter, masseur, ditch digger, bricklayer, salesman, and, when necessary, burglar. In some forgotten roadside lunchroom in Arizona where he earned a living washing glasses, he had written a short story which a leftist magazine accepted for publication. . . . Through his stories, you got the feeling that he claimed no rights on life and that nevertheless he had always had a passionate desire to live. I liked that mixture of modesty and eagerness.' Like the author, Anne loves the American novelist but finally chooses to return to her life with 'the mandarins'.

FATHER BROWN

G. K. Chesterton, *The Innocence of Father Brown* (1911), *The Wisdom of Father Brown* (1914), *The Incredulity of Father Brown* (1926), *The Secret of Father Brown* (1927), *The Scandal of Father Brown* (1935)

Father John O'Connor (1870–1952)

On his first appearance, in the 1910 story 'The Blue Cross', G. K. Chesterton's divine detective Father Brown is conspicuous by his singular appearance: 'he had a face as round and dull as a Norfolk dumpling; he had eyes as empty as the North Sea; he had several brown-paper parcels which he was quite incapable of collecting. . . . He had a large shabby umbrella, which constantly fell on the floor.' Father Brown goes on to outwit Flambeau, the 'colossus of crime'; and to astonish Valentin, 'the greatest detective alive'. When asked for the secret of his success he says 'a man who does next to nothing but hear men's real sins is not likely to be wholly unaware of human evil'.

Father Brown was (apart from the moon face) closely modelled on Father John O'Connor. An Irishman, he was curate at St Anne's, at Keighley in Yorkshire, when he wrote a fan letter to Chesterton in 1903. The following year Chesterton met Father O'Connor and the two became firm friends. O'Connor (like Father Brown) wore a flat black hat, frequently carried brown-paper parcels and sported a 'large shabby umbrella'. One evening he revealed to Chesterton how much he knew about human sin and suffering, whereupon Chesterton conceived the idea of 'constructing a comedy in which a priest should appear to know nothing and in fact know more about crime than the criminals'. The priest had a great influence on the author's life and when, on 30 July 1922, Chesterton was received into the Roman Catholic Church he made his confession to Father O'Connor. In 'The Sins of Prince Saradine' Chesterton describes Father Brown as 'an oddly sympathetic man. . . . He had that knack of friendly silence which is so essential to gossip.' Father O'Connor's gift was recognized and he was made a Privy Chamberlain to Pope Pius XI and a Monsignor.

INSPECTOR BUCKET

Charles Dickens, *Bleak House* (1852)

Inspector Charles F. Field

Inspector Bucket is the detective officer used by Tulkinghorn and Lord Dedlock. It is Bucket's skill which finally unravels the mysteries which form the structure of the central plot of *Bleak House*, the murder of Tulkinghorn, and the discovery of Lady Dedlock. He finds out that the killer of Tulkinghorn was Hortense (see HORTENSE) the French maid and not George Rouncewell or Lady Dedlock. He seems to have the power to come and go without normal locomotion. Mr Snagsby suddenly sees: 'a person with a hat and stick in his hand, who was not there when he himself came in, and has not since entered by the door or by either of the windows . . . this person stands there, with his attentive face, and his hat and stick . . . and his hands behind him, a composed and quiet listener. He is a stoutly built, steady-looking, sharp-eyed man in black, of about the middle-age.'

This is Inspector Field. He was an Inspector in the Greenwich Division of Metropolitan Police in 1833 and later promoted to the Detective Force. Dickens's friend, the journalist George Augustus Sala, wrote that: 'There was something . . . of Dickens's Inspector Bucket about Inspector Field; and I venture to think that he was a much acuter and astuter detective in *Bleak House* than he was in real life.' Dickens wrote several times about Field. In one article in *Household Words* he is described as 'a middle-aged man of a portly presence, with a large, moist, knowing eye, a husky voice, and a habit of emphasizing his conversation by the aid of a corpulent forefinger'. Elsewhere he says he is 'of a burly figure', 'sagacious, vigilant . . . polite and soothing'. He had that capacity for being everywhere at once, knowing everyone and every place. Dickens wrote that Field's eye 'is the roving eye that searches every corner of the cellar as he talks. . . . Every thief cowers before him, like a schoolboy before his schoolmaster.' Field conducted Dickens through some of the worst London slums.

NATTY BUMPPO

James Fenimore Cooper, *The Pioneers* (1823), *The Last of the Mohicans* (1826), *The Prairie* (1827), *The Pathfinder* (1840), *The Deerslayer* (1841)

Daniel Boone (1734–1820)

James Fenimore Cooper's hero Natty Bumppo, a 'man of the forest', declares himself in *The Pioneers* as an archetypal loner: 'I have lived in the woods for forty long years, and have spent five at a time without seeing the light of a clearing bigger than a wind-row in the trees.' Natty, known as Hawk-eye in *The Last of the Mohicans*, and Leatherstocking elsewhere, has an appropriately odd appearance: 'His moccasins were ornamented after the gay fashion of the natives, while the only part of his underdress which appeared below the hunting frock was a pair of buckskin leggings that laced at the sides, and which were gartered above the knees with the sinews of a deer.'

As a fiercely independent individual who pushes back frontiers and impresses his rugged personality on the American soil, Natty was modelled on 'the venerable patriarch' Daniel Boone – as Cooper acknowledged in *The Prairie*, the third Leatherstocking tale. Boone, born near Reading, Pennsylvania, fought in the French and Indian War. In 1767 and, more spectacularly, in 1769, he explored Kentucky to which he returned in 1775 as an agent for the Transylvania Company. Boone led a group of settlers to Kentucky and erected a fort at what was to become Boonesborough. Captured by the Shawnees at the Lower Blue Licks in 1778 he escaped in time to warn Boonesborough of an imminent Indian attack which was thereby resisted in a long siege. The following year he brought more settlers to Kentucky and, when Kentucky was made a county of Virginia, Boone was made a lieutenant-colonel in the militia, was chosen for the legislature, and was (in 1782) appointed sheriff and county lieutenant. However his claims on land in Kentucky were invalidated as he had not registered them properly, so he left the county in 1788 going first to Point Pleasant and then to Missouri where he lived on land given to him by Congress.

BILLY BUNTER

Frank Richards, *Magnet* (issue numbers 1–1683)

Lewis Ross Higgins (1885–1919)

On 15 February 1908 the halfpenny paper *Magnet* made its first appearance with a hero, Harry Wharton, and a school, Greyfriars in Kent. Wharton goes to Study No 1 along with Billy Bunter, 'a somewhat stout junior with a broad face and a large pair of spectacles'. Bunter's weekly adventures continued until 1940 when the paper closed down with *Magnet* issue number 1683. After the war Bunter appeared in books and (in 1952) on BBC television. He was an unforgettable character with his Fat Owl face, his faith in the imminent appearance of a postal order (on the strength of which he borrowed), his addiction to 'tuck', and his stock phrases 'Yarooh!', 'Oh, crumbs' and 'Oh, crikey'.

Frank Richards, the astonishingly prolific author who created Bunter, acknowledged his original: 'His extensive circumference came from an editorial gentleman who . . . seemed to overflow the editorial chair and almost the editorial office.' This was Lewis Ross Higgins who edited the comic paper *Chuckles* from 1914 until his death. He was a Welshman who, on account of his great girth, was sometimes mistaken for G. K. Chesterton; in addition to his work as editor, cartoonist and illustrator he wrote art criticism for *Punch*.

Two other sources were tapped to complete the picture of Bunter. The large spectacles came from Richards's sister Una who was 'wont to peer . . . somewhat like an Owl in boyhood days'. The celebrated postal order was 'a reincarnation of a cheque which a certain person constantly expected but which did not often materialise', the certain person being Richards's brother Alex whose literary submissions frequently resulted in rejection slips rather than the hoped-for cheques.

BUNTHORNE

Opera, *Patience* (1881, libretto by W. S. Gilbert,
music by A. S. Sullivan)

Oscar Wilde (1854–1900)

Bunthorne, the leading character in Gilbert and Sullivan's comic operetta which attacks the aesthetic movement, is given a splendid character which portrays an aesthetic young thing who 'walked down Piccadilly with a poppy or a lily in his medieval hand'.

This is a picture of Oscar Wilde, who was then leading quite a flamboyant life and was often seen in Piccadilly in what was perceived as fancy dress. The craze for an almost feminine sartorial elegance, offset with flowers and a touch of medievalism, was under vehement attack from such philistine quarters as *Punch*. *Patience* struck a chord in the British middle-class soul: 'Then a sentimental passion/of a vegetable fashion/must excite your languid spleen,/An attachment à la Plato/for a bashful young potato,/or not-too-French French bean!/ Though the philistines may jostle,/you will rank as an apostle/ in the high aesthetic band,/If you walk down Piccadilly/with a poppy or a lily/in your medieval hand./And everyone will say,/As you walk your flowery way,/"If he's content with a vegetable love/which would certainly not suit me,/Why, what a most particularly pure/young man this pure young man must be!"'

Wilde had an answer for it, of course. Anybody could have walked down Piccadilly like that, he claimed, but: 'The difficult thing to achieve was to make people believe that I had done it.' His lecture tour of the United States coincided with the staging of *Patience* in America. He lectured on the 'Principles of Aestheticism'. Tour and opera were mutually successful. Wilde had been a brilliant student at Oxford, and easily achieved fame as essayist, attender at 'first-nights', conversationalist and dandy. Wilde was the leader of the art-for-art's sake movement and a poseur with the intention of outraging the bourgeoisie; he triumphed in America and Paris. *The Picture of Dorian Gray* (1891) struck a slightly more sinister note, foreshadowing characteristically flamboyant decadence. He produced brilliant comedies in the 1890s and then his trial in 1895, following his association with Lord Alfred Douglas, brought to an end one of the most spectacular literary careers. He died in Paris.

Sir Harold Beauchamp

Several of Katherine Mansfield's stories are drawn from her experiences as a member of a prosperous New Zealand family. She was the third daughter of Harold and Annie Beauchamp who had two further children so that Kezia, as Katherine appears in the stories, was the child in the middle. In 1893, when Katherine was five, the family moved from Wellington to Karori and this shift from a town to a country house is the subject of Mansfield's most distinctive story, 'Prelude', so called because it was conceived as the prelude to a projected novel entitled *Karori*. 'Prelude' presents Kezia's father, Stanley Burnell, as a strong physical presence 'so delighted with his firm, obedient body that he hit himself on the chest and gave a loud "Ah"'. In 'At the Bay' Stanley is still endearingly energetic – 'a figure in a broad-striped bathing-suit [who] flung down the paddock, cleared the stile, rushed through the tussock grass into the hollow' – but in 'The Little Girl' the father-figure is a domestic tyrant.

Harold Beauchamp, Katherine Mansfield's father and the Stanley Burnell of the stories, was a successful businessman who became, in 1907, Chairman of the Bank of New Zealand. The following year he agreed to pay his daughter an allowance (initially of £100 a year) to enable her to live in England and pursue her literary ambitions. He provided her with an income for the rest of her life though he frequently disapproved of the company she kept and thought her husband John Middleton Murry was 'a perfect rotter'. For his services to the Dominion of New Zealand, Harold Beauchamp was knighted in 1923, the year his daughter died. Shortly after her death he bequeathed a large sum of money towards the encouragement of the arts in New Zealand, a demonstration of the sensitivity his wife noted in 'At the Bay'.

MADAM BUTTERFLY

Opera, *Madam Butterfly* (1900, music by Giacomo Puccini, libretto by Giacosa and Illica)

Japanese wife of Thomas Blake Glover

Lieutenant Pinkerton of the US navy goes through the formalities of marrying the young Japanese, Cio-Cio-San ('Madam Butterfly'). She has renounced her religion to marry him as she is really in love with him. She is convinced that he will return to her, not realizing that he embarked on the 'marriage' without sincerity, intending eventually to marry an American girl. Three years pass. The American Consul, Sharpless comes to tell Butterfly that Pinkerton is returning, and that he is now married to an American. Butterfly is so thrilled at hearing of his return that Sharpless has not the heart to tell her he is married. When Butterfly learns the truth she stabs herself just as Pinkerton enters, calling her name. The house is empty except for Butterfly's child by Pinkerton.

Puccini's tear-jerker was based on David Belasco's one-act melodrama (1900). This was a one-act version of a story he had read in an American magazine by J. L. Long. Long had borrowed the story from a romance by an officer in the French navy, Pierre Loti (real name L. M. Julien Viaud, 1850–1923). Loti's story was called *Madame Chrysanthème* (1887). It may have been in part autobiographical; at one time he had proposed it be subtitled *Le Mariage de Loti*. He spent a great deal of his professional life in the East and was at Nagasaki when Japan was first opened up to the trade with the West. He doubtless heard the story of the successful trader and gunrunner, Glover, who was based in Nagasaki after 1859 (six years after Perry and the American fleet came to Tokyo Bay) and who married a Japanese girl. Sharpless was probably based on Townsend Harris, American Consul at Shimoda, who arrived in 1856. In Nagasaki the house where Glover lived is now called Butterfly House, and features 'Cio-Cio-San's Garden' – bamboo fences, ponds, bridges, cherry trees and all. Harris's journals survive and record that he knew Glover well. Harris died in Japan in 1886, a year after Loti's story appeared.

ROY CALVERT

C. P. Snow, *Strangers and Brothers* (1940), *The Light and the Dark* (1947), *Time of Hope* (1949), *The Masters* (1951)

Charles Allberry (1912–43)

Roy Calvert, the tormented hero of C. P. Snow's novel *The Light and the Dark*, is an academic who lives his life at a ferocious pace. Lewis Eliot comes to Cambridge as a fellow in 1933 and has rooms near Calvert, so he is able to study the young man who is poised to achieve an international reputation as an orientalist. Eliot notices, however, that Calvert's nature threatens any long-term achievement: 'He was born with this melancholy; it was a curse of fate, like a hereditary disease. It shadowed all his life.' Eliot also admits that 'my friendship with him became the deepest of my life'. Calvert's linguistic work brings him to Berlin where he is briefly impressed by Nazism; when the war comes he becomes a bomber pilot and is reported missing after going on one of his regular raids.

Calvert's character is closely modelled on Charles Allberry who was the youngest fellow at Christ's College when Snow worked at Cambridge in the 1930s. Allberry was athletically accomplished as well as intellectually dazzling and was considered to be one of Cambridge's brightest men; at the age of twenty-seven he was already considered to be among the finest orientalists in Europe. As Germany became more menacing Allberry affected an indifference to it all, in deference to the German professor in Berlin who was his collaborator; when war was declared, though, he volunteered as a bomber pilot. On 3 April 1943 he left for a raid on Essen and was later reported missing. In a letter to his brother, C. P. Snow wrote 'His loss is harder to bear than that of any other of my friends would be. I learned from him more of the adventures and solitariness of the spirit than from anyone else; in some ways he was the most gifted & the most remarkable of all of us, and the most unhappy.'

TONY CAMONTE

Film, *Scarface* (1932, directed by Howard Hawks, written by Ben Hecht, based on the novel by Armitage Triall, starring Paul Muni)

Al Capone (1899–1947)

Scarface traces the rise and fall of a gangster, and resembles a Chicago gangland version of the story of the Borgias, including the very strong suggestion of incest between Tony Camonte and his sister. The script contained at least fifteen killings, including a brief reference to something akin to the St Valentine's Day massacre, the shooting of a character called Big Louie Costillo in a telephone booth and the attempted slaying of one Johnny Lovo. Tony has a taste for high culture and Italian opera. He goes to a performance of *Rain*. 'I like to see shows like that,' he says, 'Serious.' Half way through he is called out to see to the killing of a mobster rival. Afterwards he asks what happened in the play. A fellow gunman who stayed for the show says: 'She climbed back in the hay with the Army.' Tony Camonte retorts: 'That's-a fine, she's-a smarta girl.' There is something engagingly child-like about Camonte. When he picks up his first tommy gun he says: 'I'm going to write my name all over this town in big letters. Outta my way, I'm spittin'.' He is deeply jealously protective of his sister and resents to an unnatural degree any association with males on her part. He is finally tracked down and killed by the police after he has shot and killed a fellow gangster who had seduced his sister.

This is clearly the life story of Al Capone. Both gangsters had facial scars and the narrative of the film has several key parallel moments – the killing of Big Louie is the killing of Big Jim Colosimo and Johnny Lovo is really Johnny Torrio. Capone was called 'Scarface Al' in the tabloids of the day. Although all spoken references to the city of Chicago were removed from the soundtrack, the parallels were obvious, and to a well-established extent *Scarface* was made with Capone's cooperation. Capone worked originally for Colosimo, and when he was killed, for Johnny Torrio. Torrio, who himself was nearly killed, retired as Capone became Mr Big, controlling Chicago's vice, gambling and bootlegging on a syndicate basis, with the law rendered powerless by bribery. He was finally imprisoned for tax offences and died in 1947.

SISTER CARRIE

Theodore Dreiser, *Sister Carrie* (1900, unexpurgated edn
1981)

Emma Wilhelmina Dreiser

Theodore Dreiser's *Sister Carrie* shows the inexorable rise of
the heroine at the expense of the men in her life, particularly
Hurstwood who steals for her. Dreiser based the story on his
sister Em's adventures with, first, a Chicago architect, and then
L. A. Hopkins, a saloon-manager. Dreiser described Emma
Wilhelmina, his sister, as a 'showy, erotic' woman, 'one of the
most attractive of all the girls in our family'. She had none of
her brother's literary interests and, as such, she is introduced
with critical caution as Caroline in the novel: 'Caroline, or
"Sister Carrie" as she had been half affectionately termed by
the family, was possessed of a mind rudimentary in its power
of observation and analysis. Self-interest with her was high,
but not strong. It was nevertheless her guiding characteristic.
Warm with the fancies of youth, pretty with the insipid
prettiness of the formative period, possessed of a figure which
tended towards eventual shapeliness and an eye alight with
certain native intelligence, she was a fair example of the middle
American class – two generations removed from the emigrant.
Books were beyond her interest – knowledge a sealed book.'

When Em met L. A. Hopkins in Chicago they became lovers
and were found in bed by a detective acting on behalf of
Hopkins's wife. In 1886 Hopkins took some three thousand
dollars from the safe of the saloon he managed and eloped with
Em to Montreal. Eventually they came to New York where
fact parted from fiction. Hopkins set up in style on the proceeds
of his corrupt connections with local government; however,
when Dreiser joined Em and Hopkins in 1894 as a boarder, the
couple were far from happy. Hopkins was given to bouts of
violence and once suggested to Em that they rent out their
rooms for prostitution. Dreiser observed all this and then
advised his sister to leave Hopkins, which she did.

EDWARD CASAUBON
George Eliot, *Middlemarch* (1872)

Dr Robert Henry Brabant

Dorothea Brooke, the heroine of George Eliot's *Middlemarch*, has an exaggerated idea of duty and feels that the 'really delightful marriage must be that where your husband was a sort of father, and could teach you even Hebrew, if you wished it'. Her marital philosophy is put to a severe test when she marries the Revd Edward Casaubon, a man thirty years her senior. Casaubon is soon revealed as a tiresome pedant whose abiding interest is his projected (but never completed) work of religious scholarship: 'Mr Casaubon, too, was the centre of his own world [for] he was liable to think that others were providentially made for him, and especially to consider them in the light of their fitness for the author of a *Key to all Mythologies*.' Only after his death can Dorothea resume her own life.

In 1843 Mary Ann Evans (George Eliot) was a bridesmaid at the wedding of her friends Charles Hennell and Elizabeth Rebecca Brabant – who had been nicknamed Rufa in some verses by Coleridge, once her father's patient. Dr Robert Henry Brabant considered himself to be a great scholar, despite his lack of actual scholarship, and claimed to be writing a definitive work dealing with the supernatural aspects of Christianity. After Rufa's wedding Dr Brabant took Mary Ann home with him to Devizes where she was to assist him in his literary labours. He called her Deutera, his second daughter, and she wrote to her friend Cara Bray to say 'I am in a little heaven here, Dr Brabant being its archangel. . . . We read and walk and talk together, and I am never weary of his company.' However the arrangement was not to the liking of Dr Brabant's blind wife and her sister Susan Hughes pressurized Mary Ann into returning to Coventry after only two weeks. Mary Ann was mortified and never forgave the pedant who promised so much yet constantly failed to deliver.

LADY CASTLEWOOD
William Makepeace Thackeray, *The History of Henry Esmond*
(1852)

Jane Brookfield (1821–95)

When young Harry Esmond, the hero of Thackeray's *The History of Henry Esmond*, first sees Rachel, Lady Castlewood – the woman he is eventually to marry – he is enchanted. As Thackeray writes 'The instinct which led Henry Esmond to admire and love the gracious person, the fair apparition of whose beauty and kindness had so moved him when he first beheld her, became soon a devoted affection and passion of gratitude, which entirely filled his young heart. . . . There seemed, as the boy thought, in every look or gesture of this fair creature, an angelical softness and bright pity – in motion or repose she seemed gracious alike; the tone of her voice, though she uttered words ever so trivial, gave him a pleasure that amounted almost to anguish.'

Thackeray himself conceived such a passion for Jane Brookfield, wife of his friend William Henry Brookfield, an eccentric and theologically daring preacher. Brookfield's lofty indifference to his wife's sensitivity offended Thackeray who offered Jane his devotion – as he demonstrated by portraying her first as Amelia in *Vanity Fair* (1848) then as Lady Castlewood. Thackeray called on Jane frequently, to the consternation of Brookfield, and believed she was in love with him. Then in 1849 he was shocked to learn that Jane was pregnant – by her husband. Jane had encouraged Thackeray to assume that her marriage was a loveless ordeal so he was consumed by jealousy at the thought of Brookfield's intimacy with his wife. In 1851 Thackeray told Brookfield what he thought of him and his treatment of his wife; the result was an angry scene leading to a break between the Brookfields and the celebrated author. Thackeray admitted 'I have loved his wife too much, to be able to bear to see her belong even to her husband any more – that's the truth.'

ANNE CATHERICK, THE WOMAN IN WHITE

Wilkie Collins, *The Woman in White* (1860)

The case of the **Marquise de Douhault** (1787)

The opening of *The Woman in White* is supposed to be based on Wilkie Collins's own experiences. Out walking one evening he heard a young woman scream. Then he saw a female figure, dressed in flowing white, running from a large house. He ran to her aid and discovered from her own account that she had been held a prisoner there under hypnotism for several years. She became Collins's mistress and he used her story as the basis of his classic thriller, which opens in the dead of night as a stranger, walking alone down a moonlit road, is touched suddenly on the shoulder by 'a solitary woman, dressed from head to foot in white'. Thus is the life of Walter Hartright, a drawing master, changed for ever. The young woman appears to be demented and to have escaped from an asylum. Her name is Anne Catherick. She bears a strong resemblance to Laura Fairlie, daughter of Hartright's employer. Hartright falls in love with Laura, and leaves the country in despair when she marries Sir Perceval Glyde, of Blackwater Park. Glyde is really after the Fairlie family fortunes, and has planned to get Laura to sign a document in which she surrenders her wealth to him, and then to get her confined to the asylum as Anne Catherick, who has died in the meantime. When Anne dies she is to be buried as Lady Glyde and the wicked Sir Perceval will thus gain her wealth. Glyde's plot is revealed by the hero, and it is even discovered that the villain has no right to the title as he was born out of wedlock. He dies in a fire at the church where he is attempting to forge evidence by tampering with the parish register.

Wilkie Collins used as the outline for this plot the real-life case of the Marquise de Douhault. She came to Paris in 1787 to take the necessary legal steps to regain from her brother, a shifty and dishonest type, properties which were hers by right, as they had been left to her by her father. Her brother had her kidnapped, and kept her drugged and confined for years, until she managed to smuggle out a letter to friends which eventually effected her release and the exposure of her brother's villainy.

CHARLIE
John Le Carré, *The Little Drummer Girl* (1983)

Charlotte Cornwell

John Le Carré's *The Little Drummer Girl* opens explosively with the impact of a Palestinian terrorist bomb-attack on Jews in Germany. As a counter-terrorist move Israeli intelligence decides to infiltrate a Palestinian group by using a double agent. The girl they choose for this work, Charlie, is an actress who naturally sees herself as a heroine in search of a strong, dramatic political role: 'Her name was actually Charmain but she was known to everyone as "Charlie", and often as "Charlie the Red" in deference to the colour of her hair and to her somewhat crazy radical stances, which were her way of caring for the world and coming to grips with its injustices. . . . Charlie was not the prettiest of the girls, by any means, though her sexuality shone through, as did her incurable goodwill, which was never quite concealed by her posturing.' Recruited by the Israelis she proves to be an effective double agent though at the end of the book she has cause to dwell on the implications of her role-playing.

Le Carré based the character on his sister Charlotte Cornwell, the Shakespearean actress, who acknowledges that 'politically there are great similarities. When I was younger I was lured towards several extreme left-wing groups of people. I was desperate to find a place where I could hang [my beliefs and ideals] on a hook somewhere.' Le Carré recalls seeing his sister, when touring with the Royal Shakespeare Company, performing at the Camborne sports centre: 'It was pouring with rain, the most unbelievable noise on the roof. Charlotte was really having to belt it out and I thought she was very good but she was over the top, I mean she was booming in order to defeat the rain. It was actually the moment when I thought, yes, I'll have Charlotte for my character, at least as the raw material.'

COUNTESS OF CHELL
Arnold Bennett *The Card* (1911)

Duchess of Sutherland (1851–1913)

One of Denry Machin's funniest exploits is to get himself invited, while still a humble solicitor's clerk, to the ball given by the Countess of Chell (see DENRY MACHIN). The Countess is known locally as 'Interfering Iris' for very good reasons; she is a local do-gooder and busybody.

Bennett based her on a local Hanley celebrity, the Duchess of Sutherland, known as 'Meddlesome Millie'. She took a great interest in affairs of the day, and was forever opening bazaars, church fetes, bring-and-buy sales and fund-raising functions for good causes. She spoke at school prize-givings, lectured on Benjamin Constant and infant mortality, lead poisoning in the pottery trade (a matter of considerable local interest in the pottery towns!) and expressed her concern at the widespread incidence of phthisis in the area and advocated the teaching of Gaelic. She had a finger in every pie and was involved in every fad and passing fashion.

Bennett was later to suffer the considerable personal embarrassment, perhaps well-deserved, of meeting the Duchess of Sutherland at a dinner in London. The identification of the Countess of Chell with the Duchess of Sutherland was well-established and the Lady herself was aware of it. She later returned to France and Arnold Bennett wrote to her there, saying he was: 'admiring, apologetic, and unrepentant'. She was a well-known eccentric and Frank Harris records an anecdote about her complaining in public that Queen Victoria's English syntax had been ruined by the German influence of her husband, and this unfortunate awkwardness rendered royal messages 'not being so pure as they used to be'. Arthur Balfour, to whom the complaint was made, bravely answered: 'I had nothing to do with it. . . . It doesn't matter much.' He was Prime Minister at the time.

LORD CHILTERN
Anthony Trollope, *Phineas Finn* (1869)

Thomas Pitt, Second Baron Camelford
(1775–1804)

When Phineas goes to London and leaves Mary Flood Jones, he is soon deeply attracted by Lady Laura Standish, who is a very beautiful young woman who takes to him also. She has a brother, younger than her, Lord Chiltern. These two are 'related to almost everybody who was anybody among the high Whigs'. When Phineas first notices him he sees: 'something in the countenance of the man which struck him almost with dread, something approaching ferocity'. Laura is very attached to her brother, saying that: 'he is not half so bad as people say he is. In many ways he is very good – very good. And he is very clever.... I think he loves me.' But Lord Chiltern is a violent character and drinks a great deal. He brings disgrace upon his family: 'He had fallen through his violence into some terrible misfortune at Paris, had been brought before a public judge, and his name and his infamy had been made notorious in every newspaper' in Paris and London. Chiltern grows very jealous of Finn's association with Violet Effingham, whom he had wooed without success, and he challenges Finn to a duel. It is fought in Belgium. Chiltern is killed. A radical newspaper publishes an account of the incident, attacking the principals, and commenting: 'There were old stories afloat . . . of what in a former century had been done by Lord Mohuns and Mr. Bests; but now, in 186–', etc. Trollope's reference is clearly to Lord Camelford, and there are several important clues. The first is the reference to Mr Best. Camelford was shot and killed by Best in a duel of honour, fought over the reputation of one Fanny Loveden, in 1804. The second clue is the reference to Lord Mohun. Mohun was killed in a duel in 1712, and he was the last owner of Bocconnoc, which was later bought by Thomas Pitt, Lord Camelford's illustrious ancestor. Thomas Pitt, second Baron Camelford, had a notorious reputation for violence and eccentric behaviour. While in the navy he challenged his commander to a duel, and shot and killed a fellow officer in a dispute over seniority. Anthony Trollope may have got the story of Camelford from his sister, Anne Pitt, Lady Grenville, who died in 1864.

Henrietta, Countess of Suffolk (1681–1767)

The story of Daphnis and Chloe is one of the most beloved of all pastoral romances. It is an ancient Greek tale of love. Two infants are discovered by Lamon and Dryas, who are shepherds of Mitylene. They are brought up to tend sheep and goats, and Daphnis and Chloe are constant and loyal companions whose virtue and affection serve as a model for all. It is eventually discovered that they are really the children of wealthy parents, and they are destined to live happily ever after.

Pope's treatment of this charming theme is somewhat mocking, as Chloe is presented as a shallow and cold young woman, who can neither really give nor receive love, as she totally lacks heart: 'She, while her lover pants upon her breast,/Can mark the figure on an Indian chest;/And when she sees her friend in deep despair,/Observes how much a chintz exceeds mohair. . . . Safe is your secret still in Chloe's ear;/But none of Chloe's shall you ever hear.'

This is Henrietta Howard, Countess of Suffolk, who was the mistress of George II. She was the daughter of Sir Henry Hobart, and married Charles Howard, who became the Ninth Earl of Suffolk, and they lived at Hanover. When George I came to England, she became woman-of-the-bedchamber to the Princess of Wales, and consequently came into contact with George II. Her house in Marble Hill, Twickenham, was the meeting place of the most distinguished company of the day, including Pope, Arbuthnot and Swift. She was a celebrated beauty and was admired by Charles, Third Earl of Peterborough (1658–1735) a patron of letters and science, general, diplomat and admiral. As mistress of George II she was much courted because of the power it was believed she wielded. She became Countess in 1731 and retired from court in 1734. In 1735 she married the Hon George Berkeley. This character, and that of Philomède (Henrietta, Duchess of Marlborough) were suppressed until later editions of the *Moral Essays*.

ANNA CHRISTIE
Eugene O'Neill, *Anna Christie* (1921)

Marie

Eugene O'Neill's *Anna Christie* arranges, in an affirmative manner, the bits and pieces in the life of a so-called fallen woman. Anna, 'tall, blonde, fully-developed [and] handsome after a large, Viking-daughter fashion' turns up in New York in search of her father, Christopher Christopherson, captain of a coal barge. When he last saw Anna, fifteen years before, she was a child in Sweden and he is pleased she has been raised on a Minnesotan farm away from 'dat ole davil sea'. As the heroine explains, to Marthy Owen but not to her father, she has had an unfortunately eventful life. Seduced at the age of sixteen she ran away from the farm to find work as a nursemaid; subsequently she became a prostitute and, after a raid on the brothel, received a prison sentence. After she finds her father she renews her life on his barge and ends the play in the arms of Mat Burke, an Irish stoker.

The story is a dramatic version of the life of Marie, mistress of O'Neill's closest drinking-friend Terry Carlin (the original of Larry Slade in *The Iceman Cometh*). Marie was a nursemaid before she took to prostitution and was in despair when rescued and restored by Terry. After living with him she left to find herself in the hills of California and a letter she wrote provided O'Neill with the basis for Anna's sense of euphoria. 'I am intoxicated by all this beauty,' wrote Marie to Terry, 'and love the very air and earth. . . . I feel newborn and free. The air is scented with balsam and bay, and a pure crystal stream flows through this valley between two hills covered with giant redwood trees. . . . At night I sleep as I have never slept – a deep dreamless slumber. I awake to a cold plunge in the stream. Oh, it just suits me! . . . Everything in the past is dead . . . I have become happy, healthy, and free, free without hardness . . . I will now lave myself with the pure crystal waters and make myself clean again, and then look on the sun once more.'

CHRISTOPHER ROBIN

A. A. Milne, *When We Were Very Young* (1924), *Winnie the Pooh* (1926), *Now We Are Six* (1927), *The House at Pooh Corner* (1928)

Christopher Milne (born 1920)

The name Christopher Robin is immortalized in the poems A. A. Milne assembled in *When We Were Very Young* and its sequel *Now We Are Six*, and in the two books of prose that celebrate Christopher's adventures with 'a Bear of Very Little Brain' – *Winnie the Pooh* and *The House at Pooh Corner*. In 'Buckingham Palace' there is spectacle for 'They're changing guard at Buckingham Palace – /Christopher Robin went down with Alice' and in 'Vespers' there is pathos in 'Hush! Hush! Whisper who dares!/Christopher Robin is saying his prayers.'

Christopher Robin is Milne's son Christopher Robin Milne (1920–   ). In 1925 A. A. Milne bought Cotchford Farm, Sussex, which provided the setting for the Pooh books. Pooh was Christopher's teddy bear; Christopher would invent adventures for Pooh and his father would develop them as stories. The illustrator E. H. Shepard studied the teddy bear before making his first Pooh drawings. Shepard's drawings of Christopher Robin are an accurate portrayal of Christopher Milne as a boy, and in his autobiography *The Enchanted Places* (1974) Christopher explained his appearance: 'I suspect that, with my golden tresses, I reminded my mother of the girl she had always wanted to have. And I would have reminded my father of the boy with long, flaxen hair he once had been.' Later in life Christopher Milne resented the little-boy image associated with him and felt that 'Christopher Robin was . . . a sore place that looked as if it would never heal up.' Occasionally he thought his father 'had filched from me my good name and had left me with nothing but the empty fame of being his son'. However he learned to live with the problem and in 1951 opened a bookshop in Dartmouth where he is still approached by visitors wishing to shake hands with the original Christopher Robin who still 'fills me with acute embarrassment'.

CLARENCE, EARL OF EMSWORTH

P. G. Wodehouse, *Summer Lightning* (1929), *Blandings Castle* (1935), *A Pelican at Blandings* (1969), etc

Spencer Compton Cavendish, Marquess of Hartington and Eighth Duke of Devonshire (1833–1908)

Lord Emsworth, leading character in the Blandings Castle stories of P. G. Wodehouse, and proud owner of the Empress of Blandings – the greatest prize pig in English fiction, has many interesting parallels with the Eighth Duke of Devonshire.

He was the eldest son of the Seventh Duke of Devonshire and was awarded his MA at Cambridge in 1854. Three years later he was elected Liberal MP for North Lancashire. He travelled to the United States, where he met President Lincoln and held various government positions including Under Secretary at the War Office, Postmaster General, Chief Secretary for Ireland, Secretary of State for India, and with Joseph Chamberlain he founded the Liberal-Unionist party. He served under Gladstone, Lord Russell and Lord Salisbury and three times refused the premiership himself. He was, in turn, MP for North Lancashire, the Radnor boroughs, North-East Lancashire and Rossdale. When Victoria congratulated him on his appointment as Minister for War he replied that there would not be much for him to do, and the Queen noted in her diary on 6 May 1885 that he was 'rather amusing about Britain's friendlessness'. He presided over the Cabinet when the decision was made to send Gordon to Khartoum. Chamberlain called him 'Rip Van Winkle'. He was a keen sportsman, generous landlord and public-spirited benefactor. He entertained King Edward VII frequently, though on one occasion he invited him to dinner and then forgot and went out to dine at the Turf Club. The King arrived at Devonshire House to find his host absent. Devonshire was also known to walk past his Cabinet colleagues so absent-mindedly that he did not seem to recognize them. When made Grand Commander of the Victorian Order he complained that the award would 'only complicate his dressing'. He was late for Edward VII's coronation. He genuinely preferred baggy old clothes and casuals to formal attire, notoriously neglected his guests and avoided 'bores'. Once when a fellow peer was going on in the Chamber about 'the greatest moment in his life' Devonshire opined: 'My greatest moment was when my pig won first prize at Skipton Fair.' Was this a reference to the Empress of Blandings?

COMUS

John Milton, *Comus, A Masque, presented at Ludlow Castle, 1634, before the Earl of Bridgewater, Lord President of Wales*

James Touchet, Second Earl of Castlehaven
(executed 1631)

Comus was written to celebrate the Earl of Bridgewater's entry to the presidency of Wales. The name 'Comus' does not appear in the title of the first three printed editions. The name is taken from one of the leading characters in the masque, Comus, a pagan god. Comus is an invention of Milton's, and is the son of Bacchus and Circe. Comus waylays travellers and attempts to enchant them with a magic drink which changes their faces to those of beasts. A lady is parted from her two brothers one night in the forest and is discovered by Comus. He is disguised as a shepherd. She allows herself to be led off to his cottage. Her brothers, aided by the good Attendant Spirit, find her in time. Comus is pressing an enchanted cup upon her, but her goodness and purity enable her to resist. But in part Comus's evil powers are effective, as she cannot move from the enchanted chair: 'Beauty is natures coyn, must not be hoorded,/But must be currant, and the good thereof/Consists in mutual and partak'n bliss'. She is only finally freed by the powers of Sabrina, goddess of the River Severn.

Lord Castlehaven was executed for abominable crimes in 1631, after being exposed by his eldest son, James Touchet (1617–84) who became Third Earl of Castlehaven. The Touchet family were kin of the Bridgewaters, for whom *Comus* was written. Lady Alice Bridgewater played the Lady in the original production. She was a cousin of a girl who had suffered horribly at the hands of her stepfather, the Second Earl of Castlehaven. The Castlehaven scandal was widely discussed at the time, especially as the exposure of the Earl by his eldest son was such a dramatic feature of the case. Thus Lady Alice Egerton, daughter of the Earl of Bridgewater, is the original of the Lady in Milton's *Comus*: 'Let us fly this cursed place,/Lest the Sorcerer us entice/With some other new device', would strike home with fearful relevance to those who knew about the dreadful Castlehaven scandal.

HARRY CONINGSBY
Benjamin Disraeli, *Coningsby* (1844)

George Augustus Frederick Percy Sydney Smythe, Seventh Viscount Strangford and Second Baron Penshurst (1818–57)

Harry Coningsby is the young hero whose life story holds together the various threads of interest in *Coningsby* – Disraeli's belief in the social duties and responsibilities of the aristocracy, the need to return to the chivalrous values of the past, the empty nature of Peelite Conservatism and the evils of the factory system. Harry stands for the ideals of the young generation. The name 'Coningsby' was probably suggested to Disraeli by his reading of Sir Philip Sidney. Sidney was a central influence in Disraeli's thinking. Sir Thomas Coningsby was a companion of Sidney's.

Harry Coningsby's countenance is described as: 'radiant with health and the lustre of innocence. . . . The expression of his deep blue eyes was serious . . . the face was one that would never have passed unobserved. His short upper lip indicated a good breed; and his chestnut curls clustered over his open brow.' We follow his career through Eton and Cambridge, his marriage with Edith, daughter of Oswald Millbank, a rich manufacturer, the disinheritance by his aristocratic grandfather, Lord Monmouth (see LORD MONMOUTH), and a career in the law. He is finally elected an MP at Darlford, Millbank's constituency. We are told the exact date of Coningsby's birth, 1818, the year Lord Strangford was born. There is also the important link with the Sidneys of Penshurst.

Strangford went to Eton and St John's College, Cambridge and wrote promising verse. He was an MA *jure natalium* in 1840, and MP for Canterbury and a leading member of Disraeli's Young England party. He supported Peel in the Corn Law issue and broke with Disraeli, who remained a protectionist, but this was after *Coningsby* was published. His wife said of him: 'He loved to recall the grandeur of the ancient nobility . . . to sing the days of chivalry . . . and together with his friend, Lord John Manners, he dreamed of a powerful aristocracy and an almsgiving church.' Young England personified.

CONRAD
Lord Byron, *The Corsair* (1814)

Jean Lafitte (1780–1826)

Conrad is the pirate chief hero of Byron's poem. In a note to the 1815 edition the poet admitted that he had in mind Jean Lafitte, the French privateer, whose notorious exploits against the British and Spanish would have been daily reading in contemporary newspapers. There are strong parallels between Lafitte's devil-may-care character and the Byronic hero – 'there was a laughing Devil in his sneer' – as well as similarities in the pirate colony of Barataria run by Lafitte, and Conrad's pirate community on the Aegean island described by Byron.

Conrad has only one virtue – chivalry – but many vices. He learns that Seyd, the Turkish Pasha, is preparing to attack his Aegean community, and resolves to strike the first blow. Disguised as a Dervish, and having bidden farewell to his beloved Medora, he gains access to Seyd by claiming that he himself has recently escaped the pirates. His plot misfires as Conrad's men prematurely fire on the Pasha's ships. Conrad is wounded and captured but helped by Gulnare, the Pasha's leading slave-girl, who stabs Seyd in his sleep. The two then escape although Conrad is repulsed by Gulnare's violent act. He returns to his pirate island to find that Medora had died of grief, believing him slain. Conrad's adventures are continued in the sequel (see LARA).

Lafitte's early career is obscure until his exploits around New Orleans made him famous during the war of 1812. He and his privateers lived in a pirate colony on the Baratarian Gulf, off the coast of Louisiana. They earned their living by preying on Spanish and other vessels and trading in New Orleans. Efforts to destroy them failed, including one mounted by the US Navy commanded by Commodore Patterson. The Baratarian Gulf was strategically important in giving access to New Orleans and in 1814 the British offered Laffite £30,000 and a commission in the Royal Navy to cooperate against the US. Lafitte handed over these papers to the US authorities in exchange for a general pardon. His offer of help against the British was accepted by Andrew Jackson and the privateers played a significant part in the defeat of the British. Their pardon was proclaimed by President Madison. He continued to operate from a base in Texas until the US government was pursuaded to act against him. He then left with his best ship, the *Pride*.

VITTORIA COROMBONA

John Webster, *The White Divel* (1608)

Vittoria Accoramboni (1557–85)

Webster's tragedy, *The White Divel*, is a wild, thrilling and rhetorical drama of adultery, murder, bloodshed and betrayal, which has the sound and fury of early Verdi opera. The Duke of Brachiano is married to Isabella, who is the sister of the Duke of Florence. He is tired of her and lusts after Vittoria, who is already married to Camillo. Vittoria's brother, Flamineo, helps Brachiano in his sister's seduction, and assists in the killing of her husband, Camillo. In the meantime, Brachiano gets Isabella poisoned. Vittoria is accused of adultery and murder and sentenced to be confined. Her escape is effected and she is married to Brachiano. Flamineo and his brother, the virtuous young Marcello, quarrel, and Flamineo kills him. Isabella's brother, the Duke of Florence, avenges the death of his sister by poisoning Brachiano. Lodovico and Gasparo, dependants of the Duke of Florence, finally kill Vittoria and Flamineo. A significant aspect of the play's great fascination is Webster's exploitation of the tension which exists between the heroine's fair-seeming exterior and the black wickedness of which she is the centre. Monticelso, the cardinal, at her trial says: 'You see, my lords, what goodly fruits she seems;/Yet like those apples travellers report/To grow where Sodom and Gomorrah stood,/I will but touch her, and you straight shall see/She'll fall to soot and ashes.'

The real Vittoria Accoramboni was also famous for her great beauty and the violence and tragedy of her life. She was born in Rome and married Francesco Peretti in 1573. He was the nephew of Cardinal Montalto, who was expected to become Pope. She was admired by many men, in particular by Orsini, Duke of Bracciano. Her brother Marcello, hoping to see his sister married to Bracciano, had Peretti murdered in 1581. Bracciano and Vittoria were then married. Orsini was already suspected of murdering Vittoria's husband, as his name was associated in the murder of his first wife, Isabella de Medici. Vittoria was imprisoned and there was pressure to have the marriage annulled. In 1585 Cardinal Montalto became Pope and was determined to have vengeance on Bracciano and Vittoria for the death of Francesco Peretti, his nephew. They fled to Salo, where Bracciano died. Here Vittoria was put to death in December 1585 by Lodovico Orsini, a relation of Bracciano, who hoped to gain from the division of the property. This terrible story was also used by Ludwig Tieck in his novel *Vittoria Accoramboni* (1840).

Henry Fauntleroy (1785–1824)

Bulwer Lytton's splendid melodrama *The Disowned* is, on the surface at least, the story of the young hero – Clinton L'Estrange – who is rejected by his father, Lord Ulswater. Ulswater believes that the boy is not really his son. In the end, father and son are reconciled, and Clinton's legitimacy established. But the most fascinating character in the book is the villain, Richard Crauford, swindler, forger and master of disguise. He nearly escapes justice and flees to Paris, under the successfully assumed identity of the Revd Dr Stapyton. Immediately before his arrest we find him at an inn in Dover, eating and drinking like a true *gourmand*, unconscious of the fact that the detective is on his tail: 'A pleasant trip to France!' he cries, filling a bumper, 'That's the land for hearts like ours . . . we will leave our wives behind us, and take, with a new country, and new names, a new lease of life. What will it signify to men making love at Paris what fools say of them in London? Another bumper . . . a bumper to the girls!' But, his triumphs are over: 'On the very day on which the patent for his peerage was to have been made out – on the very day on which he had afterwards calculated on reaching Paris – on that very day was Mr Richard Crauford lodged in Newgate, fully committed for a trial of life and death.' He is brilliant at his trial, having become a figure of public admiration and fame, he fully exploits these qualities, and the whole audience dissolve into tears. It is to no avail, he is sentenced to death and executed.

Crauford is based on the banker and forger Henry Fauntleroy. He was a partner in his father's bank, Marsh, Sibbald and Company in London, from 1807 until his arrest in 1824. He was accused of fraudulently selling stock in 1820 and for forging the trustees' signatures to a power of attorney. He defended his actions by claiming they were motivated by his desire to maintain the credit of the banking house. Many petitions were signed to gain him clemency, but Fauntleroy was executed in 1824.

ROBINSON CRUSOE

Daniel Defoe, *The Life and Strange Surprising Adventures of
Robinson Crusoe* (1719), *The Farther Adventures of Robinson
Crusoe* (1719)

Alexander Selkirk (1676–1721)

Defoe's masterpiece describes, to cite the full title of the first
part of the novel published on 25 April 1719, 'The Life and
Strange Surprising Adventures of Robinson Crusoe of York,
Mariner.' Defoe narrates the book in the first person and comes
alive as the resourceful young sailor cast away on an island in
the Caribbean Sea where he survives thanks to his ingenuity
and the devotion of 'My man Friday'.

The extraordinary narrative was based on the life of Alexander
Selkirk, a Scotsman from Largo in Fife. As sailing master of
the *Cinque Ports* galley, Selkirk sailed from the Downs to
Brazil in 1703. When the captain of the *Cinque Ports* died in
Brazil he was replaced by Thomas Stradling whose authority
was undermined by Selkirk's hostility. After many quarrels
Selkirk was, at his own request, put ashore in September 1704
on the island of Juan Fernandez where he lived, alone, for more
than four years. Captain Woodes Rogers anchored the *Duke*
off the island on 2 February 1709 and took Selkirk aboard as
mate before returning to England.

Later Rogers published his journal, *A Cruizing Voyage round
the World* (1712), and described Selkirk's life on the island:
'After he had conquered his melancholy, he diverted himself
sometimes with cutting his name on the trees, and the time of
his being left, and his continuance there . . . he came, at last, to
conquer all the inconveniences of his solitude, and to be very
easy.' From this principal source Defoe built up his adventure
which is full of brilliantly inventive touches and so Selkirk the
celebrity became Crusoe the hero of a classic fiction.

William Cowper was also inspired by the story of Selkirk and
wrote 'Verses Supposed to be Written by Alexander Selkirk'
beginning 'I am monarch of all I survey,/My right there is
none to dispute.'

Chief Inspector Jonathan Whicher

The Moonstone is the precious diamond which had once stood in the forehead of a Hindu moon-god. It has passed into the possession of Miss Verinder on her eighteenth birthday as a result of the disposition of its original possessor, John Herncastle, an English officer serving at Seringapatam. The diamond mysteriously disappears the same night. It has been taken by Franklin Blake, her lover, while in an opium trance. Three Indian jugglers, recently seen in the vicinity, are suspected. The villain, Godfrey Ablewhite, who is Blake's rival for Miss Verinder's love, manages to gain the Moonstone. He is murdered in mysterious circumstances, while engaged in a contest of cunning with the three Indians. The novel is complicated by the use of several differing points of view in the narration, and by the fact that Blake does not realize what he has done while in a trance. Suspicion is thrown on various innocent people in the household and the whole complication is finally resolved by the brilliant detective work of Sergeant Cuff.

Cuff is based on Jonathan Whicher, who had become famous as a result of his solving of the Roadhill House mystery, in Wiltshire in 1860. The three-year-old son of Samuel Kent was found murdered in the outside privy at Roadhill House and Whicher when called in to solve the crime concluded that it must have been committed by someone in the household. His theory was based on the fact that no bloodstained garment was found, yet the murderer must have been stained with the crime which was a very bloody one. A nightdress belonging to Constance Kent, the boy's sister, aged sixteen, was missing. Constance Kent later confessed to the crime in July 1865, was found guilty and sentenced to life imprisonment. She was released in 1885. She stated that she had committed the murder of the child on her own and 'unaided'. What made Whicher's reputation was the fact that he had suspected Constance Kent initially on the basis of the missing bloodstained garment, and had applied for a warrant to have her arrested as early as 19 July 1860, but the girl was discharged for lack of evidence. Bungling by the local police had allowed the bloodstained nightdress to be disposed of. Early in the case Whicher and his theories were ridiculed but the subsequent confession and trial fully vindicated him. Collins makes use of the missing garment incident and portrays Whicher as Cuff.

ADOLPHUS CUSINS
George Bernard Shaw, *Major Barbara* (1905)

Gilbert Murray (1866–1957)

Adolphus Cusins, engaged to the heroine of Shaw's *Major Barbara*, ends the play by changing his name to Andrew Undershaft and, as befits a foundling, inheriting a hugely profitable armaments business from Barbara's father. Throughout the play Adolphus, a professor of Greek, argues morality with Undershaft who calls him 'Euripides'. Shaw describes Adolphus in a typically precise stage-direction: 'His sense of humour is intellectual and subtle, and is complicated by an appalling temper. The lifelong struggle of a benevolent temperament and a high conscience against impulses of inhuman ridicule and fierce impatience has set up a chronic strain which has visibly wrecked his constitution. He is a most implacable, determined, tenacious, intolerant person who by mere force of character presents himself as – and indeed actually is – considerate, gentle, explanatory, even mild and apologetic, capable possibly of murder, but not of cruelty or coarseness.'

Shaw created Cusins as a caricature of his friend Gilbert Murray who was something of an irascible pedagogue. Murray was highly respected as a professor of Greek (in the universities of Glasgow and Oxford) who produced scholarly editions of the Greek classics. More influentially, and controversially, he produced popular verse translations of the tragedies of Sophocles, Aeschylus and Euripides. Shaw admired Murray's erudition and political tenacity and has Cusins declare at the end of the play: 'As a teacher of Greek I gave the intellectual man weapons against the common man. I now want to give the common man weapons against the intellectual man.'

Murray's political interests led him to become Chairman of the League of Nations Union from 1923 to 1938 and to publish books on pacifism. Although best known for his advocacy of Euripides his international reputation was broadly based and in 1926 he was Professor of Poetry at Harvard.

Lord Byron (1788–1824)

Mr Cypress calls at Nightmare Abbey to bid farewell to Scythrop Glowry, before leaving the country. They had been friends since college days and he is now a famous poet. He is described as 'a lacerated spirit' – brooding, melancholy, disillusioned, slightly Satanic with a strong affection for the Greek world: 'The mind is restless,' he says, 'and must persist in seeking, though to find is to be disappointed. Do you feel no aspirations towards the countries of Socrates and Cicero? No wish to wander among the venerable remains of the greatness that has passed for ever?' He affects the fashionable pessimism of the time: 'I have no hope for myself or for others. Our life is a false nature; it is not in the harmony of things; it is all-blasting upas, whose root is earth, and whose leaves are the skies which rain their poison dews upon mankind. We wither from our youth; we gasp with unslaked thirst for unattainable good; lured from the first to the last by phantoms – love, fame, ambition, avarice – all idle, and all ill – one meteor of many names, that vanishes in the smoke of death.'

This is a comically exaggerated picture of Byron, in Wordsworth's phrase, 'the mocking bird of our Parnassian ornithology'. It contains direct quotation from Byron's *Childe Harold*, which had made him famous throughout the land ('I awoke one morning and found myself famous' he wrote after the poem first appeared).

Byron created an alien and mysterious persona – gloomy, passionate, and world weary. He was born in London and educated at Aberdeen, he succeeded to the title and estates in 1798, was sent to Harrow and Cambridge, where he lived wildly and extravagantly. He travelled widely in Europe and achieved fame as satirist and poet. But it was *Childe Harold* which put before the public that personality forever associated with him. He separated from Lady Byron and left England, never to return, in 1816. He lived in Italy and died fighting with Greek insurgents against the Turks in 1824.

MRS DALLOWAY
Virginia Woolf, *The Voyage Out* (1915),
Mrs Dalloway (1925)

Kitty Maxse (1867–1922)

Virginia Woolf's novel *Mrs Dalloway* was born when Kitty
Maxse died after a fall at her London home. In her diary for 8
October 1922 Virginia wrote about 'visualising her – her
white hair – pink cheeks – how she sat upright – her voice –
with its characteristic tones [and] her earrings, her gaiety, yet
melancholy; her smartness: her tears, which stayed on her
cheek.' Six days later she wrote that 'Mrs Dalloway has
branched into a book'.

In the novel, Clarissa is preparing for an evening party at her
home when a series of coincidences brings back vivid memories of her life before her marriage to Richard Dalloway, MP.
Whereas the past unfolds dynamically, her present life seems
devoid of surprises: 'She had the oddest sense of being herself
invisible [making] this astonishing and rather solemn progress
with the rest of them, up Bond Street, this being Mrs Dalloway; not even Clarissa any more; this being Mrs Richard
Dalloway.'

Virginia's mother Julia Stephen was friendly with Kitty's
mother and Julia was responsible, in 1890, for matching Kitty
in marriage with Leopold Maxse, owner-editor of *The National Review*. After Julia's death, in 1895, Kitty took a maternal
interest in Virginia and her sister Vanessa and helped to bring
them on in smart London society. Virginia respected Kitty but
could never feel at ease with her and her cultivation of the
social graces. For her part Kitty had reservations about Virginia
and she was not amused when the Stephen sisters moved from
fashionable Kensington to bohemian Bloomsbury. Towards
the end of the novel it is suggested that 'Clarissa was at heart a
snob – one had to admit it, a snob' but also that 'Clarissa was
pure-hearted'. After the book was published Virginia wrote in
her diary (for 18 June 1925) that the distaste she felt for Mrs
Dalloway was 'true to my feeling for Kitty'.

D'ARTAGNAN

Alexandre Dumas, *The Three Musketeers* (1844), *Twenty Years After* (1845), *The Man in the Iron Mask* (1848–50)

Charles de Batz de Castelmore (1623–73)

D'Artagnan, the swashbuckling hero celebrated by Alexandre Dumas, makes an ungainly first entrance on a pony in *The Three Musketeers* though his quality still shines through: 'face long and brown; high cheek-bones, a sign of sagacity; the maxillary muscles enormously developed . . . the eye open and intelligent; the nose hooked, but finely chiselled'. He soon meets the three musketeers Athos, Porthos, Aramais whose 'appearance, although it was not quite at ease, excited by its carelessness, at once full of dignity and submission, the admiration of D'Artagnan, who beheld in these two men demigods, and in their leader [Athos] an Olympian Jupiter, armed with all his thunders'. Subsequently D'Artagnan becomes the greatest musketeer of all.

Dumas came across his hero in the fanciful *Mémoirs d'Artagnan, capitaine, lieutenant des grands Mousquetaires* (1700) by Gatien Courtilz de Sandras. With the assistance of historian Auguste Maquet, Dumas recreated the career of D'Artagnan in a spectacular manner. The historical D'Artagnan was born Charles de Batz de Castelmore in 1623 and inherited the estate of Artaignan. Commissioned in the Grey Musketeers he was entrusted with various daring exploits such as the arrest of Fouquet, the Finance Minister, in 1661. By 1667 D'Artagnan had become a captain and gradually he became involved in administrative work, first as Marshal of the Royal Camps and Armies then as military governor of Lille. He returned to active service in 1673 when, on behalf of the Duke of Monmouth, he led the storming of Maestricht. The action was ill-advised and D'Artagnan was killed along with more than a hundred of his musketeers. His three stout-hearted companions in the Dumas novels were also historically based – on the Gascon noblemen Armand Athos d'Auterielle, Isaac de Portau and Henri d'Aramitz.

Helen Walker (1712–91)

The source of the sentimental story that is at the heart of Sir Walter Scott's *The Heart of Midlothian* came to him in a letter from an admirer, Mrs Helen Goldie, who told the tale of Helen Walker: 'She had been left an orphan, with the charge of a sister considerably younger than herself, and who was educated and maintained by her exertions. Attached to her by so many ties, therefore, it will not be easy to conceive her feelings, when she found that this only sister must be tried by the laws of her country for child-murder, and upon being called as principal witness against her.' Scottish law stipulated that, in the case of a child being dead or missing, a woman who gave birth without seeking assistance should be charged with infanticide and executed if found guilty. Helen Walker could have spared her sister the death sentence if she had testified to her preparation for the birth but she declared 'It is impossible for me to swear to a falsehood; and, whatever may be the consequence, I will give my oath according to my conscience.' When her sister was duly sentenced to death Helen had a petition drawn up, then set out on foot to London to present herself (as Mrs Goldie told Scott) 'in her tartan plaid and country attire, to the late Duke of Argyle, who immediately procured the pardon she petitioned for, and Helen returned with it, on foot, just in time to save her sister'.

From this moral tale Scott fashioned the character of plain Jeanie Deans who, by a similar strategy, saves her beautiful half-sister from execution in Edinburgh in whose Tolbooth prison (known as the Heart of Midlothian) Effie is confined at the beginning of the book. Jeanie, daughter of the staunchly presbyterian Douce Davie Deans, rises to the moralistic occasion by saying 'I will bear my load alone – the back is made for the burden.'

Towards the end of his life Scott provided – in Irongray churchyard, Dumfriesshire – a tombstone to the memory of Helen Walker.

CYRANO DE BERGERAC

Edmond Rostand, *Cyrano de Bergerac* (1897)

Savinien Cyrano de Bergerac (1620–55)

Cyrano de Bergerac is the hero of Rostand's romantic play. He is a dashing and brave young officer, with a reputation for wit, panache and daring. Unfortunately, he has a monstrously large nose, which stands in the way of his romantically fulfilling the true potential of his soul. He loves the beautiful Roxane but knows that his facial disfigurement will always prevent her loving him. From the deep generosity of his heart, he enables another to woo and to win her, in the course of which romance he actually pens the love-letters. The wit and romance of Cyrano's character comes through in some of the sharp exchanges of Rostand's dialogue, even in translation: 'Twirling my wit as it were my moustache,/The while I pass among the crowd, I make/Bold truths ring out like spurs'; ' 'Tis my soul/That I thus hold erect as if with stays,/And decked with daring deed instead of ribbons'; 'Your name hangs in my heart like a bell's tongue'; 'To offend is my pleasure; I love to be hated'; 'A kiss, when all is said, what is it?/. . . a rosy dot/Placed on the "i" in loving; 'tis a secret/Told to the mouth instead of to the ear.'

Savinien Cyrano de Bergerac is the original of this hero. He was a French dramatist and romance-writer, born in Paris, and studied at the College de Beauvais, in company with Henri Lebret, who was later his biographer. Cyrano joined the guards and earned a reputation for dare and dashing, fighting some thousand duels and writing tragedies in the classical mode and several romances. His unique mixture of science and romance was later imitated by Voltaire, Swift and Poe. He was seriously injured by falling timber at the house of his patron, the Duke of Arpajon in 1654. He was persecuted as a free thinker and sought refuge with friends. He died in Paris.

JOHN DERRINGHAM
Elinor Glyn, *Halcyone* (1912)

George Nathaniel Curzon, Marquess Curzon of Kedleston (1859–1925)

John Derringham is the hero of Elinor Glyn's sentimental and poignant romance *Halcyone*. He is a brilliant and ambitious politician who meets and falls in love with Halcyone and agrees to marry her. The marriage will have to be kept secret for the time for political reasons. At the same time a cunning rich American widow is scheming to capture his attentions. Before they can marry, he suffers an accident and is separated from Halcyone. His engagement to Mrs Cricklander is announced in the papers and Halcyone is brokenhearted. His party falls from office and Mrs Cricklander, not wishing to marry an opposition leader, passes him over for a radical. After much tension on the heart strings, Derringham and Halcyone are reunited. Derringham is described as a tall, 'lanky, rather distinguished young Englishman'. He is brilliant, and got a double first at Oxford. He is 'full of ambitions in the political line, and he has a fearless and rather caustic wit'.

This is a portrait of Curzon. Derringham, like Curzon, was a fine scholar, and had been captain of the Oppidans at Eton. They shared an aristocratic descent obscured by poverty as well as tearing political ambition. Derringham, like Curzon, had already been Foreign Under-Secretary. They have less attractive qualities in common; both are selfish egotists who put their own ambitions above everything else. Elinor Glyn knew Curzon personally; in fact, he was a fan of hers, and made her a gift of the celebrated tiger skin, immortalized in the lines: 'Would you like to sin/with Elinor Glyn/on a tiger-skin?/Or would you prefer/to err/with her/on some other fur?' Curzon was an intensely ambitious Conservative politician, a brilliant scholar and master of foreign affairs. A distinguished Viceroy of India, he was bitterly disappointed not to have been Prime Minister. He acknowledged his copy of *Halcyone* by pointing out two spelling mistakes in the author's accompanying letter.

DIDO, QUEEN OF CARTHAGE.
Virgil, *Aeneid* (circa 29 BC)

Cleopatra, Queen of Egypt, Cleopatra VII
(69–30 BC)

Virgil's masterpiece narrates the story of Aeneas, the Trojan hero, after the destruction of Troy. Aeneas and his followers are luxuriously entertained by Dido after they are shipwrecked at Carthage, and Aeneas returns to her after escaping from Troy. Here occurs the deep love between them. He is summoned to return to establish Rome and deserts the Queen, who takes her own life: 'Deep entered in her side/The piercing steel, with reeking purple dyed,/Clogged in the wound the cruel weapon stands,/The spouting blood came streaming on her hands./Her sad attendants saw the deadly stroke,/And with loud cries the sounding palace shook.'

Virgil's life spanned a period of considerable political upheaval, and his aim in the *Aeneid* was to portray the destiny of Rome as a civilizing and law-giving power, fully realized under the Emperor Augustus. He was twenty-five when Julius Caesar was assassinated. Then followed civil wars, the triumvirate of Antony, Lepidus and Octavius, the tension brought about in international stability by the relationship between Antony and Cleopatra, and the terrible threat posed to Roman power from the east which was ended by the battle of Actium in 31 BC.

The theme, so stressed in Virgil, of the need for a powerful central authority in the Mediterranean world, finds its parallel in the triumphant career of Octavius, who became the Emperor Augustus. The luxury of Carthage, Aeneas's fascination with Dido, the tension between love and duty, the suicide of the Queen, are all echoes of the exotic world of Egypt, Antony's infatuation with Cleopatra, his neglect of Roman duties and the suicide of the Queen of the Nile. It was while Antony was enamoured of Cleopatra that Octavius was able to consolidate his power in the western part of the Roman world. Cleopatra had already fascinated Julius Caesar, and now enchanted Antony. After they met in 41 BC she bore him three sons. The war between Octavius and Antony was decided at Actium, a sea battle fought in 31 BC off the west of Greece. Cleopatra fled with sixty of her ships and Antony followed. When besieged in Alexandria, Antony stabbed himself and Cleopatra died of the sting of a serpent.

LUCKY JIM DIXON
Kingsley Amis, *Lucky Jim* (1954)

Philip Larkin (born 1922)

English fiction was treated to a new sense of irreverent fun
when Kingsley Amis presented the adventures of *Lucky Jim* as
a university lecturer in a Department of History presided over
by the pompous Professor Welch. The reader sympathizes
with Jim Dixon as he endures the absurd pretensions of the
academic establishment around him. Professor Welch's idea of
a musical event is not, for example, Jim's: 'he disclosed that the
local composer and the amateur violinist were going to "tackle"
a violin sonata by some Teutonic bore, that an unstated number
of recorders would then perform some suitable item, and that
at some later time Johns might be expected to produce music
from his oboe'.

The dread of cultural bores is something Kingsley Amis shares
with his friend Philip Larkin who combines a great poetic gift
with an enthusiasm for traditional jazz. *Lucky Jim* is dedicated
to Larkin who was Amis's contemporary at wartime Oxford
where they both read English at St John's College. In a tribute
to the poet, included in Anthony Thwaite's *Larkin at Sixty*
(1982), Amis wrote: 'Jim Dixon's surname has something to
do with ordinariness, but at the outset had much more to do
with Dixon Drive, the street where Philip lived [in Leicester].
Yes, for a short time it was to be his story.' As Amis points out,
Jim Dixon differs from Larkin. Whereas Larkin is tall and lean,
Dixon is 'on the short side, fair and round-faced'. Moreover,
Larkin worked as a librarian not a lecturer. Lucky Jim Dixon
retains, though, some Larkinesque attitudes for he distrusts
those in authority, dislikes stuffiness and is temperamentally
inclined to endorse Larkin's dread (in 'Vers de Société') of
'Asking that ass about his fool research.'

Edward F. Ricketts (died 1948)

John Steinbeck's *Cannery Row* is dedicated to 'Ed Ricketts who knows why or should' since, as the central character Doc, he dominates the book and gives it its human warmth. All the life that thrives on Cannery Row is drawn to Doc, owner and operator of the Western Biological Laboratory. Doc's existence is an example to others: 'He wears a beard and his face is half Christ and half satyr and his face tells the truth. . . . He became the fountain of philosophy and science and art. . . . Doc would listen to any kind of nonsense and change it for you to a kind of wisdom. His mind had no horizon – and his sympathy had no warp. He could talk to children, telling them very profound things so that they understood. He lived in a world of wonders, of excitement. He was concupiscent as a rabbit and gentle as hell.'

In 1930 John Steinbeck and his wife Carol moved to a cottage in Pacific Grove on the Monterey Peninsula. There, on Cannery Row in Monterey, Steinbeck met Ed Ricketts, owner of the Pacific Biological Laboratory. Steinbeck's wife worked in the laboratory, which collected and sold West Coast biological specimens, and Steinbeck himself became fascinated by the ecological implications of Ricketts's research into marine biology. He adopted Ricketts as his guru and collaborated with him on a book *The Sea of Cortez* (1941).

Driving across the Southern Pacific tracks in 1948 Ricketts was killed when his car was struck by the evening train from San Francisco. Steinbeck wrote to a friend: 'there died the greatest man I have known and the best teacher. It is going to take a long time to reorganize my thinking and my planning without him. It is good that he was killed during the very best time of his life with his work at its peak and with the best girl he ever had. I am extremely glad for that.'

PAUL DOMBEY
Charles Dickens, *Dombey and Son* (1848)

Harry Burnett (died 1848)

Little Paul Dombey is his father's son and heir. Mr Dombey thought the world of his son. His mother died in bringing him into the world and he is cared for by Polly Toodle and Mrs Wickham. He is sent to Mrs Pipchin's establishment at Brighton and then on to Dr Blimber's academy. His father always had great plans for him and was all for pushing him forward and setting him great tasks. But Paul is thoughtful and 'old fashioned' child, devoted to his sister Florence, the unwanted and neglected daughter of Mr Dombey, who is about ten when the novel opens. He is naturally delicate, and often in frail health: 'Every tooth was a breakneck fence, and every pimple in the measles a stone wall to him. He was down in every fit of the whooping-cough, and rolled upon and crushed by a whole field of small diseases. . . . Some bird of prey got into his throat instead of the thrush; and the very chickens turning ferocious – if they have anything to do with that infant malady to which they lend their name – worried him like tiger-cats.' But he is always wise beyond his years and has a disconcerting way of cutting right through cant and artifice with a directness and ruthlessness which adults find quite unstoppable. He tells Mrs Pipchin that there is nobody like his sister Florence. 'Well!' retorted Mrs Pipchin, shortly, 'and there's nobody like me, I suppose'. 'Ain't there really though?' asked Paul, leaning forward in his chair, and looking at her very hard. 'No,' said the old lady. 'I am glad of that,' observed Paul, 'that's a very good thing.' Paul is taken seriously ill when he is nine and dies soon afterwards, in one of the most famous of Dickens's child-death scenes.

This episode was written in January 1847. Paul was based on the frail and crippled son of Dickens's sister, Frances, who married Henry Burnett, the musician and actor. Frances was to die some months before her son, and she spoke to Charles Dickens 'about an invention she had heard of that she would like to have tried for the deformed child's back'.

DON ARMADO
William Shakespeare, *Love's Labours Lost* (1598)

Sir Walter Raleigh (1552–1618)

Don Adriano de Armado is a fantastical Spanish warrior and self-consciously romantic figure of great pomposity and arrogance. The major element in his comicality lies in his grandiloquent and extravagant language. He is in love with the country wench Jaquenetta and is rivalled by Costard. A love letter he writes to her is given by mistake to Rosaline, the clever young lady-in-waiting to the Queen of France. He portrays Hector in the pageant of the Nine Worthies in Act V (see HOLOFERNES). It has been suggested that this is a satiric portrait of Gabriel Harvey (see MOTH) but the parallels and references to Sir Walter Raleigh are more convincing.

Raleigh was a soldier, poet, navigator, explorer and the Queen's leading favourite until he made the tragic mistake of marrying one of her ladies-in-waiting. He was a court rival to the Earl of Essex, who was supported by Shakespeare. Raleigh was a major figure in the group known as the School of the Night, a fellowship of intellectuals who had ambitions similar to those of the King of Navarre and his friends in *Love's Labours Lost* – to abjure the company of women and to spend their time in study and pursuits of the mind. Raleigh's associates included Thomas Harriot, Henry Percy, Matthew Roydon and George Chapman, whose poem *The Shadow of Night* (1594) glorified the life of contemplation and study in contrast to the shallow entertainments of society and female company. Shakespeare's comedy contains a direct reference to the group: 'Black is the badge of hell,/The hue of dungeons and the school of night' (Act IV, Scene 3, lines 254–5).

Raleigh was tried for conspiracy against James I, found guilty but reprieved in 1603. He undertook an expedition up the Orinoco in 1616 when he was given strict orders not to make war against the Spanish. The Spanish settlement at San Tomas was burned and his punishment was demanded by the Spanish minister. He was executed in 1618. He wrote: 'What is our life? a play of passion;/Our mirth, the music of division;/Our mothers' wombs the tiring-houses be/Where we are dressed for this short comedy./Heaven the judicious sharp spectator is,/That sits and marks still who doth act amiss;/Our graves that hide us from the searching sun/Are like drawn curtains when the play is done./Thus march we playing to our latest rest;/Only we die in earnest – that's no jest.' Raleigh may also be portrayed as Tarquin in the *Rape of Lucrece*, 'for his excessive pride surnamed Superbus'.

DON GIOVANNI

Opera, *Don Giovanni* (1787) music by Wolfgang Amadeus
Mozart, libretto by Lorenzo da Ponte

Giovanni Jacopo Casanova (1725–98)

Although the Don Juan story is widely spread in European
literature, the figure was definitively placed in Western con-
sciousness by Mozart's opera. When the composer and his
librettist wanted expert advice they called in Casanova. Not
only do they share first names, there are other fundamental
and unmistakable parallels. The existence of an original person,
Don Juan Tenorio, has long been discredited, but what is
certain is Don Juan's first appearance in European literature in
a play attributed to Tirso de Molina, *El Burlador de Sevilla y
convidado de piedra,* printed in Barcelona in 1630. The story of
the blaspheming profligate who invites a dead man to supper
and is dragged off to hell is found much earlier and seems to be
a universal type.

The opera opens with the Don attempting to seduce Donna
Anna, daughter of the Commendatore. Giovanni is disturbed
by Anna's father and then kills him in a sword fight. Giovanni
flees with his servant, Leporello. Donna Elvira, Giovanni's
discarded mistress, now appears only to be told – in the famous
'catalogue' aria – by Leporello, that she is wasting her time in
pursuing Giovanni, as the Don has numerous conquests and is
always seeking new game. Giovanni further attempts to seduce
the peasant girl Zerlina, already betrothed. Mockingly Giovanni invites the statue of Anna's father, which stands on his
grave, to supper. It arrives at the banquet and drags him to
hades.

Casanova's autobiography, *Histoire de Ma Vie* (in twelve
volumes!) catalogues amours in strikingly similar vein to
Leporello's 'catalogue' aria. Leporello tells Elvira his master's
adventures number 2,065 : 640 in Italy, 231 in Germany, 100
in France, 91 in Turkey and in Spain some 1,003. Casanova
claimed well over 130 women, including conquests of Italian,
French, Swiss, German, English, Greek, Spanish, Polish, Dutch,
Russian, African and Portuguese women of all ranks of society
from the ages of eleven to over fifty, married, single and
widowed, dark, blond and brown, involving sexual activities
of all imaginable kinds. He was, like Don Giovanni, a connois-
seur, genuinely believing in the passion of love. 'I was not born
a nobleman,' he asserted, 'I achieved nobility.'

DON JUAN
Lord Byron, *Don Juan* (1819–24)

Lord Byron (1788–1824)

Although Byron believed his satiric poem *Don Juan* might have been 'too free for these very modest days' it is in fact a parody, or an inversion of the Don Juan legend – far from being an arch seducer from whose advances no woman is secure, Byron's hero is a naive and Candide-like innocent who is constantly seduced almost against his will. Juan is given a strictly academic education by his mother, Donna Inez (a satiric portrait of Byron's wife, Annabella) which totally fails to equip him for the moral complexities of life. In his teens he is seduced by Donna Julia, a young married woman: 'Juan she saw, and, as a pretty child,/caressed him often – such a thing might be/Quite innocently done, and harmless styled,/When she had twenty years, and thirteen he;/But I am not so sure I should have smiled/When he was sixteen, Julia twenty-three.' This is followed by exploits in Seville, the Greek islands, Constantinople, Russia and England.

To a very large extent *Don Juan* is self-confessional. Juan's precocious sexuality is a reflection of Byron's own. A very close friend, John Cam Hobhouse, related that when Byron was nine, 'a free Scotch girl used to come to bed to him and play tricks with his person'. His amours continued at Harrow and Cambridge and in seemingly inexhaustible profligacy in London, Greece, Albania and Asia Minor. He enjoyed a tempestuous affair with Lady Caroline Lamb, wife of the future prime minister, Lord Melbourne, and a liaison with Jane Elizabeth Scott, the wife of the Earl of Oxford. As well as numerous whores, he seduced his half-sister, Augusta Leigh, who bore him a daughter. His astonishing personal magnetism worked like enchantment. Women seemed to throw themselves at him – which is an experience shared by his hero Don Juan. Such a sacrificial victim was Claire Clairmont, half-sister of Shelley's wife, who gave him a daughter. 'I never loved nor pretended to love her,' Byron wrote, 'but a man is a man, and if a girl of eighteen comes prancing to you at all hours, there is but one way. . .' (letter dated 12 January 1817). Scandal forced him into exile in Italy, where his free-wheeling sexuality found free rein. He said that he had enjoyed some two hundred women, 'Perhaps more, for I have not kept count.' His affair with the nineteen-year-old Countess Guiccoli, whose husband he cuckolded in his own house (closely paralleled in the poem) dates immediately prior to its composition.

Prince Vlad Dracula (1431–76)

In Bram Stoker's novel *Dracula* the Count is seen, in his coffin, as a being bloated with the blood of others: 'the mouth was redder than ever, for on the lips were gouts of fresh blood, which trickled from the corners of the mouth and ran over the chin and neck. . . . It seemed as if the whole creature were simply gorged with blood; he lay like a filthy leech, exhausted with his repletion.' Stoker's Dracula is a vampire who terrorizes Transylvania with his nocturnal habits. The historical Dracula was, if anything, more bloodthirsty than the fictional Count; he was not, however, a vampire.

Prince Vlad Dracula was the ruler of Wallachia at a time when the land that is now Romania was occupied by Wallachia, Moldavia and Transylvania; Vlad's father was called Dracul, or Dragon, so the name Dracula means 'son of the dragon'. As a child Vlad was imprisoned by the Turks and would bribe his guards to bring him birds which he first mutilated then impaled on sticks. As an adult he refined this practice and earned the name Vlad Tepes (*tzepa* = spike) or Vlad the Impaler. In his campaign against the infidel Turk he indulged in his favourite torture; his victims were pressed on to the oiled point of a stake and left as the weight of their bodies forced the point through them in an agonizing death that could take hours. After one triumph against the Turks, in 1456, Vlad impaled twenty thousand prisoners. Vlad Dracula's reputation was embellished in Romanian folklore and he was accused of unspeakable acts of cruelty such as forcing mothers to eat their babies and of being a 'wampyr'. In recreating Vlad as a vampire, Stoker seized on the images associated with Dracula and gave him an aura of elegant evil: 'The mouth, so far as I could see under the heavy moustache, was fixed and rather cruel looking, with peculiarly sharp white teeth.'

ROSIE DRIFFIELD

W. Somerset Maugham, *Cakes and Ale* (1930)

Sue Jones (1883–1948)

In 1906 Somerset Maugham met and fell in love with Sue Jones, the original of Rosie Driffield in *Cakes and Ale*. Sue was the daughter of popular dramatist Henry Arthur Jones and made her debut as an actress in 1897 in her father's play *The Manoeuvres of Jane*. She married a theatrical producer in 1902 but that marriage ended in divorce. When she met Maugham she was twenty-three and, as he described her in *A Writer's Notebook,* 'a woman of ripe and abundant charms, rosy of cheek and fair of hair, with eyes as blue as the summer sea, with rounded lines and full breasts'.

The second Mrs Driffield tells the narrator of *Cakes and Ale,* Willie Ashenden, that Rosie was 'a nymphomaniac', a thought which must have occurred to Maugham who was at first disturbed by Sue's promiscuity. Yet he came to endorse Ashenden's considered opinion: 'She was naturally affectionate. When she liked anyone it was quite natural for her to go to bed with him. She never thought twice about it. It was not vice; it wasn't lasciviousness; it was her nature. She gave herself as naturally as the sun gives heat or the flowers their perfume. It was a pleasure to her and she liked to give pleasure to others.'

After some hesitation Maugham decided to propose marriage to Sue and travelled to Chicago where she was acting in 1913. She turned him down in characteristic fashion by telling him, so he recalled in *Looking Back,* 'If you want to go to bed with me, you may, but I won't marry you.' Instead Sue married Angus McDonnell, second son of the Sixth Earl of Antrim, who became a colonel in the First World War and handled public relations for the British ambassador to Washington in the Second. During the Second World War, Maugham was engaged in official work for the British government and was in touch with the embassy in Washington but he scrupulously avoided contact with the woman he had loved to distraction.

HENRY DRUMMOND

Film, *Inherit the Wind* (written by Nathan E. Douglas and Harold Jacob Smith, based on the play by Jerome Lawrence and Robert E. Lee, directed by Stanley Kramer, 1960)

Clarence Darrow (1857–1938)

A schoolmaster in a small town in the southern United States is accused of teaching the theory of evolution to his pupils. The fundamentalists get him put on trial. The prosecution is led by a supporter of the Old Style Religion, Martin Harrison Brady, and the schoolmaster is defended by a brilliant liberal advocate Henry Drummond. The whole trial becomes a *cause célèbre* and public interest is fanned by its regularly being reported by E. R. Hornbeck, a cynical newspaper reporter, who is sent to cover the proceedings. The film provided starring roles for Frederick March (Brady), Spencer Tracy (Drummond) and Gene Kelly (Hornbeck).

This was based on the infamous Scopes trial in Tennessee in 1925, in which the courtroom confrontation of William Jennings Bryan (1860–1925) and Clarence Darrow was reported by H. L. Mencken in the *American Mercury*. Clarence Darrow was a famous defence attorney. His defence of Eugene Debs and the American Railway Union in 1894 made his name a household word. He represented the coalminers in the anthracite strike of 1902, William Haywood and other 'Wobblies' on the charge of murdering a former governor of Idaho. ('Wobblies' was the popular name for the Industrial Workers of the World, a labour organization founded in 1905, a coalition of left-wing trade unionists and political theorists. Their policy was the destruction of capitalism by direct action, similar to syndicalism in Europe.) Darrow was a long-term opponent of capital punishment, and secured life imprisonment for Richard Loeb and Nathan Leopold in the Chicago youth-slaying case. This case was the basis of the film *Compulsion* in which the role of the defence lawyer, a portrait of Clarence Darrow, was played by Orson Welles. Darrow once said: 'I don't believe in God because I don't believe in Mother Goose.' This would hardly endear him to his opponent, William Jennings Bryan, who was a devout supporter of Protestant fundamentalism. Scopes was convicted, but Bryan died at the end of the trial. Darrow went on to defend eleven blacks who were accused of the murder of a Klu Klux Klansman in Detroit, and in 1934 was chosen by Franklin D. Roosevelt to head a commission to study the operation of the National Recovery Administration.

THE DUCHESS OF MALFI

John Webster, *The Duchess of Malfi* (1614)

Giovanna, Duchess of Amalfi (died 1513)

Webster's *Duchess of Malfi* is one of the greatest Jacobean tragedies. The Duchess has recently been widowed. She reveals her love for Antonio, the steward of her court. Her two brothers – one of them a cardinal, the other the Duke of Calabria, insist that she should not marry again. Their motives are to get their hands on her property. The Duchess and Antonio secretly marry. The Cardinal and the Duke of Calabria employ espionage to watch her every move. Antonio and the Duchess separate for the time being. She is captured by Calabria, tortured and finally strangled together with her children. There is a strong suggestion of incestuous feelings by the Duke of Calabria for his sister, the Duchess of Malfi. He exclaims when he learns that she has married, contrary to his injunction: 'What'er thou art that hast enjoy'd my sister,/For I am sure thou hear'st me, for thine own sake/Let me not know thee. I came hither prepar'd/To work thy discovery; yet am now persuaded/It would beget such violent effects/As would damn us both.' He is overcome with grief when he has her murdered: 'Cover her face; mine eyes dazzle: she died young.' Her husband, Antonio, is also killed. The Duke of Calabria is driven mad and his brother, the Cardinal, is killed by the murderer who was hired by the two brothers to kill the Duchess and her husband.

The story is a true one which Webster read in William Painter's *Palace of Pleasure* (1566–67.) The historical facts are these: Enrico of Aragona, half-brother of Federico, King of Naples, had three children. Lodovico was the eldest, and he became a cardinal. The younger son, Carlo, took the title Marquis of Gerace when Lodovico became a cardinal. Giovanna, their sister, was married in 1490 to Alphonso Piccolimini. Alphonso became Duke of Amalfi in 1493 but he died in 1498. Their son, Alphonso was born in 1499, and Giovanna was to rule Amalfi during his minority. But she has secretly married Antonio Bologna, former master of her household. Both Antonio and the Duchess are killed, the latter together with her children at Amalfi in 1513. The Duchess is a truly tragic figure in the Shakespearean mould, proclaiming the stature of her soul at the moment of her death: 'I am the Duchess of Malfi still.' She stands out in the gloomy, melancholy and revengeful atmosphere of the play as a generous and powerful spirit.

DUNCE

Dunce – noun, a very dull child at school; a stupid person

Johannes Duns Scotus (1265–1308)

The original 'Dunce' was one of the greatest of medieval schoolmen. Scotus was born in Roxburghshire and joined the Franciscan order. He was educated at Oxford and lectured there on theology and philosophy, to numerous students – legend has it that his teaching attracted some thirty-thousand. He also taught at Paris and Cologne. He was the founder of a new type of scholarship – a critique of the existing union which had been maintained between Aristotelian philosophy and theology, the powerful tradition inherited from scholars such as Thomas Aquinas. Scotus maintained that Aquinas was error in subordinating the practical to the theoretical, and king in speculation the foundation of faith, instead of realizing Christianity in practical work. It was here that true theology was based. Scotus urged that theology rests in faith, which is practical, not speculative. It is an act of will.

Because he subjected the vast apparatus of theology built up by Aquinas and his followers to the most thorough and searching critical analysis, he earned the name 'Doctor Subtilis'. He supported the doctrine of the Immaculate Conception against the teaching of the Dominicans (Aquinas's order). Scotus's work in turn became the basis of a new orthodoxy, and his followers became the dominating sect, the Scotists or Dunsemen. In the 16th century they were attacked by the New Humanists and reformers, as merchants of a farrago of hair-splitting sophistry. The term Duns became synonymous with a dull obstinate person, impervious to the New Learning. In 1530 Tindale wrote: 'Remember ye not how ... the old barking curs, Dunces disciples and like draffe called Scotists ... raged in every pulpit against Greek, Latin and Hebrew.' (*Answer to More*). In 1728 Alexander Pope published the first version of his verse satire, *The Dunciad,* the epic of the Dunces.

MR EAMES

Norman Douglas, *South Wind* (1917)

John Ellington Brooks

One of the most extraordinary characters in Norman Douglas's *South Wind* is Ernest Eames who spends his life annotating a book on the antiquities of the island of Nepenthe, where the action of the novel takes place. Although he is absolutely dedicated to his scholarly work he still attracts the gossip that sweeps round the island like the sirocco. Yet Mr Eames is safe and secure in his scholarship: 'He had taken a high degree in classics, though Greek was never much to his taste. . . . But Latin – ah, Latin was different! Even at his preparatory school, where he was known as a swot of the first water, he had displayed an unhealthy infatuation for that tongue; he loved its cold, lapidary construction; and while other boys played football or cricket, this withered little fellow used to lark about with a note-book, all by himself, torturing sensible English into its refractory and colourless periods and elaborating, without the help of a Gradus, those inept word-mosaics which are called Latin verses. "Good fun," he used to say, "and every bit as exciting as algebra," as though that constituted a recommendation.'

Norman Douglas was born at Tilquhillie, on Deeside, of distinguished Scottish and German ancestry but found his spiritual home when he settled in Capri. There he came to know John Ellington Brooks who lived on his own and never travelled to the mainland. He was apparently a contented man who had his cat for company, his piano for amusement and his scholarly pursuits for passion. Brooks, the model for Mr Eames, spent his time writing original prose and poetry and translating work from the Greek and Latin. Yet he had no interest in publishing any of this work; scholarship was for him a fine end in itself. When Douglas published *Birds and Beasts of the Greek Anthology* (1927), an annotated list of the animals mentioned by the Greek poets, he used translations by Brooks and dedicated the book to him. That, and a sonnet he once sold, comprised the complete published work of John Ellington Brooks.

MARTIN EDEN
Jack London, *Martin Eden* (1909)

Jack London (1876–1916)

Martin Eden is the story of an unsuccessful writer who is rejected at first by the wealthy woman that he loves. Only Russ Brissenden, a socialist poet, really understands and properly evaluates what Martin Eden is trying to do in his writings. Eden eventually achieves success and as he becomes rich and famous the self-same people who had previously neglected him now come flocking to him and try to court his favour. He is totally disgusted and leaves civilization on a voyage to the South Seas. Totally demoralized and lacking a sense of his bearings, his personality disintegrates and he commits suicide. The writer comments: 'Had Martin Eden been a socialist, he would not have died – he would have been able to find a meaning in life.'

Martin Eden is a self-portrait. Jack London was born in San Francisco, the illegitimate son of one W. H. Chancey, an astrologist and spiritualist, and Flora Wellman, who later married John London. Jack's early days were spent in poverty and upheaval. He worked on the waterfront, sailed to Japan, prospected at the Klondike and read voraciously – Darwin, Marx, Nietzsche, Huxley, Flaubert, Kipling, Melville, Hardy, Conrad and Zola. His stories began to appear in 1900 and *The Call of the Wild,* which made him rich and famous was published in 1903. He was war correspondent in the Russo-Japanese conflict, lived in the slums of London (*The People of the Abyss* 1903) earned and spent large sums and continually undermined an iron physique with drinking. He wrote some fifty books all told – including *The Sea-Wolf* (1904), *White Fang* (1906), *The Iron Heel* (1907), *John Barleycorn* (1913), *The Valley of the Moon* (1913) and *The Star Rover* (1915). He tries to reconcile his obsession with rugged individualism in a struggle against the world, with his fundamental belief in the Marxist concept of human collective cooperation. Like Martin Eden, he committed suicide while at sea.

ELEONORA
Edgar Allan Poe, *Eleonora* (1842)

Virginia Clemm (1823–47)

Poe's *Eleonora* is a study of the torture of separation felt between two who truly love each other. It is one of those stories – so characteristic of its author – which extends the frontiers of experience from anguish even unto madness: 'I am come of a race noted for vigour of fancy and ardour of passion. Men have called me mad. . . . We will say, then, that I am mad. I grant, at least, that there are two distinct conditions of my mental existence – the condition of lucid reason . . . and a condition of shadow and doubt.' In the story the beloved Eleonora returns after death and forgives the narrator for breaking his vow of eternal love for her by marrying Ermengarde. He had loved Eleonora in his youth. She was the only daughter of his mother's only sister: 'Eleonora was the name of my cousin. . . . The loveliness of Eleonora was that of the Seraphim; but she was a maiden artless and innocent as the brief life she had led among the flowers.'

Eleonora was based on Poe's first cousin, Virginia Clemm, whom he married when she was only thirteen, on 16 May 1836. He was never able to bear the thought of parting from her, and the torture of separation at the core of *Eleonora* was the real emotion Poe experienced. It was once suggested that Virginia should leave home for a while and stay with a relative, Neilson Poe, who had married Virginia's half-sister, where she could be accommodated and have her schooling paid for. He could not bear it: 'I cannot express in words the fervent devotion I feel towards my dear little cousin – my own darling.' he wrote in a letter. She died when barely twenty-four, after a long and painful illness. It drove him nearly insane and he took to drink and often behaved in a manner friends and colleagues thought insane. The oscillation between hope and despair, sanity and madness, intoxication and sobriety, characteristic of his mood when under the stress of Virginia's illness and death, he had anticipated in the story written five years before. 'We will say, then, that I am mad.'

Germaine Necker, Madame de Stael
(1766–1817)

The hero of the novel is a brilliant young man who is the son of a member of the government of a small German principality. It is his father's ambition that Adolphe should be educated not only academically (he has just completed a splendid career at the university of Göttingen) but by the world. To this end Adolphe is dispatched to another small German state where it is hoped he will learn something of sophisticated court life. Here Adolphe meets Ellènore. She is the mistress of an aristocrat and has already borne him two children. Adolphe decides that he will seduce her and is successful. He almost convinces himself that he is in love with her, although he is conscious most of the time that his rational mind is in charge of his emotions and his activities. To some extent his feelings for Ellènore are the result of his pity for her, and these are the feelings which he sometimes mistakes for love. The dynamic tension in the novel is the result of the contrast Constant portrays between reason and emotions. He determines to leave her. At the same time Ellènore finally breaks with her lover, the count, and she is now free to follow Adolphe back to his home. His father disapproves of the relationship and makes arrangements to have Ellènore sent away. Adolphe is now precipitated, partly by affection for her and partly by pity for her, to run away with Ellènore. They travel together to Bohemia and on to Warsaw. He has now seriously tired of her and plans to leave her. The truth dawns on Ellènore and she dies, brokenhearted.

Constant was a brilliantly intelligent civil servant, courtier and political journalist who had a great weakness for women older than himself. He was seduced by an older woman when he was eighteen. *Adolphe* seems to be based on his experiences with three women: Madame de Charrière, an older woman who greatly influenced him; Anna Lindsay, whom he seduced from another lover; and Madame de Stael, who was the daughter of Louis XIV's finance minister, and a critic, philosopher and novelist. She met Constant in 1794, and their relationship lasted until 1811. She had a great hold over him although their association was severely strained by jealousies and misunderstandings. It seems that *Adolphe* is an exploration of his affair with Madame de Stael in which he exploits the narrative framework of his association with Anna Lindsay.

John Hall Stevenson (1718–85)

Eugenius is the sentimental friend of the Parson Yorick, in Sterne's comic masterpiece. The fond and tearful farewells as Yorick lies dying of a broken heart are among the immortal pages of *Tristram Shandy*: 'A few hours before Yorick breathed his last, Eugenius stept in with an intent to take his last farewell of him . . . he told him, he was within a few hours of giving his enemies the slip for ever. I hope not, answered Eugenius, with tears trickling down his cheeks, and with the tenderest tone that ever man spoke . . . Eugenius was convinced . . . that the heart of his friend was broke: he squeezed his hand . . . and then walked softly out of the room, weeping as he walked.'

John Hall met Sterne at Jesus College, Cambridge, and they became friends. He took his wife's surname – Stevenson – after 1738. He inherited Skelton Castle ('Crazy Castle') in Yorkshire from a maternal aunt, and there he formed, in imitation of John Wilkes and the Monks of Medmenham, a club of Demoniacs. He had probably been a member of Wilkes' circle, and certainly knew Wilkes and Horace Walpole. He published scurrilous libels about Sir Francis Dashwood (1701–81) – *Confessions of Sir F . . . of Medmenham* – which suggested the young lord had committed incest with his stepmother and his sisters. He was also the author of *Crazy Tales* and *Monkish Epitaphs*, and writer and avid reader of erotic prose and poetry. Laurence Sterne was a member of Stevenson's Demoniacs, and as a result of black parsonic clothes was known as 'Blackbird'. The activities of this club seem to have been a strange mixture of shooting, fishing, racing their horses along Saltburn sands, drinking, black magic and erotic practices. He wrote a continuation of Sterne's *Sentimental Journey* (1769) as well as political pamphlets and imitations of coarse French *fabliaux*.

EVANGELIST

John Bunyan, *The Pilgrim's Progress* (1678)

John Gifford (died 1655)

At the beginning of the allegorical journey that constitutes *The Pilgrim's Progress,* Christian, 'greatly distressed in his mind', is turned towards the truth by Evangelist: 'Then said Evangelist, pointing with his finger over a very wide Field, Do you see yonder Wicket-gate? The Man said, No. Then said the other, Do you see yonder shining Light? He said, I think I do. Then said Evangelist, Keep that Light in your eye, and go up directly thereto: so shalt thou see the Gate'. The spiritual trials and tribulations endured by Christian are a record of the various doubts and difficulties that assailed Bunyan in his own career.

Bunyan's mentor John Gifford, the original of Evangelist, provided Bunyan with inspirational assistance. Gifford's conversion to the Puritan cause was dramatic; he had been a major in the Royalist Army and a notorious womanizer and gambler. After losing a particularly large amount of money at cards he cursed God then suddenly felt himself reaching for religion. When he first associated with the Bedford Meeting (founded in 1650 as a rallying place for Puritans) he was a disruptive force. Gradually, though, his piety impressed others until he became an obvious candidate for the ministry: in 1653 he was presented with the living of St John's Church, Bedford. Gifford understood Bunyan's spiritual crisis and took him to his home to discuss the tenets of Puritanism and thus Bunyan was 'led from truth to truth'. Eventually Bunyan moved from Elstow to Bedford to be closer to Gifford who died in 1655. In his farewell to his flock Gifford urged Puritans to 'Salute the brethren who walke not in fellowship with you with the same love and name of brother or sister as those who do.' After Gifford's death Bunyan eloquently developed his own powers as a preacher and laid himself open to persecution and imprisonment; while a prisoner in 1675 he began work on *The Pilgrim's Progress.*

SIR JOHN FALSTAFF

William Shakespeare, *Henry IV,* Parts 1 and 2; *The Merry Wives of Windsor,* (1597–1600)

Sir John Oldcastle (died 1417); Sir John Fastolf (1378–1459)

Falstaff is the cowardly companion of Prince Hal, who later rejects him when he becomes King Henry V. The fat knight may be seen as an alternative father-figure, a gross parody on the high-flown power-political themes of the history plays, though in other respects, he is Hal's tempter. We learn of Falstaff's death in *Henry V. The Merry Wives* is a droll account of Sir John's amorous escapades.

There are several clues in the plays which suggest Sir John Oldcastle as the original Falstaff, with many qualities from Sir John Fastolf. Sir John Oldcastle was a soldier and friend of Henry V, and served in the Welsh and French wars. He was a Lollard and a martyr to the cause, imprisoned and – after an escape – party to a plot to overthrow the King. He was executed in 1417. The Falstaff character was originally called 'Oldcastle' in the Henry IV plays, taken from Shakespeare's major source, the *Famous Victories of Henry V.* Oldcastle's descendants protested, and the name was changed to Falstaff, which was derived from a slight adjustment to the name of Sir John Fastolf, who served Henry V at Agincourt, was governor of the Bastille, regent in Normandy, governor of Anjou and Main, but was groundlessly accused of cowardice during the retreat at Patay in 1429. He was a friend of John Paston and wrote a great number of the celebrated Paston letters and left funds towards the founding of Magdalen College.

The attempt to mollify the descendants of Oldcastle are apparent in the epilogue to *Henry IV Part Two*: 'if you be not too much cloy'd with fat meat, our humble author will make you merry with Fair Katherine of France; where ... Falstaff shall die of a sweat, unless already he be killed with your hard opinions; for Oldcastle died a martyr and this is not the man'.

William Brooke, Seventh Lord Cobham, (descended from Oldcastle) a powerful Elizabethan nobleman, was nicknamed Falstaff. Essex wrote to the Earl of Salisbury and referred to Cobham as 'Sir Jo. Falstaff'. Hal calls Falstaff 'my old lad of the castle'. In *The Merry Wives* Master Ford originally assumed the name 'Brooke' when he seeks Falstaff's help in testing Mrs Ford's fidelity. Falstaff appears in operas by Nicolai, Vaughan Williams, Holst and Verdi, a symphonic work by Elgar and is the subject of a novel by Robert Nye.

Thomas Robert Malthus (1766–1834)

Melincourt features several long discussions on social, economic and philosophical topics involving Sylvester Forester and Mr Fax, who is described as: 'The champion of calm reason, the indefatigable explorer of the cold clear springs of knowledge, the bearer of the torch of dispassionate truth, that gives more light than warmth. He looks upon the human world, the world of mind, the conflict of interests, the collision of feelings, the infinitely diversified developments of energy and intelligence, as a mathematician looks on his diagrams, or a mechanist on his wheels and pulleys, as if they were foreign to his own nature, and were nothing more than subjects of curious speculation.' He is a 'tall, thin, pale, grave-looking personage'. There is not an emotion which crosses the human breast, or a thought which occurs to the human mind, which Mr Fax cannot discuss in an almost dismissive and detached scientific way. Forester happens to remark that mutations of fortune are often the inexhaustible theme of history, poetry and romance, and happen in daily life as often as on the stage of Drury Lane. Fax responds: 'That the best prospects are often overshadowed is most certainly true; but there are degrees and modes of well-grounded reliance on futurity, sufficient to justify the enterprises of prudence, and equally well-grounded prospiciences of hopelessness and helplessness, that should check the steps of rashness and passion, in their headlong progress to perdition'.

This is Peacock's sarcastic portrait of Thomas Malthus, the controversial economist. He was professor of history at Haileybury and was led to evolve his celebrated theories of population and subsistence by reading Godwin's *Enquiry Concerning Political Justice*. Godwin's theories were refuted by the facts of nature, Malthus believed. His *Essay on Population* (1798) caused tremendous controversy. Population ever treads on the limits of subsistence, surplus population was wiped out by misery, consequently checks on population were necessary.

Thomas Love Peacock, *Melincourt* (1817)

Robert Southey (1774–1843)

Feathernest, one of the house-guests in *Melincourt*, is a reactionary poet and social-climber who began life as a political radical
and supporter of the French Revolution, but becomes an *ami
du prince*, who spends the morning writing odes to all the
crowned heads of Europe. He is a parasite of Lord Anophel
Achthar, who brings him to Melincourt Castle. Lord Anophel,
in the course of a pleasant conversation, asks him 'what is the
spirit of the age of chivalry?' This takes him by surprise: 'Since
his profitable metamorphosis into an *ami du prince*, he had
never dreamed of such a question. It burst upon him like the
spectre of his youthful integrity, and he mumbled a half-
intelligible reply about truth and liberty – disinterested benevolence – self oblivion – heroic devotion to love and honour –
protection of the feeble, and subversion of tyranny.' He is
naturally taken aback when his Lordship retorts: 'All the
ingredients of a rank Jacobin, Feathernest, 'pon honour!' But
he is not totally at a loss, his good friend Mr Mystic (see MYSTIC)
had taught him the value of the mysterious of transcendental
philosophy, and he calls on this for assistance, 'and overwhelmed his lordship with a volley of ponderous jargon,
which left him in profound astonishment at the depth of Mr
Feathernest's knowledge'.

This is Robert Southey, who became Poet Laureate. He was
born in Bristol and educated at Oxford. As a young man he
was sympathetic to the French Revolution and wrote his epic
Joan of Arc, in 1793. He met Coleridge and the two of them
planned to create an ideal democratic society, Pantisocracy, in
north-east America. The scheme failed to get off the ground.
Southey became an essayist and prolific poet, moving progres-
sively to the right in politics, and received a government
pension, augmented by his salary as Poet Laureate and a further
pension of £300 in 1835, after he declined a baronetcy. He
was attacked by Byron in *Don Juan*.

DR FELL

Nursery rhyme, 'I do not love thee, Dr Fell' – in Thomas
Brown, *Collected Works* (1707)

John Fell (1625–86)

The English divine and distinguished dean of Christ Church,
Oxford, is preserved in a traditional English nursery rhyme.
John Fell was born in Longworth, Berkshire and took holy
orders at Christ Church. He was a deacon by 1647 and priest
two years later. He supported the Royalist cause in the Civil
War, and fell from favour during the Commonwealth. When
Charles II was restored he was granted a succession of honours
and preferments, including successively Canon of Christ
Church, dean of Christ Church and chaplain to the King. In
1676 he was made bishop of Oxford and declined the primacy
of Ireland.

His reforms at Oxford included the restoration of respect for
authority and compulsory attendance at lectures and increasing
the efficiency of the examination system. He also put in hand
an extensive building programme, completing the quadrangle
begun by Cardinal Wolsey – admired by John Aubrey who
wrote: 'the brave designe whereof Dr John Fell hath deteriorated with his new device'. He also promoted the building of
the theatre now named after Archbishop Sheldon. Fell was a
considerable classical scholar and a formative influence in the
creation of the university press at Oxford, bringing out au-
thoritative editions of classical and theological texts.

While a student at Christ Church, John Locke earned the
displeasure of the King by his friendship with Lord Shaftes-
bury. At the King's request, Fell suspended Locke and dismissed
him without giving him a chance to defend himself. Fell later
regretted his actions. Thomas Brown, author of the rhyme
which immortalized Fell, was about to be expelled from
Oxford when Fell set him the task of an impromptu translation
of the thirty-third epigram of Martial: 'Non amo te, Sabidi,
nec possum dicere quare;/Hoc tantum possum dicere, non amo
te.' Brown responded immediately with his translation: 'I do
not love thee, Doctor Fell,/The reason why I cannot tell;/But
this alone I know full well,/I do not love thee, Doctor Fell.' Dr
Fell pardoned him.

FLORA FINCHING
Charles Dickens, *Little Dorrit* (1855)

Maria Beadnell (1810–86)

As a young man, Arthur Clennam had loved Flora. They meet in later life, when she has been widowed. Arthur now finds her to be a rather silly creature: 'Flora, always tall, had grown to be very broad too, and short of breath; but that was not much. Flora, whom he had left a lily, had become a peony; but that was not much. Flora, who had seemed enchanting in all she said and thought, was diffuse and silly. That was much. Flora, who had been spoiled and artless long ago, was determined to be spoiled and artless now. That was a fatal blow.' But in his youth he had ardently loved her and had heaped upon her 'all the locked up wealth of his affection and imagination. . . . Ever since that memorable time he had kept the old fancy of the Past unchanged, in its old sacred place.'

Dickens is here describing his youthful infatuation with Maria Beadnell, whom he had met in 1830, when she was very pretty and petite with bright eyes and ringlets. Her father worked in a bank, and eventually became a bank manager. In fact, her family did not take very kindly to Charles, who was a young newspaper reporter at this time. Her father considered him to be an unsuitable match as he was inclined to be irresponsible. He was eventually not allowed to call and see her and she was sent abroad to finishing school. Their friendship was ended by Maria, and his pride was deeply wounded. He met her again after he had become a famous novelist, with *Copperfield* and *Hard Times* behind him, and was quite shocked at what an empty chatterbox she was. He caught a severe cold from her, which must have seemed the final blow. He felt so lowered by the whole experience that he said 'nothing would do me the least good, but setting up a balloon'. Maria also appears as Dora in *David Copperfield*.

PHINEAS FINN

Anthony Trollope, *Phineas Finn* (1869), *Phineas Redux* (1873), *The Prime Minister* (1875) and *The Duke's Children* (1880)

Sir John Pope-Hennessy (1834–91)

These are a series of political novels. Phineas is a charming but poor Irish MP who leaves behind the girl who loves him, Mary Flood Jones. In the whirl of parliamentary and social life in the metropolis he becomes associated with several society ladies, Violet Effingham, Lady Standish and the widow, Madame Goesler. He is made under-secretary for the colonies, falls out with the government, resigns, and comes back home to marry Mary. She dies and he returns to London life, nearly makes it to the Cabinet, is accused of killing a political rival but is exonerated and marries Madame Goesler who has supported him. He makes minor appearances in *The Prime Minister* and *The Duke's Children,* though the main focus of attention is on the political and social life of Plantagenet Palliser and Lady Glencora. Phineas is an elaborately created character, charming on the surface, but not strong-willed, and a man who tries to be honest and principled. The main impression is of an attractive man who learns and develops.

He is based on John Pope-Hennessy, who came from the same kind of drab social background in the middle-classes as Phineas, but shone in London society and in parliament. He was the first Roman Catholic Conservative to be elected. He was MP for King's County and a barrister at the Inner Temple in 1861. In 1867–71 he was governor of Labuan, and of the Gold Coast 1872–73, of the Windward Islands 1875–76, of Hongkong 1877–82 and Mauritius 1883–89. He was returned for Killkenny in 1890 as an anti-Parnellite home-ruler. Henry Sweet Escott, first biographer of Trollope, wrote of his 'fine presence, winning manners', and said his return to St Stephens after an interval of absence suggested Phineas Finn. (see LORD CHILTERN.)

Gerald Haxton (1892–1944)

In the First World War, Somerset Maugham served in a Red Cross ambulance unit in France and there met, in the same unit, the American Gerald Haxton. Maugham fell in love with Haxton who became his secretary-companion and the passion of his life. When Haxton was, in 1915, arrested on a charge of gross indecency he was acquitted but his reputation was ruined and in 1919 he was deported from England as an undesirable alien. The fact that Haxton could not return to England prompted Maugham's own decision to live in exile; in 1928 he bought the Villa Mauresque, on the French Riviera, and lived there with Haxton. Although Haxton's heavy drinking, gambling and sexual adventuring annoyed Maugham he reluctantly accepted these foibles because of the many compensations. When Maugham and Haxton travelled it was the gregarious Gerald who would make contact with the people subsequently used as raw material for the novels. When Haxton died Maugham was heartbroken.

Haxton appeared vividly in Maugham's *Up at the Villa* (1953) as Rowley Flint, an Englishman who helps a rich English widow to get rid of a body and then blackmails her into marrying him. The description of Rowley as a scoundrel is a detailed portrayal of Gerald: 'He had a tolerable figure, but he was of no more than average height, and in clothes he looked thick-set. He had not a single feature that you could call good: he had white teeth, but they were not very even; he had a fresh colour, but not a very clear skin; he had a good head of hair, but it was of a vague brown between dark and fair; his eyes were fairly large, but they were of the pallid blue that is generally described as grey. He had an air of dissipation and people who didn't like him said he looked shifty.... He was in short a young man with a shocking reputation which he thoroughly deserved.'

Samuel Taylor Coleridge (1772–1834)

Nightmare Abbey puts before the reader a satiric portrait of some of the leading figures of English romanticism, who are friends and associates of the young Scythrop Glowry (see GLOWRY). Among the visitors to Nightmare Abbey is the poet and philosopher Ferdinando Flosky, 'a very lachrymose and morbid gentleman, of some note in the literary world, but in his own estimation of much more merit than name'. He has a very fine sense of the grim and the tearful: 'No one could relate a dismal story with so many minutiae of supererogatory wretchedness. No one could call up a *rawhead and bloody bones* with so many adjuncts and circumstances of ghastliness. Mystery was his natural element. He lived in the midst of that visionary world in which nothing is but what is not. He dreamed with his eyes open, and saw ghosts dancing round him at moontide.' As a young man, Flosky had been an enthusiast for Liberty, 'and had hailed the dawn of the French revolution as the promise of a day that was to banish war and slavery . . . from the face of the earth'. Because this faith had not been realized, he was convinced that nothing had been achieved, and became a reactionary, and wished to recreate the world of the past and ensure that there would be no loopholes such as had previously allowed in the light. To this endeavour he called on Kantian metaphysics ' and lay *perdu* several years in transcendental darkness, till the common daylight of common sense became intolerable to his eyes'.

This is an uncharitable thumbnail sketch of Coleridge, who, having earlier associated himself with radical causes and the hope of building utopia as Pantisocracy on the banks of the Susquehanna, failed in marriage, took to opium and soaked himself in the philosophy of Kant, notorious at the time for the obscurity of its terminology and style. Kant achieved a philosophical system which was an attempt to answer scepticism and empiricism. This was transcendental idealism, which made a prime distinction between *noumenon* (object of purely intellectual intuition) and *phenomenon* (object perceived or experienced). Coleridge's attempts to promulgate Kantian theory were considered by many incomprehensible. He was also associated with the Gothic and the gloomy — main targets in *Nightmare Abbey*. (See also MYSTIC.)

FLUELLEN
William Shakespeare, *Henry V* (1600)

Sir Roger Williams (1540–95)

Fluellen is a Welsh officer in the army of Henry V which goes to France and defeats the enemy in the battle of Agincourt. He is a thoroughly efficient and professional soldier and a colourful portrayal of what Shakespeare perceived as the Welsh character. He is very talkative, and the dramatist goes to a lot of trouble to get the sound and tone of his accent fully worked out – he repeats the phrase 'look you' and among his mannerisms is the tendency to pronounce b as p ('poys') but the general effect is of a loquacious, almost bullying character, without a shred of humour. He is frequently engaged in arguments with other officers, and has a very assertive manner which easily topples into the ridiculous. He makes out a case for Henry's similarity to Alexander the Great, though one was born in Macedon and the other in Monmouth: 'if you look in the maps of the 'orld, I warrant you sall find, in the comparisons between Macedon and Monmouth, that the situations, look you, is both alike. There is a river in Macedon; and there is also moreover a river at Monmouth; it is called the Wye at Monmouth, but it is out of my prains what is the name of the other river; but 'tis all one.'

Roger Williams was a Welsh soldier, who began his career as a page in the household of the First Earl of Pembroke, and served in Flanders in the army of Thomas Morgan, and was lieutenant to Sir John Norris. He later commanded with distinction under Leicester. He was knighted in 1586, and served at Zutphen and Sluys. During the threat of the Spanish invasion he was master of horse at the camp in Tilbury (1588). He served in France, accompanying Willoughby to Dieppe in 1589 and served in the cause of Henry of Navarre. He succeeded Essex when he was recalled to England in 1592 and Williams then became commander of the English troops before Rouen, and fought with great valour at the siege of Rue in the same year. His book, *A Brief Discourse of War*, was published in 1590. Some of Fluellen's Welsh regional characteristics may also be based on Lewis (or Ludowick) Lloyd (1573–1610) a well known figure at court, sergeant-at-arms to Elizabeth I and James I, a classical scholar and author. The allusions to ancient history with which Fluellen colours his discourse may be an echo of Lloyd.

SEBASTIAN FLYTE
Evelyn Waugh, *Brideshead Revisited* (1945)

Hugh Lygon (1904–36)

When Evelyn Waugh arrived at Oxford in 1922 he was about
to have the time of his life as his novel *Brideshead Revisited*
affirms. Waugh became a member of the Hypocrites, an
undergraduate drinking club presided over by Lord Elmley,
son of Lord Beauchamp. Greatly impressed by Elmley's social
credentials Waugh became friendly with the whole family,
including Lord Beauchamp's second son Hugh Lygon who
took him to the family seat of Madresfield Court in Worces-
tershire. After Oxford, Waugh and Hugh Lygon remained
good friends. In a letter written to Hugh's sisters, Lady Mary
and Lady Dorothy, in 1932 Waugh says, 'Well I hate to say it
but the truth is that Hugh had been at the bottle and he was
walking about the house with a red candle saying he thought
the lights might go out.' In 1934 Waugh visited Lord Beauchamp's London house, found Hugh 'in the library drinking
gin', and decided to accompany his friend on an Arctic expedition to Spitzbergen. Two years later Hugh Lygon went to
Germany on a motoring tour; when he got out of the car,
probably weakened by sunstroke, he fell and fractured his
skull. He died the same night, 19 August 1936.

Brideshead Revisited recreates Hugh as Sebastian Flyte who
begins the novel as an irrepressible undergraduate clutching
his teddy bear for comfort; and ends it as an irresponsible
drunk in a North African monastery. Even then he is 'completely charming' and the narrator Charles Ryder conjures up
an image of 'an arctic hut and a trapper alone with his furs and
oil lamp and log fire' before the sun causes a block of ice to
come down on the hut and obliterate the occupant. Although
known for his cynicism there is no reason to doubt Waugh's
sincerity when he wrote to Lady Mary Lygon, on hearing of
Hugh's death, 'It is the saddest news I ever heard. I shall miss
him bitterly.'

IRENE FORSYTE
John Galsworthy, *The Forsyte Saga* (1922)

Ada Galsworthy (1864–1956)

Describing the heroine of *The Forsyte Saga* John Galsworthy presented a seductive image of womanhood: 'A tall woman, with a beautiful figure, which some member of the family had once compared to a heathen goddess . . . Her figure swayed, so balanced that the very air seemed to set it moving. . . . But it was at her lips – asking a question, giving an answer, with that shadowy smile – that men looked; they were sensitive lips, sensuous and sweet, and through them seemed to come warmth and perfume like the warmth and perfume of a flower.'

So Galsworthy must have seen Ada, the wife of his first cousin Major Galsworthy, when they met in Paris in 1895. Later that year Galsworthy and Ada became lovers and for the rest of his life his work was made in the image of the woman who became his wife in 1905 and his Irene in *The Man of Property* (1906).

Ada Nemesis Pearson Cooper was born in 1864, the illegitimate child of Anna Julia Pearson and the adopted child of Dr Emanuel Cooper who delivered her. She married Major Galsworthy in 1891 but was unable to share his military enthusiasm and turned to the more compatible John Galsworthy. Ada was convinced that Galsworthy had great literary talent and made it her life's work to encourage him as a novelist. She also persuaded Galsworthy to see her as the embodiment of the long-suffering heroine and thus she appears in his fiction. Galsworthy was dependent on Ada and their marriage was an extremely close companionship rather than an intensely physical relationship. Ada's experience of Major Galsworthy had made her wary of men and one of her reasons for choosing to live with Galsworthy was undoubtedly her admiration for his undemanding nature. Galsworthy was eternally grateful to Ada and when he was briefly attracted to a young actress he was consumed by guilt at the thought of betraying Ada. At the end of his life he explored the possibility of making spiritual contact with Ada after his death.

SOAMES FORSYTE
John Galsworthy, *The Forsyte Saga* (1922)

Major Arthur Galsworthy

The Man of Property the first stage in *The Forsyte Saga* (which eventually comprised nine novels) is dominated by the figure of Soames Forsyte, a solicitor whose passion is for property. As a monument to his materialism he buys land at Robin Hill, outside London, and employs an architect to build a suitably impressive home. When the architect falls in love with Soame's beautiful wife Irene, Soames shows a rage for revenge. His appearance is as formidable as his personality: 'Soames Forsyte, flat-shouldered, clean-shaven, flat-cheeked, flat-waisted, yet with something round and secret about his whole appearance . . . the buttoned strictness of his black cut-away coat, conveyed an appearance of reserve and secrecy'.

Soames was modelled on Galsworthy's first cousin Major Arthur Galsworthy whose wife Ada was the woman the author eventually married. Major Galsworthy was a member of the Essex Yeomanry, not a professional soldier. He married Ada in April 1891 and the fact of her illegitimacy may well have hindered his hopes for a distinguished military career. Ada soon regretted her marriage to Major Galsworthy whose interests were confined to military matters. In 1900 Major Galsworthy had to accept the complete breakdown of his marriage and in 1904 he finally instituted divorce proceedings against Ada and John Galsworthy.

Soames as portrayed by Galsworthy is Major Galsworthy as seen by Ada, a version the author accepted as authentic. When Major Galsworthy died Ada wrote, in an undated letter to a friend, '[yesterday I had] news of the death of "Soames" (Major Galsworthy) [and heard] that two days before his death the local parson called and wished to ministrate. But the Major said: "No, and tell him the funeral will be at three." Witty to the last.' Despite Galsworthy's wish to make Soames a complete villain the character developed a life of its own and attracted the sympathy of readers.

FRA DIAVOLO

Opera, *Fra Diavolo* (1830, music by Daniel François Esprit Auber, libretto by Eugène Scribe)

Michele Pezza (1771–1806)

Fra Diavolo was first performed at the Opera Comique, Paris, in January 1830, and remained for many years one of the most popular operas in the French repertory, with a leading role, the bandit chief, which was a favourite of Alessandro Bonci, Tito Schipa and Nicolai Gedda. Fra Diavolo is a kind of Robin Hood who operates round Naples. He is chivalrous and takes from the rich to give to the poor. The plot involves Fra Diavolo in duping an English milord, attempting to seduce his wife, stealing his money, hiding in his room in a country inn and making one miraculous escape after another. He is finally accidentally betrayed and is captured by the carabinieri and shot. There is an alternative ending in which he is forgiven and the opera ends in general forgiveness and rejoicing – happy endings are a requirement of *opera comique*. The tune of the carabinieri, featured in the overture, is the regimental call of the British dragoon regiment, the 3rd Carabiniers.

This almost Hollywood-style romantic tarradiddle is based on the life story of the Italian brigand and patriot, Michele Pezza. He was originally a monk who turned to the life of an outlaw – hence his nickname, Fra Diavolo ('Father Devil'). When Naples was invaded by the French in 1799, Pezza was appointed by Cardinal Ruffo to help in its recovery. Pezza organized 'bands of the Holy Faith' which were gangs of peasants, convicts, brigands and the poor. They were fully exploited by Pezza in a series of raids and expeditions to harass the French, cause them trouble and waste their time and effort. The complications in the plot of *Fra Diavolo* arise because a reward of ten thousand piastres is placed on his head, and then Lord Cockburn, whose wife's honour is liable to be compromised by Fra Diavolo, offers six thousand 'scudi' reward for him. In real life, when Joseph Bonaparte came to the throne of Naples he put a price on the head of Pezza, who was captured and shot in 1806.

Konrad Dippel (1673–1734)

According to Mary Shelley's account of 1831 the genesis of
her novel *Frankenstein* was relatively simple. In the summer
of 1816 Shelley and Mary lived near Lord Byron at Geneva.
After reading a Gothic anthology, *Fantasmagoriana* (1812),
Byron declared 'We will each write a ghost story.' At first
unable to oblige, Mary was disturbed one night when Byron
and Shelley discussed the principle of life; when she went to
sleep she had a nightmare in which she saw 'the hideous
phantasm of a man stretched out, and then, on the working of
some powerful engine, show signs of life, and stir with an
uneasy, half vital motion'. Mary omitted to say that when she
eloped with Shelley in 1814 the couple sailed down the Rhine
and probably spent the night somewhere near Castle Frankenstein near Darmstadt. Castle Frankenstein, which still stands,
dates from the thirteenth century and was sold by the Frankenstein family in 1662.

When Konrad Dippel was born in the castle it was used as a
hospital for the war-wounded. So the boy grew up, as Radu
Florescu says in *In Search of Frankenstein* (1975), 'among the
disfigured and amputated soldiers'. Dippel enrolled at the
University of Giessen as 'Franckensteina' and went on to gain
a formidable reputation as an alchemist in which capacity he
was employed by the Landgrave of Hesse. Dippel was convinced (so Florescu records) that 'the body was an inert sub-
stance animated by an errant spirit that could leave it at any
time to infuse life into another' and he offered to supply the
Landgrave of Hesse with a vital secret in exchange for Castle
Frankenstein which he wanted for his own experiments in
distilling blood and bones. Negotiations broke down and
Dippel died, but his audacious character was resuscitated by
Mary Shelley in the person of Victor Frankenstein.

BARBARA FRIETCHIE
John Greenleaf Whittier, *In War Time* (1864)

May Quantrell

John Greenleaf Whittier's celebrated Civil War poem 'Barbara Frietchie', from *In War Time*, describes the all-American spirit of the heroine who defies the might of the Southern troops. In Frederick town, 'by the hills of Maryland', General Lee's men ride in and take down all Union flags. Old Barbara, 'Bravest of all Frederick town', takes up a flag and flies it from her attic window. When Stonewall Jackson sees this he has it shot at but Barbara snatches the flag, shakes it defiantly and utters her famous lines: '"Shoot, if you must, this old grey head,/But spare your country's flag," she said.' Deeply moved, Stonewall Jackson orders his men to march on and leave Barbara with her flag.

The story was told to Whittier by novelist Emma D.E.N. Southworth but she got it wrong: when the Southern troops entered Frederick on 6 September 1862 Stonewall Jackson was elsewhere, recovering from an injury; his troops did not pass Barbara's house; moreover, Barbara was ninety-six and on her deathbed. The real heroine was May Quantrell who waved a Union flag at the Confederate troops led by General Ambrose P. Hill. Incensed, some of the soldiers broke the staff – whereupon Mrs Quantrell obtained another flag. Hill told his men to let the lady keep her flag and so, as in Whittier's poem, 'ever the stars above look down/On thy stars below in Frederick town'. The story quickly passed into folklore and fact became confused with fiction when Barbara was given credit for an act actually performed by her near-neighbour May Quantrell.

HEDDA GABLER
Henrik Ibsen, *Hedda Gabler* (1890)

Emilie Bardach (1873–1955)

When Ibsen's heroine makes her entrance in *Hedda Gabler* she is a sensuous image of self-assurance: 'Hedda . . . is a woman of twenty-nine. Her face and figure show breeding and distinction. Her complexion is pale and opaque. Her eyes are steel grey and express a cold, unruffled repose. Her hair is an agreeable medium brown, but not especially abundant. She wears a tasteful, somewhat loose-fitting negligee.' Despite her enticing appearance Hedda is unhappy – bored by her middle-class marriage and frustrated at her failure to achieve her potential. Her efforts to change her life end tragically – 'everything I touch becomes ludicrous and despicable' she cries – and she shoots herself just before the final curtain.

Ibsen wrote the play when he was still under the erotic influence of Emilie Bardach, an eighteen-year-old Viennese girl he met in Gossensass in 1889 at a reception to celebrate the naming of the Ibsenplatz after him. When she became ill Ibsen called on her and she recorded her feelings in her diary: 'The obstacles! How they grow more numerous, the more I think of them! The difference of age! – his wife! – his son! – all that there is to keep us apart! Did this have to happen?' There is no doubt that the sixty-one-year-old writer was infatuated with Emilie and even tempted to abandon everything for a new life with her. Still, he settled down to the reality of the situation and consoled himself through correspondence. On 30 December 1889 he wrote to Emilie 'I beg you, for the time being, not to write to me again. When conditions have changed, I will let you know. I shall soon send you my new play. Accept it in friendship – but in silence.' After the 'new play', *Hedda Gabler,* there was no further contact between Emilie and Ibsen until she sent him a telegram of congratulation on his seventieth birthday and he replied saying 'The summer in Gossensass was the happiest, most beautiful in my whole life.'

THE GREAT GATSBY

F. Scott Fitzgerald, *The Great Gatsby* (1926)

Max Gerlach

F. Scott Fitzgerald's *The Great Gatsby* disturbs the American dream of innocent affluence. Installed in his Long Island mansion, Jay Gatsby seems the perfect symbol of success, having unlimited wealth to enjoy an endless round of parties: 'On weekends his Rolls-Royce became an omnibus, bearing parties to and from the city.' The great peacock display, however, is to attract one girl, for Gatsby is a romantic hopelessly in love with a married woman, Daisy Buchanan, whose cousin Nick narrates the novel. When Nick first meets Gatsby he is surprised by his 'elaborate formality of speech': Gatsby uses the old-worldly phrase 'old sport' which contrasts with the rumours of his criminal past.

From 1922 to 1924 Scott and Zelda Fitzgerald rented a house in Great Neck, Long Island, and Scott observed a convivial neighbour Max Gerlach. Shortly before her death, in 1948, Zelda recalled that Gatsby was modelled on 'a neighbour named Von Guerlach or something who was said to be General Pershing's nephew and was in trouble over bootlegging'. In the Fitzgeralds' scrapbook there is a newspaper photograph of Scott and Zelda with a note of 20 July 1923: 'En route from the coast – Here for a few days on business – How are you and the family old Sport? Gerlach.' As Matthew J. Bruccoli writes in *Some Sort of Epic Grandeur* (1982) 'Here is Gatsby's characterizing expression, *old sport*, from the hand of Gerlach. Attempts to fill in the history of Max Gerlach have failed; the only clue is a 1930 newspaper reference to him as a "wealthy yachtsman".' As 'yachtsman' was period slang for rum-runner Gerlach remains a shady, mysterious figure like the character he inspired.

MARGUERITE GAUTIER
Alexandre Dumas, fils, *La Dame aux camélias* (1852)

Rose Alphonsine Plessis, 'Marie Duplessis' (1824–46)

Alexandre Dumas's drama *La Dame aux camélias*, which was based on his novel of the same name (1848), has a straightforward plot. A young Parisian courtesan of great beauty, Marguerite Gautier, has many lovers from the top end of society. A young man of good family, Armand Duval, falls deeply in love with her and implores her to abandon her life in Paris and live with him in the country. They live blissfully together for some time and then Armand's father arrives and explains to Marguerite that the forthcoming marriage of his daughter is being seriously jeopardized by the scandal of the relationship between Armand and Marguerite. She now loves Armand and cannot really bear to lose him but his father tells her the boy is bound to tire of her and that the liaison is not blessed by heaven. She agrees to leave him. She returns to her life in Paris, knowing that she is dying of consumption. Armand misunderstands her motives, but they are briefly reconciled before she dies in his arms.

The real life Rose Alphonsine Plessis was the daughter of a pedlar, whose mother died when she was nine. By the age of thirteen she had been seduced by a man of seventy and later abandoned in Paris. She supported herself working as a corset maker, a messenger and street walker. By the age of sixteen she was in great demand, leading a life of luxury and supported by several wealthy lovers, among them the Count de Stackelberg, Russian ambassador to Vienna, who was eighty when they met. In *La Dame aux camélias* he appears as the Duc de Mauriac.

She met Dumas in 1842 and they fell in love. She was ill with consumption and he persuaded her to come and live with him in the healthier atmosphere of the countryside. She was not only a vital and attractive woman, but was also very intelligent. She had dark hair and a fine complexion. In appearance, her face was somewhat Asiatic, as she had long lacquer-like eyes. Dumas described her as 'à la virginité du vice'. Their affair was very passionate but brief. She left him to return to her life in Paris, but her illness worsened and she died at the age of twenty-three. Dumas came to see her body laid to rest in Paris in a monument engraved with marble camelias. He wrote a novel based on her life, but it was the play *La Dame aux camélias* which made her story famous. Verdi saw it in Paris in 1852 and based his opera 'La Traviata' on the story of 'Marie Duplessis'.

LUCIAN GAY
Benjamin Disraeli, *Coningsby* (1844)

Theodore Hook (1788–1841)

In Disraeli's political novel, *Coningsby*, we find this portrait of Lucian Gay: 'Nature had intended Lucian Gay for a scholar and wit; necessity had made him a scribbler and buffoon. He had distinguished himself at university; but had no patrimony, nor those powers of perseverance which success in any learned profession requires. He was good looking, had great animal spirits, and a keen sense of enjoyment, and could not drudge. Moreover, he had a fine voice, and sang his own songs with considerable taste, accomplishments which made his fortune in society, and completed his ruin. In due time he extricated himself from the bench and merged into journalism.'

This is a portrait of Theodore Hook, author, journalist and wit. He was the son of James Hook (1746–1827) who wrote many popular songs. Theodore's musical and literary gifts showed themselves at an early age, and he became the pet of green room circles. Educated at Harrow and Oxford, he did not graduate. Success came easily to him, and his comic opera *The Soldier's Return*, written when he was sixteen, made him famous, and a leading socialite. He had peerless powers of mimicry and was an astounding raconteur. He perpetrated some of the most famous practical jokes in history: the Berners Street hoax which involved the Lord Mayor, regiments of cavalry, the Chancellor of the Exchequer and other dignitaries all foregathering at the same address in London at the same time; and bringing a production of *Hamlet* to a standstill by coming on stage in Elizabethan costume and handing Hamlet a letter during the grave-diggers' scene. Such was his esteem as a socialite that the Prince Regent declared 'Something must be done for Hook!' and he was made Accountant General and Treasurer of Mauritius in 1813. He became the life and soul of the island but some £12,000 went missing and Hook was brought back home, for what he wittily termed: 'a disorder in his chest'. Journalism and miscellaneous writing sustained him for a time but he was eventually arrested for debt, whereupon he wrote a series of rollicking stories which still read well.

JOHN GILPIN

William Cowper *The Diverting History of John Gilpin* (1782)

William Beyer (1692–1791)

John Gilpin is a citizen 'of credit and renown' who has devoted his life to a prosperous trade and to public service, and has neglected his wife of some twenty years. The 'linen-draper bold' of Cheapside resolves to celebrate the twentieth anniversary of their wedding with a trip to the 'Bell' at Edmonton. He is to travel there on a horse he borrows, while his wife, her sister and the children will go there in a chaise and pair. The bold burgher loses control of the horse: 'So "Fair and softly," John he cried,/But John he cried in vain;/That trot became a gallop soon,/In spite of curb and rein.' The more he tries to restrain the beast, the wilder the horse becomes: 'Away went Gilpin, neck or nought;/Away went hat and wig;/He little dreamt, when he set out,/Of running such a rig.' Dogs bark, children scream with excitement, crowds gather thinking it is a race or an event of some kind. He gallops on to Edmonton and ten miles beyond it, on to Ware, and back again. His wife sends after him, and a hue and cry is raised with people calling out: 'Stop thief! stop thief! – a highwayman!' He is the first to arrive back home again, at the end of an eventful wedding anniversary.

The story is a true one, and the events happened to William Beyer, a linen-draper, who lived at the Cheapside corner of Paternoster Row. He died in 1791 at a ripe old age. William Cowper was a religious maniac, who suffered recurring bouts of depression and melancholia. He was befriended by Lady Anne Austen, widow of Sir Robert Austen, in 1781. She was a neighbour of his at Olney. During one of his attacks of almost suicidal depression she told him the story of poor Mr Beyer, who owned land near Olney. She had heard the story as a child. It is said that on the night in 1782 when Cowper was entertained by Lady Austen's narrative of Beyer's wedding anniversary adventures, he was kept awake all night with laughter at it, and turned it into the famous ballad which was published first in the *Public Advertiser* on 14 November 1782.

SCYTHROP GLOWRY
Thomas Love Peacock, *Nightmare Abbey* (1818)

Percy Bysshe Shelley (1792–1822)

Nightmare Abbey concerns the amorous entanglements of Scythrop Glowry, the young son of a gloomy misanthrope. One
of his ancestors hanged himself, and Scythrop's father has the
skull made into a drinking cup in his honour. Scythrop is sent
to public school, 'where a little learning was painfully beaten
into him,' and from there, to university: 'where it was carefully
taken out of him; and he was sent home like a well threshed
ear of corn, with nothing in his head.' But he did learn to drink
deep. He is early disappointed in love, and is driven half
distracted. It preys very deeply on his sensitive spirit. His father
attempts to console him by enlarging on a text from *Ecclesiastes*: 'One man among a thousand have I found, but a woman
amongst all those have I not found.' Scythrop asks why he
should have expected it, when 'the whole thousand were
locked up in his seraglio? His experience is no precedent for a
free state of society like that in which we live.' They are always
locked up, his father assures him, and vanity and interest keep
the key. 'I am sorry for it,' retorts Scythrop, 'But how is it that
their minds are locked up? The fault is in their artificial
education, which studiously models them into mere musical
dolls, to be set out for sale in the great toy-shop of society.'

These radical views of sexual politics had made Shelley notorious, and this is Peacock's portrait of young Shelley. He had
been sent down from Oxford as a result of his atheism, had
married Harriet Westbrook and left her for Mary Godwin.
He believed in 'free love' and his poem, *Queen Mab*, published
in 1813, put forward the theory that humankind was corrupted by human society, institutions and 'morality'. Peacock
shows Shelley at heart a reformer: 'Scythrop now became
troubled with the *passion for reforming the world*. He built many
castles in the air, and peopled them with secret tribunals. . . .
As he intended to institute a perfect republic, he invested
himself with absolute sovereignty over these mystical dispens-
ers of liberty.' Shelley was by no means offended, but told
Peacock he was 'delighted' with *Nightmare Abbey*.

EUGENIE GRANDET

Honoré de Balzac, *Eugénie Grandet* (1834)

Maria du Fresnay/Madame Hanska

The heroine of Balzac's *Eugénie Grandet*, a mixture of naivety and nobility, is deprived of love as a result of her father's appalling avarice. Eugénie is a portrait that combines two of the women in Balzac's life: Maria du Fresnay and Madame Hanksa. In October 1833 Balzac wrote to his sister: 'I have fathered a child, that's another secret for you, the sweetest and most naive of beings who fell at my feet like a flower from heaven, who came to me secretly, refused to let me write to her, and asks for nothing from me except "Love me for a year. I will love you all my life".'

Little is known of Maria du Fresnay beyond the fact that she was married when she met Balzac; Marie, the child she had by Balzac, lived from 1834 to 1930. Still, Balzac dedicated his novel to Maria: 'May your name be set on this book, whose fairest ornament is your portrait.'

Physically, Eugénie is formidable, 'built on such a generous scale', and the description fits Madame Evelina Hanska, the Polish countess Balzac was to marry five months before his death. Madame Hanska first wrote anonymously to Balzac in 1832 then, encouraged by him to correspond, wrote a second letter telling him 'You elevate woman to her true dignity; love in her is a celestial virtue, a divine emanation.' This notion of nobility was in his mind as he composed *Eugénie Grandet* during 1833. Accustomed to the exercise of authority Madame Hanska, an enormously wealthy woman, demanded that Balzac write to her every week about his activities but he had, eventually, to put his work before this woman. When Mme Hanska's husband died in 1842 Balzac wrote to 'my angel, my heavenly flower' proposing marriage but she had turned against him on account of his infidelities. It was only when it became obvious that Balzac was dying that Madame Hanska agreed to marry him in a ceremony conducted at Berdichev on 14 March 1850.

DORIAN GRAY

Oscar Wilde, *The Picture of Dorian Gray* (1891)

Father John Gray (1866–1934)

Oscar Wilde's novel *The Picture of Dorian Gray* is a sumptuously told tale of a vain young man who exchanges his soul so he will retain his youth while his portrait ages instead. Gray is a collector of exquisite experiences and, for example, 'the Roman ritual had always a great attraction for him. . . . The fuming censers, that the grave boys, in their lace and scarlet, tossed into the air like great gilt flowers, had their subtle fascination for him. . . . He had a special passion, also, for ecclesiastical vestments, as indeed he had for everything connected with the service of the Church.'

Although Dorian Gray never succumbs formally to the call of the Roman Catholic Church, John Gray – the friend Wilde referred to as 'Dorian' – eventually became Father John Gray of St Peter's Church, Edinburgh. Gray was introduced to Wilde in 1889 at a session of the Rhymers' Club. Wilde felt that Gray had all the markings of the perfect disciple for he was good-looking and wrote suitably decadent poems. After Wilde met Lord Alfred Douglas in 1891 he lost interest in John Gray but felt guilty enough about this to pay for the cost of publication of Gray's first collection of poems, *Silverpoints* (1892). Gray decided to enter the priesthood after the arrest of Oscar Wilde in 1895 and instructed a barrister to attend Wilde's trial to take action should his name be mentioned. In a letter, written to Lord Alfred Douglas from Reading Gaol, Wilde said 'When I compare my friendship with you with such still younger men as John Gray and Pierre Louys, I feel ashamed. My real life, my higher life was with them and such as they.'

Williamina Belsches (1775–1810)

When Alan Fairford, the autobiographical hero of Sir Walter
Scott's *Redgauntlet*, comes face to face with the mysterious
Green-Mantle, alias Lilias Redgauntlet, he is impressed: 'she
was a very pretty young woman . . . and the slight derange-
ment of the beautiful brown locks which escaped in natural
ringlets from under her riding-hat, with the bloom which
exercise had brought into her cheek, made her even more than
usually fascinating.'

As a young advocate (called to the Scottish Bar in 1792) Scott
felt he had found the love of his life in Williamina Belsches
(1775–1810), an heiress whose father Sir John had squandered
his own inheritance and was several thousand pounds in debt.
Scott declared his love in a letter to Williamina in 1795 and
her reply was ambiguous enough to give Scott hopes of an
eventual match. Scott's father, however, felt Williamina too
highly placed for the young advocate and wrote to Sir John to
say so. In 1796 Williamina was shown a copy of Scott's first
book, *The Chase, and William and Helen*, and was duly delighted though her praise of the author was dutiful not emotional. A rival had raised his financially irresistible head:
William Forbes, son of a great banker. Since Sir John Belsches
was becoming hopelessly in debt the marriage of Williamina
and young Forbes, in 1797, solved his financial problems. Scott
was shattered, 'broken-hearted for two years . . . but the crack
will remain till my dying day.' On the rebound Scott married
a French girl, Charlotte Charpentier, and embarked on thirty-
nine years of marriage which was 'something short of love in
all its fervour'. Scott never forgot his infatuation for Williamina and so portrayed her fondly as Green-Mantle. In his
Journal of 1827 Scott confessed that the thought of Williamina
was still enough to 'agitate my heart'.

When he met Williamina's mother in Edinburgh, the real
Green-Mantle had been dead for seventeen years and Scott
'fairly softened myself, like an old fool, with recalling stories,
till I was fit for nothing but shedding tears and repeating verses
for the whole night'.

CLYDE GRIFFITHS
Theodore Dreiser, *An American Tragedy* (1925)

Chester Gillette (1881–1908)

Early in Theodore Dreiser's *An American Tragedy* there is a
glimpse of Clyde Griffiths as a twelve-year-old boy who seems
apart from the little group he walks with: 'The boy moved
restlessly from one foot to the other. . . . A tall and yet slight
figure, surmounted by an interesting head and face – white
skin, dark hair – he seemed more keenly observant and decid-
edly more sensitive than most of the others – appeared indeed
to resent and even to suffer from the position in which he
found himself.' Clyde longs to escape from the evangelical
atmosphere associated with his parents who run a mission for
misfits. After being involved in an accident resulting in the
death of a child, Clyde goes to Chicago where he works as a
bellboy in a club. There he meets his rich uncle Samuel who
gives him a job in his shirt factory in Lycurgus. Two women
now dramatically enter Clyde's life: Roberta Alden, who
works in Clyde's department at the shirt factory; and Sondra
Finchley, a beautiful society girl. When Roberta becomes
pregnant Clyde attempts to simplify his life by drowning her
– which he finally does more by accident than intention. He is
found guilty of murder in the first degree and executed.

The story thus sticks closely to Dreiser's source in a murder
case of 1906. Chester Gillette was brought up in the American
West by his parents who ran a mission. He moved to Cortland,
New York, where his uncle gave him a job as a supervisor in
his skirt factory. Gillette seduced one of the factory girls, Grace
'Billy' Brown, and her pregnancy threatened his relationship
with a local debutante. In July 1906 Gillette persuaded Billy
to go on a holiday with him and, on Big Moose Lake, hit her
over the head with a tennis racket and watched as she drowned.
During the trial much was made of the heartbreakingly tender
letters written by Billy to Gillette and these were integrated
into Dreiser's novel. Gillette went to the electric chair in 1908
without ever acknowledging his guilt.

GUNGA DIN
Rudyard Kipling, *Barrack Room Ballads* (1892)

Juma

Rudyard Kipling was born in Bombay and, after schooling in England, returned to India in 1882 to work on the Lahore *Civil Military Gazette*. In the course of his journalistic work he picked up many stories of local life which he was able to retell with soldierly slang. His poem 'Gunga Din', from *Barrack Room Ballads* (1892), is a tribute from a Cockney soldier to a low-caste water-carrier (or bhisti): 'Now in Inja's sunny clime,/ Where I used to spend my time/A-servin' of 'Er Majesty the Queen,/Of all them blackfaced crew/The finest man I knew/ Was our regimental bhisti, Gunga Din.'

Kipling based Gunga Din on Juma, the regimental bhisti, with the Corps of the Guides, a crack fighting unit comprising native soldiers and British officers. Low-caste Indians like Juma were excluded from actually joining the Corps on the grounds that experience of servility would prevent a man acquiring the necessary ferocity to fight. At the siege of Delhi in 1857 Juma distinguished himself over two months by disregarding his own safety in order to bring water to the wounded. As a result of this the soldiers themselves cited his humble heroism: 'This man is the bravest of the brave, for without arms or protection of any sort he is in the foremost line. If anyone deserves the star for valour, this man does.' On the recommendation of the fighting men of the Guides, Juma was himself enlisted and awarded the star for valour, the highest honour given to an Indian soldier. Subsequently Juma became an officer in the Guides and earned further honours for his displays of courage in the Afghan War of 1878.

OLIVER HADDO

W. Somerset Maugham, *The Magician* (1908)

Aleister Crowley (1875–1947)

At the Chat Blanc, in Paris in 1905, Somerset Maugham met the notorious Satanist Aleister Crowley and soon began the process of transforming him into a fictional character. Oliver Haddo, as Crowley is called in Maugham's *The Magician*, is an unbearably arrogant individual with an aesthetic turn of phrase. When he arrives at the Chien Noir (as the Chat Blanc is renamed in the novel) he tells the waitress 'Marie, disembarrass me of this coat of frieze. Hang my sombrero upon a convenient peg.' Subsequently the story becomes more sinister as Haddo, whose activities include the making of test tube beings, pursues a young woman against her wishes and offers her as a human sacrifice.

Crowley, the Great Beast (as he called himself after the beast in Revelation), was attracted to the occult as a young man and formed his own secret society, the Astrum Argentinum (Silver Star) in London. As his infamy grew he began to travel in search of disciples and outrageous experiences. His *The Book of the Law*, dictated to him (so he said) by his guardian angel Aiwass, preached the message 'Do what thou wilt shall be the whole of the Law.' Drawing further on his fondness for Rabelais (who had used the motto in *Gargantua and Pantagruel*) Crowley founded, in 1920, his Abbey of Thelema on the northern coast of Sicily, but rumours of sexual perversion and sacrifice disturbed Mussolini who ordered Crowley out of the country in 1923. Crowley's career ended ingloriously with the Great Beast selling a patent medicine of his own concoction. Crowley was furious when Maugham's novel appeared, noting that the author had fictionalized 'some of the most private and personal incidents of my life, my marriage, my exploration, my adventures with big game, my magical opinions, ambitions and exploits [and] added a number of the many absurd legends of which I was the central figure'.

RICHARD HANNAY

John Buchan, *The Thiry-Nine Steps* (1915), *Greenmantle* (1916), *Mr Standfast* (1919), *The Three Hostages* (1924), *The Island of Sheep* (1936)

William Edmund Ironside, First Baron Ironside (1880–1959)

Richard Hannay, John Buchan's most popular hero, is a no-nonsense, get-up-and-go man of action who is at his best when on the move since, as he said in *Memory Hold-The-Door* (1941), Buchan was 'especially fascinated by the notion of hurried journeys'. Hannay is a Scotsman who has spent most of his life as a speculator and copper-engineer in South Africa. When *The Thirty-Nine Steps* opens he regrets leaving South Africa and reckons himself to be 'the best bored man in the United Kingdom' – at which point Franklin P. Scudder enters his life and then, with 'a long knife through his heart', leaves Hannay to save Britain.

Buchan went to South Africa in 1901 to work for Lord Milner, High Commissioner for South Africa; in this capacity he met Lieutenant Edmund Ironside who was doing Intelligence work in German South-West Africa. Ironically known as 'Tiny' because of his height of six foot four inches, Ironside was a brilliant operator with fourteen languages at his command. Using one of these languages – *taal* or Cape Dutch – Ironside disguised himself as a Boer transport-driver, accompanied a German military expedition against the Hereros (a nomadic Bantu-speaking people living in South-West Africa) and was awarded a German military medal before going back to British South Africa. When Buchan, confined to bed at Broadstairs in 1914 with a duodenal ulcer, wrote his 'shocker' *The Thirty-Nine Steps,* he made Hannay in the resourceful image of Ironside and gave him a similar combination of determination and panache. Ironside was Chief of the Imperial General Staff from 1938 until Dunkirk, and then for two months Commander-in-Chief, Home Forces. He was created Field Marshal in 1940 and a baron in 1941.

GWENDOLEN HARLETH

George Eliot, *Daniel Deronda* (1876)

Miss Leigh, Lord Byron's grandniece

Daniel Deronda is a love story. Gwendolen Harleth is a
vivacious, confident young woman, who marries Harleigh
Grandcourt. He is a wealthy and sophisticated man, and she is
attracted to him for the security he seems to offer. But she is
aware that another woman exists and that there are children
of this relationship. She learns to explore her own character
and question her own motives when she comes under the
influence of Daniel Deronda, a high-principled and noble
character. She feels particularly guilty when Grandcourt is
killed, as she has found herself wishing his death as she hopes to
be able to turn to Daniel, but he marries Mirah, after discovering his Jewish origins and devoting himself to the ideal of a
home for the Jewish race. Gwendolen learns to accept her life.
We are first introduced to Gwendolen when she is in her mid-
twenties, and she is in a gambling salon at Leubronn: 'one of
those splendid resorts which the enlightenment of ages has
prepared for the same species of pleasure at heavy cost of gilt
mouldings, dark toned colour and chubby nudities. . . . There
was deep stillness, broken only by a light rattle, a light chink,
a small sweeping sound, and an occasional monotone in
French.' Daniel looks at her, and asks himself: 'Was she beautiful or not beautiful?'

The seed which grew into *Daniel Deronda* was planted in
George Eliot's imagination when, in September 1872, she
watched Miss Leigh, Byron's grandniece, at the roulette table
in Homburg. She wrote in a letter: 'The saddest thing to be
witnessed is the play of Miss Leigh, Byron's grandniece, who
is only twenty-six years old, and is completely in the grasp of
this mean, money-making demon. It made me cry to see her
young fresh face among the hags and brutally stupid men
around her.' She had in fact lost £500, and looked hot and
excited by her play. In the novel she wrote: 'the vice of
gambling lay in losing money at it . . . while every single
player differed markedly from every other, there was a certain
uniform negativeness of expression which had the effect of a
mask'.

CAPTAIN HARVILLE
Jane Austen, *Persuasion* (1818)

Frank Austen (1774–1865)

One of the most persuasive moments in Jane Austen's *Persuasion* occurs when two characters, Captain Benwick and Louisa, are brought together in Lyme at the home of Captain Harville. Jane Austen's description of Captain Harville suggests a creature of infinite goodwill, which helps in his crucial discussion with the heroine towards the end of the novel. 'Captain Harville was a tall, dark man, with a sensible, benevolent countenance,' writes Austen, 'a perfect gentleman, unaffected, warm, and obliging.' With his wife he lives in a cottage near an old pier and, as a result of a wound, spends much time indoors where 'a mind of usefulness and ingenuity seemed to furnish him with constant employment within. He drew, he varnished, he carpentered, he glued, he made toys for the children, he fashioned new netting-needles and pins with improvements; and if everything else was done, sat down to his large fishing-net at one corner of the room.'

Captain Harville is Jane's affectionate portrait of her elder brother Frank Austen who was known to busy himself obsessively when indoors. As a boy of twelve, Frank entered the Royal Naval Academy in Portsmouth then served as a midshipman at home and abroad. He became Captain Austen in 1800 and helped blockade Boulogne in 1804 when Napoleon hoped to invade England. Subsequently he served as flag-captain to Nelson's second-in-command; diverted to Gibraltar for supplies he just missed the battle of Trafalgar and regretted losing 'all share in the glory'. After helping to defeat the French at St Domingo, Frank came home and in 1807 married Mary Gibson. He organized the disembarkation of Sir John Moore's troops in the Peninsular War, saw action against the French and Americans and was awarded the Companion of the Order of the Bath in 1815. After Jane's death (in 1817) Frank's career continued with distinction: he became Rear-Admiral in 1830 and Commander of the Fleet in 1863.

MISS HAVISHAM
Charles Dickens, *Great Expectations* (1860)

Martha Joachim (1788–1850)

Miss Havisham is a former beauty and heiress. She was jilted by Compeyson and has lived ever since her bridal morning in complete seclusion in Satis House, Rochester. She has brought up an adopted child, Estella, to despise the male sex. Pip, the stepson of the local blacksmith, is called in to play with Estella, who is cruel to him. He longs to become a gentleman so that he may be worthy of her. When he is told he is a young man of great expectations and is to be sent to London to learn the *bon ton*, he assumes it is part of Miss Havisham's plans to bring him and Estella together. The first sight of Miss Havisham understandably greatly impresses young Pip: 'She was dressed in rich materials . . . all of white. Her shoes were white . . . she had a long white veil . . . her hair was white . . . everything within my view which ought to be white . . . had lost its lustre, and was faded and yellow . . . the bride within the bridal dress had withered like the dress.' In Satis House time has stopped. The hands of the clocks are stopped. No sunlight enters. Miss Havisham lives in the past.

In January 1850 *Household Words*, a journal edited by Dickens, carried a report on the inquest on Martha Joachim, 'a wealthy and eccentric lady' who had died in York Buildings, Marylebone, aged sixty-two. 'It was shown in evidence that on the 1st. June 1808, her father, an officer in the Life Guards, was murdered and robbed . . . the murderer was apprehended. . . . In 1825, a suitor of the deceased, whom her mother rejected, shot himself. . . . From that instant she lost her reason . . . she had led the life of a recluse, dressed in white, and never going out.' There was another woman-in-white who fascinated Dickens, the White Woman of Berners Street, Oxford Street, whom he had seen in his childhood. He wrote about her in an essay, *Where We Stopped Growing*: 'she was constantly on parade in that street. . . . She is dressed entirely in white. . . . She is a conceited old creature, cold and formal in manner, and evidently went simpering mad on personal grounds. . . . This is her bridal dress. She is always walking up here, on her way to church.'

HEATHCLIFF
Emily Brontë, *Wuthering Heights* (1847)

'Welsh' Brunty

The passionate love story of Catherine Earnshaw and the gipsy foundling taken in by her father is the main narrative thread of this wild and romantic novel. Heathcliff is brought back from Liverpool, 'a dirty, ragged, black-haired child, big enough both to walk and talk ... its face looked older than Catherine's; yet when it was set on its feet it only stared round, and repeated over and over again some gibberish that nobody could understand'.

There is an interesting source for this story. Patrick Brontë, father of Emily, Charlotte and Anne, was born on the 17 March 1777, the son of Hugh Brunty and Alice Eleanor Brunty, in Drumballyroney, County Down. Hugh's grandfather had a farm near the Boyne. On a trip cattle-dealing to Liverpool, he picked up a dark, dirty and ragged foundling and adopted him. His dark complexion made them believe he was either Welsh or a gipsy, so he was named 'Welsh'. Though he was a morose and cunning lad, he learned the business and went everywhere with Mr Brunty and Brunty's own children grew very resentful of him. When Brunty died suddenly Welsh took over the farm, and made it clear he was determined to marry Brunty's daughter, Mary. He tried all his cunning to get the Brunty family in his grasp, but failed, though eventually he managed to manipulate Mary into marrying him. They were a childless couple and adopted Hugh Brunty, whose father lived in the south of Ireland, on condition that his father was never to communicate with him again. The journey was deliberately elongated so Hugh would never recall the way home. Hugh was badly treated by Welsh and made to work hard on the farm. Welsh had a second in command, a sullen bible-thumping peasant, similar to Joseph in *Wuthering Heights*, and Hugh's best friend was a farm dog, Keeper. Emily Brontë's favourite dog was called 'Keeper'. Hugh's aunt Mary, 'Welsh' Brunty's wife, told Hugh the whole story, as she was sorry for him. Hugh lived in Ireland and eloped with Alice McClory in 1776. Their son, Patrick, passed on the story to the children of his marriage to Maria Branwell. It is echoed in Charlotte's story of Willie Ellin.

PHILIP HERRITON
E.M. Forster, *Where Angels Fear to Tread* (1905)

Edward J. Dent (1876–1957)

Like Philip Herriton, his fictional counterpart, the musicologist Edward J. Dent believed that the cultural climate of Italy improved the individual. Herriton's Italian experience in E.M. Forster's first novel *Where Angels Fear to Tread*, however, turns out to be traumatic rather than triumphant: he becomes entangled in the aftermath of a marriage between his sister-in-law Lilia and Gino, a dentist's son. Philip is presented as an awkward man with the saving graces of aesthetic appreciation and good humour: 'The sense of beauty developed first. It caused him at the age of twenty to wear parti-coloured ties and a squashy hat. . . . At twenty-two he went to Italy with some cousins, and there he absorbed into one aesthetic whole olive-trees, blue sky, frescoes, country inns, saints, peasants, mosaics, statues, beggars.' As Dent, who knew Forster at Cambridge, spent his own holidays in Italy (in musical research) he encouraged his friend to follow suit, so in 1901 Forster visited San Gimignano, the model for the fictional Monteriano.

When he began to write the novel, Forster based Philip firmly on Dent who (so Forster said in an interview) 'knew this, and took an interest in his own progress'. When the novel was accepted for publication Forster's original title, *Monteriano*, was rejected and Dent supplied the title Forster finally used. Dent went on to achieve great distinction as a scholar and brilliant translator of Italian opera into English; his superbly singable versions of Mozart made opera more accessible to English audiences. In 1919 Dent helped found the British Musical Society and in 1923 became the first President of the International Society for Contemporary Music. From 1926 to 1941 he was Professor of Music at Cambridge. On 22 March 1950 Forster wrote to Dent to say he was conscious 'of how much I owe you'.

HIAWATHA
Henry Wadsworth Longfellow, *Hiawatha* (1855)

Haion 'hwa 'tha and 'Manabozho'
(circa 1550)

Longfellow's poem tells the story of the life and death of
Hiawatha, an Indian chief of miraculous descent among the
Iroquois. He was sent to earth to teach men the arts of peace
and good civilization. He is the son of Wenonah, a beautiful
Indian woman, and the West Wind. Hiawatha is brought up
by his grandmother, Nokomis, the daughter of the Moon.
From all his adventures Hiawatha accumulates great wisdom,
and he is able to avenge his mother against the West Wind, his
father. He becomes the leader of his people, teaching humankind that maize is their food and teaching them the skills of
navigation and the science of medicine. Tribes should live in
peace with each other, and with the white man, was his
message. In doing this people followed the wishes of the Great
Spirit, Manitou, whom all Indians worshipped: 'On the Mountains of the Prairie/Gitche Manitou the mighty . . ./Stood erect
and called the nations/Called the tribes of men together.'

Longfellow got his subject matter from the researches of Henry
Rowe Schoolcraft (1793–1864) an American explorer (he
discovered the source of the Mississippi), ethnologist and
scholar. His six-volume work, *Information Respecting the Indian
Tribes of the United States,* 1851–57, was the result of a commission by Congress. In 1839 he published *Algic Researches,* in
two volumes, revised in 1856 as *The Myth of Hiawatha.*
Schoolcraft married Jane D. Johnston, granddaughter of an
Indian chief, who aided his researches into Indian myth and
history. Schoolcraft confuses the Iroquois Hiawatha, Haion
'hwa 'tha, who was an historical figure, with the legendary
hero of the Algongquin, 'Manabozho'. North American Indian
culture was devoid of writing and time systems and consisted
entirely of legendary traditions, which may have had factual
bases. Schoolcraft encumbered the historical Hiawatha with
the traditional exploits which accumulated round the name of
Manabozho. Longfellow follows him in these errors, and sets
the narrative on Lake Superior, but it belongs in central New
York.

HENRY HIGGINS
George Bernard Shaw, *Pygmalion* (1912)

Henry Sweet (1845–1912)

In George Bernard Shaw's *Pygmalion* Professor Henry Higgins describes his apparently astounding powers of linguistic observation as perfectly logical: 'Simply phonetics. The science of speech. That's my profession: also my hobby. . . . You can spot an Irishman or a Yorkshireman by his brogue. *I* can place any man within six miles. I can place him within two miles in London. Sometimes within two streets.'

As Shaw acknowledged enthusiastically in his preface to the play, Higgins was based on the character and career of Henry Sweet the philologist who invented a phonetic shorthand. Sweet was born in London and studied for some time in Germany where he acquired an interest in the scientific study of language. His books, such as *A History of English Sounds* (1874) and *A Handbook of Phonetics* (1877), established him as the leading phonetist of his time. However his scorn for his colleagues made him an isolated figure and Oxford could accommodate him only by creating for him (in 1901) a special Readership in Phonetics. In Shaw's play Henry Higgins transforms Eliza Doolittle into a lady by linguistic methods. According to Shaw, Sweet too could have achieved stunning results had his personality been more practical: 'With Higgins's physique and temperament Sweet might have set the Thames on fire. As it was, he impressed himself professionally on Europe to an extent that made his comparative personal obscurity, and the failure of Oxford to do justice to his eminence, a puzzle to foreign specialists in his subject.' Shaw also noted that Sweet lacked 'sweetness of character: he was about as conciliatory to conventional mortals as Ibsen or Samuel Butler. His great ability as a phonetician (he was, I think, the best of them all at his job) would have entitled him to high official recognition . . . but for his Satanic contempt for all academic dignitaries and persons in general who thought more of Greek than phonetics.'

HIGHLAND MARY
Robert Burns, *Poetical Works* (1904)

Mary Campbell (1763–86)

'Will ye go to the Indies, my Mary,/And leave auld Scotia's
shore?/Will ye go to the Indies, my Mary,/Across the Atlantic's
roar?': like many of his contemporaries Robert Burns frequently thought of seeking his fortunes overseas from Scotland.
In 1786 he had good reason to contemplate a new life; he had
got a girl, Jean Armour, pregnant and been rejected as a possible
son-in-law by a man who disliked his behaviour and deplored
his lack of prospects. Accordingly Burns accepted a job as a
plantation book-keeper in Jamaica and turned his bruised
affections to another girl – Mary Campbell, a Coilsfield dairy-
maid. On the second Sunday of May 1786, the couple met 'in
a sequestered spot by the Banks of Ayr' and exchanged Bibles
over the Faile stream. Then, as Burns put it, they 'spent the day
in taking farewell, before she should embark for the West
Highlands to arrange matters among her friends for our
projected change of life'.

It seems that they intended to marry and emigrate to Jamaica
together; the publication of Burns's first book would alleviate
his financial worries for he was well on the way to raising the
necessary subscriptions. *Poems, Chiefly in the Scottish Dialect*,
published on 30 July 1786, was an immediate success. Burns
was scheduled to meet Mary Campbell at Greenock in September so they could both sail for Kingston; meanwhile he went
to Mossgiel farm where he heard that Jean Armour had given
birth to twins. Then, from Greenock, came the shattering news
of Mary Campbell's death – Burns claimed she died from a
'malignant fever' but there is a possibility that she died in
childbirth. Suddenly the journey to Jamaica seemed pointless
and Burns headed, instead, for Edinburgh where he was lion-
ized as a cultural phenomenon. Burns, in 'Highland Mary',
wrote: 'But still within my bosom's core/Shall live my Highland Mary.'

HOBBINOL
Edmund Spenser, *The Shepherd's Calendar* (1579)

Gabriel Harvey (1545–1630)

The Shepherd's Calendar, is a pastoral poem in twelve eclogues (sections) which Spenser dedicated to Sir Philip Sidney. It has a prefatory letter addressed to Gabriel Harvey and detailed notes by 'E.K.' (generally identified as Edward Kirke 1553–1613, a friend of the poet's at Pembroke College, Cambridge). Spenser uses classical models – Theocritus, Virgil – as well as Mantuan, Sannarzaro, Marot and early Tudor poets such as Barclay and Googe. The eclogues are subdivided into three types – plaintive (love poems, with compliments to several persons); moral (satiric of religious abuses); and recreative (purely entertaining). The main theme holding the *Calendar* together is the narrative of the hopeless love of Colin Clout (= Spenser) for the cold and distant shepherdess, Rosalind (who has never satisfactorily been identified). Colin's close friend is Hobbinol, who is certainly the poet's dear friend Gabriel Harvey: 'the person of some his very special and most familiar friend, whom he entirely and extraordinarily beloved' as E.K. explains. In some ways there is a tension between Colin's affection for Rosalind and his love for Hobbinol: 'It is not Hobbinol wherefore I plaine,/Albee my love he seek with dayly suit;/His clownish gifts and curtsies I disdaine,/His kiddes, his cracknelles, and his early fruit./Ah, foolish Hobbinol! thy gyfts bene vayne;/Colin them gives to Rosalind againe.' As E.K. explains, the relationship might even seem somewhat of a homosexual nature: 'seemeth to be some savour of disorderly love, which the learned call *paederastice*'.

Harvey was a Cambridge scholar and met Spenser as a student. They became very good friends. Harvey was lecturer in Greek and professor of rhetoric, and became engaged in the celebrated Greene/Harvey/Nashe controversy, which really was a debate about the changing role of the writer in Elizabethan society, with Harvey on the side of the academic, traditionalist and classical model. He was on the receiving end of Nashe's *Have With You to Saffron Walden*, and was notorious in his efforts to dissuade Spenser from writing *The Faerie Queene*. With Philip Sidney the three formed the *Areopagus* – a literary club aimed at adapting classical metres to English verse.

PRINCE HOHENSTIEL-SCHWANGAU

Robert Browning, *Prince Hohenstiel-Schwangau, Saviour of Society* (1871)

Charles Louis Napoleon Bonaparte, Napoleon III (1808–73)

In Browning's monologue, the Prince is a deposed European autocrat, who picks up a girl in the Haymarket. In a tea-room he confides to the girl that he has seen better days: 'And worse too, for they brought me no such bud-mouth/As yours to lisp "You wish you knew me!"' He goes on to defend his political career, which was based on the principle of expediency, of taking things as they were, not seeking radical change, tolerating 'change' only insofar as the basic structure of society was not altered; though in terms of philosophy, the Prince was able to seem 'modern' by toying with fashionable ideas of the day, such as Darwinism. The shallow decadence of his empire is delineated, together with its latent propensity for war: 'tired of the illimitable line on line/Of boulevard-building, tired o' the theatre/With the tuneful thousand in their thrones above,/ For glory of the male intelligence,/And Nakedness in her due niche below,/For illustration of the female use.'

This is Louis Napoleon, then living in exile after the French defeat in the Franco-Prussian war. He was born in Paris, the third son of Louis Bonaparte and Hortense de Beauharnais, the brother and stepdaughter, respectively, of Napoleon I. He attempted to gain political power on two early occasions, and was imprisoned in 1840. He escaped in 1846 and lived in London but took advantage of the revolution of 1948 to return to France. He was elected President of the Republic and built up support by claiming to uphold stability and religion against the threat of revolution. He achieved a coup d'état in 1851 and within a year proclaimed himself Emperor. He perceived overseas war as a means of securing a sense of glory for his regime, and France entered the Crimean War, engaged in war against Austria in 1859 and attempted to create an imperial colony in Mexico 1863–67. At home, opposition forced him to make democratic concessions and corruption was rife. His *Vie de César* was not well received. Suspecting the loyalty of the army, he allowed himself to think war might rekindle national ardour and was pushed by Bismarck into the Prussian War in 1870. His empire collapsed after his surrender at Sedan, with 83,000 men.

SHERLOCK HOLMES

Sir Arthur Conan Doyle, *A Study in Scarlet* (1887), *The Sign of Four* (1890), *The Adventures of Sherlock Holmes* (1892), *The Memoirs of Sherlock Holmes* (1894), *The Hound of the Baskervilles* (1902), *The Return of Sherlock Holmes* (1905), *The Valley of Fear* (1915), *His Last Bow* (1917), *The Case-Book of Sherlock Holmes* (1927)

Dr Joseph Bell (1837–1911)

When Arthur Conan Doyle settled down, in March 1886, to write *A Study in Scarlet* he determined to create a detective who would outdo in ingenuity his own favourite – Edgar Allen Poe's 'masterful detective, M. Dupin'. As a medical student in Edinburgh in the 1870s, Doyle had been hugely impressed by the deductive skills of Dr Joseph Bell who was consulting surgeon at Edinburgh Infirmary, professor at Edinburgh University, and editor of the *Edinburgh Medical Journal*. In creating Sherlock Holmes, so he writes in his *Memories and Adventures* (1924), Doyle 'thought of my old teacher Joe Bell, of his eagle face, of his curious ways, of his eerie trick of spotting details'. Writing to Dr Bell on 4 May 1892 Doyle declared 'It is most certainly to you that I owe Sherlock Holmes. . . . I do not think that his analytical work is in the least an exaggeration of some effects which I have seen you produce in the out-patient ward.'

Doyle served as Bell's out-patient clerk and prepared notes before each patient was presented to Bell for diagnosis. In one example recorded by Doyle, Bell deduced that a patient had recently served in a Highland regiment as a non-commissioned officer stationed at Barbados. 'You see, gentlemen,' Bell explained, 'the man was a respectful man but did not remove his hat. They do not in the army, but he would have learned civilian ways had he been long discharged. He has an air of authority and he is obviously Scottish. As to Barbados, his complaint is elephantiasis, which is West Indian and not British.' Bell himself, though flattered by the compliment Doyle had paid him, had a different view of the origins of the great detective and told Doyle 'You are yourself Sherlock Holmes, and well you know it.'

HOLOFERNES

William Shakespeare, *Love's Labours Lost* (1594)

Alexander Aspinall (died 1624)

In Shakespeare's early comedy *Love's Labours Lost,* the pedantic village schoolmaster, Holofernes, suggests that a dramatic presentation of the Nine Worthies is given for the entertainment of the Princess of France. He casts himself as Judas Maccabaeus, other village notables appear as Pompey, Alexander, Hector, Hercules etc. Holofernes is portrayed in the comedy as a pompous schoolmaster anxious to display his book-learning, who can never say anything directly, nor without showing off his command of the classics. Of a deer that is shot in the hunt he says: 'The deer was, as you know, sanguis, in blood; ripe as the pomewater, who now hangeth like a jewel in the ear of caelo, the sky, the welkin, the heaven; and anon falleth like a crab on the face of terra, the soil, the land, the earth.' He is admired for this, the curate, Nathaniel, answers: 'Truly, Master Holofernes, the epithets are sweetly varied, like a scholar at the least' and asserts that Holofernes' talent for learning and versifying are remarkable. Holofernes agrees with him: 'This is a gift that I have, simple, simple; a foolish extravagant spirit, full of forms, figures, shapes, objects, ideas, apprehensions, motions, revolutions. These are begot in the ventricle of memory, nourished in the womb pia mater, and delivered upon the mellowing of occasion. But the gift is good in those in whom it is acute, and I am grateful for it.' The elaborate masque of the heroes of the ancient world which Holofernes designed fails to give him the starring role he clearly had in mind for himself, and the audience constantly interrupt the performance and he is laughed off the stage.

Alexander Aspinall was the schoolmaster at Stratford grammar school from 1582 until the time of his death. He was born in Lancashire and educated at Brasenose, Oxford, where he gained his BA in 1575 and his MA in 1578. He was a notable citizen of Stratford, as he married a wealthy widow and went into trade while continuing as schoolmaster, later becoming successively burgess, alderman, and chamberlain of the ward where Shakespeare lived. The dramatist modelled Holofernes on Aspinall, who was a noted Stratford worthy, an 'ancient Master of Art and a man learned', according to one of his contemporaries. Shakespeare composed a posy for him when in middle age he went a-wooing with a pair of gloves for his beloved: 'The gift is small:/The will is all:/Alexander Aspinall.' This is recorded in Sir Francis Fane's commonplace book, with the comment: 'Shaxpaire upon a peaire of gloves that Master Aspinall sent to his mistris.'

FELIX HOLT
George Eliot, *Felix Holt the Radical* (1866)

Gerald Massey (1828–1907)

Felix Holt deals with the career, political ambitions and romantic complications of the lives of Felix Holt and Harold Transome. Holt is the son of a family which makes its living selling quack medicines. He develops into a noble young man with very high and sincere political ambitions to make the world a better place. He puts his ideas into practice by deliberately choosing a humble existence and the life of a working man in order to demonstrate to his fellows in the working classes that their amelioration lies in the direction of education and learning to think for themselves, rather than simply in hoping that improvement will come about in society as the result of the benevolence of the law-makers. He is contrasted with Transome, who is an honest enough young man, but a career politician who is not above using the system to get on. Romantic complications result from the choice that the heroine, Esther, has to make between them – either a life of ease, comfort and success with Transome, or hardship, poverty and good works with Holt. She chooses Felix Holt. Felix is a rough and ready man, with no trimmings. We first see him through the eyes of the minister of the town of Treby Magna : 'accustomed to the respectable air of provincial townsmen, and especially to the sleek well-clipped gravity of his own male congregation, felt a slight shock as his glasses made perfectly clear to him the shaggy-headed, large-eyed, strong-limbed person of this questionable young man, without waistcoat or cravat'.

This was based on Gerald Massey, of Tring, who worked from the age of eight, was self taught, became a poet and joined the Chartist movement and was a devout Christian Socialist, intimate of Maurice and Kingsley. He published much poetry and popular Egyptology, became a mystic and spiritualist. Massey was also a successful lecturer and journalist, and travelled in the USA.

Maria Manning (1821–49)

Hortense is a French maid, in the service of Lady Dedlock. She is thirty-two years old and from somewhere in the southern country about Avignon and Marseilles: 'a large-eyed, brown woman with black hair who would have been handsome, but for a certain feline mouth, and general uncomfortable tightness of face, rendering the jaws too eager, and the skull too prominent . . . she has a watchful way of looking out of the corners of her eyes without turning her head . . . especially when she was in an ill-humour and near knives.' She works for Lady Dedlock for five years and then is dismissed through becoming jealous of another servant, Rosa. But Hortense has found out something of Lady Dedlock's secret – that she had had a child by Captain Hawden – and tries to get money out of Tulkinghorn, the lawyer. She fails and murders him. She then tries to put the blame on Lady Dedlock. Inspector Bucket (see BUCKET) solves the crime and she is arrested.

Hortense was based on the Belgian murderess, Maria Manning. She and her husband George Manning murdered their lodger, Patrick O'Connor, for his money. The unfortunate O'Connor was invited to a dinner of roast goose. When he arrived they shot him and put his body in quicklime below the floor while they went on to enjoy their meal. At the trial she called out: 'There is no law nor justice to be got here!' – 'Base and degraded England!' In prison she was violent and abused the staff. She also attempted suicide. Dickens saw their execution on 13 November 1849, and subsequently wrote a letter to *The Times* about the harmfulness of public executions. Maria Manning had been lady's maid to the Duchess of Sunderland, and she was arrested by Inspector Field. He traced her to her lodging, tapped quietly on the door and said: 'Only me – Charley Field – so just open the door quietly, Maria.'

THE HOUSE OF THE SEVEN GABLES

Nathaniel Hawthorne, *The House of the Seven Gables* (1851)

The first sentence of Nathaniel Hawthorne's *The House of the Seven Gables* describes the novel's central symbol: 'Halfway down a bystreet of one of our New England towns stands a rusty wooden house, with seven acutely peaked gables, facing towards various points of the compass, and a huge, clustered chimney in the midst.' Condemned as a wizard, Matthew Maule casts a curse from the scaffold on his tormentor, Colonel Pyncheon: 'God will give him blood to drink!' Still, Pyncheon builds the House of the Seven Gables over Maule's log-built hut: 'His home would include the home of the dead and buried wizard, and would thus afford the ghost of the latter a kind of privilege to haunt its new apartments, and the chambers into which bridegrooms were to lead their brides, and where children of the Pyncheon blood were to be born.' Colonel Pyncheon is found dead, his beard 'saturated' with blood, and Maule's curse hangs over the House for three generations.

Hawthorne was born and brought up in Salem, Massachusetts, and was a frequent visitor to the House of the Seven Gables which was owned by his cousin, Miss Susannah Ingersoll. Built in 1668 by Captain John Turner, the House was extended in the 1690s by John Turner II, so that it had the seven gables. Miss Susannah liked to tell Hawthorne tales of their ancestors, including Major William Hathorne (as the surname was spelt before Hawthorne altered it); among the Quakers he persecuted was one John Maule. In 1692, during the notorious witch hysteria, Hawthorne's ancestor John Hathorne acted as an examiner of persons accused. According to Salem folklore the curse 'God will give you blood to drink' was uttered in 1692 by a condemned witch. From his intimate knowledge of the House itself, and from stories of Salem, Hawthorne created his romance. In 1908 Caroline O. Emmerton bought the House and had it restored to the original design with the seven gables; since 1910 it has been open to the public.

Delmore Schwartz (1913–66)

Charlie Citrine, the playwright-narrator of Saul Bellow's *Humboldt's Gift*, finds that his life is inextricably connected with the rise and fall of the poet Von Humboldt Fleisher. Humboldt, Citrine explains, was a poetic sensation of the 1930s, an instant celebrity whose 'picture appeared in *Time* without insult and in *Newsweek* with praise'. He was good-looking, eloquent, erudite: 'The guy had it all.' After all his promise, though, Humbolt had degenerated into drunkenness, despair and madness: 'He dropped dead in a dismal hotel off Times Square,' Citrine writes. At about 3 a.m. Humboldt had a heart attack: 'Fighting for breath, he tore off his shirt. When the cops came to take the dead man to the hospital his chest was naked. . . . At the morgue there were no readers of modern poetry. . . . So he lay there, another derelict.'

This description of the death of Humboldt is an exact account of the fate of Brooklyn-born Delmore Schwartz whose first volume of poems and stories, *In Dreams Begin Responsibilities* (1938), had been greatly applauded by the critics. Schwartz was, like Humboldt, a manic-depressive whose instability led to hospitalization in Bellevue. When Saul Bellow organized a collection to pay for psychiatric help, the disturbed poet turned against the successful novelist; this cycle of jealousy and love-hatred is recreated in Bellow's novel. Although Bellow stresses the comic aspects of Humboldt the book is a deeply felt tribute to Schwartz: 'He was a lovely man, and generous, with a heart of gold. . . . For after all Humboldt did what poets in crass America are supposed to do. He chased ruin and death even harder than he had chased women. He blew his talent and his health and reached home, the grave, in a dusty slide.'

PAUL JAGO

C.P. Snow, *The Light and the Dark* (1947), *The Masters* (1951), *The Affair* (1960)

Canon Charles Earle Raven (1885–1964)

The Masters by C.P. Snow is a study of a struggle for the control of a Cambridge college. In a claustrophobically close environment two candidates emerge as possible successors to the Master who is dying of cancer. Redvers Crawford represents the interests of science whereas Paul Jago, senior tutor, is a traditionalist devoted to Cambridge and 'the only one of the present college who had been born into the academic life'. Crawford triumphs in the interests of pragmatism but the reader's sympathy is directed towards Jago: 'Many [people] disliked his love of display. Yet they were affected by the depth of his feeling. Nearly everyone recognized that, though it took some insight to perceive that he was not only a man of deep feeling, but also one of passionate pride.'

According to Philip Snow's *Stranger and Brother* (1982), Jago is 'a superbly drawn portrait' of Canon Charles Earle Raven who was Professor of Divinity at Cambridge from 1932 to 1950. Raven's greatest ambition was to become Master of Christ's College where C.P. Snow was a fellow from 1930. When the mastership election was held in 1939 Raven (unlike his fictional counterpart) was successful and C.P. Snow, who took a dim view of Raven's pacifism, wrote to his brother: 'I think if I had gone all out I could probably have kept him out. . . . You should have seen him on the morning of his election, when it was fairly certain that he would get it. He kept walking round the Court, only keeping himself from smiling by an effort; and, though he kept his mouth from smiling, he couldn't control his eyes.' Once Master, Raven basked in the glory of the position by dining almost every night and showing a proprietorial pride in fellows and furnishings. Snow's novel was resented by the college and for some time after the publication of the book the author was, in the words of his brother, '*persona non grata* among certain fellows'.

JEANIE WITH THE LIGHT BROWN HAIR

Stephen Foster, *'Jeanie with the Light Brown Hair'* (1854)

Jane McDowell

Stephen Foster's song 'Jeanie with the Light Brown Hair' expresses great tenderness: 'I long for Jeanie with the day-dawn smile,/Radiant in gladness, warm with winning guile.' It was composed at a time when Foster was living apart from his Jeanie – Jane Denny McDowell. Foster was born in Lawrenceville, Pittsburgh, and went to Cincinnati in the 1840s to work as a book-keeper for his brother Dunning Foster. He returned to his home town in 1850 and on 22 July married a beautiful local girl, Jane McDowell.

Like Foster, Jane was of Scottish-Irish pioneer stock; but as the daughter of a leading Pittsburgh physician she was accustomed to a higher standard of living than Foster could provide though in the first years of his marriage he produced such classic songs as 'Old Folks at Home'. On 18 April 1851 Marion, the only child of Stephen and Jane Foster, was born and the marriage seemed secure. Yet Stephen's drinking bouts distressed Jane and the couple separated in 1853. While his wife and daughter stayed in Pittsburgh, Foster went to New York so it was at an emotional and geographical distance from his wife that the self-taught songwriter created 'Jeanie with the Light Brown Hair'. The sentiment seemed to bring Stephen and 'Jeanie' together again and Foster returned to Pittsburgh to be with his family. In 1860 he brought his wife and daughter to New York but was unable to support them and Jane returned to work for the Pennsylvanian Railroad at Greensburg, near Pittsburgh. Alone in his room, in the Bowery of New York, Foster drank heavily; on 10 January 1864 he collapsed and seriously injured himself. He died in Bellevue Hospital seven days later and Jane, his 'Jeanie', came to New York to bring his body back to Pittsburgh.

DR JEKYLL

Robert Louis Stevenson, *The Strange Case of Dr Jekyll and Mr Hyde* (1886)

William Brodie (1741–88)

In the summer of 1879 W.E. Henley stayed with Robert Louis Stevenson at Swanston village, Edinburgh, and the two men worked on a drama based on the life of William Brodie, Deacon of the Wrights (or cabinet-makers). By day, Deacon Brodie was a businessman, town councillor and prominent member of the Edinburgh establishment; by night he set his gang of burglars loose on the city. Brodie's most ambitious job, the break-in at the General Excise Office of Scotland, led to his downfall for the Brodie gang were caught in the act. Brodie, on hearing this, fled to Holland but he was brought back, put on trial, and hanged. After his escape from Edinburgh, Brodie wrote to a friend: 'Were I to write to you all that has happened to me and the hairbreadth escapes I made from a well-scented pack of bloodhounds, it would make a small volume.' The Henley-Stevenson play, *Deacon Brodie*, was not a success; it was privately printed in 1880 and produced in 1882.

However, in 1885 Stevenson had a nightmare about a man 'being pressed into a cabinet when he swallowed a drug and changed into another'. This insight into human duality was given an allegorical dimension, at the suggestion of Stevenson's wife Fanny, and written up as *The Strange Case of Dr Jekyll and Mr Hyde*. Though the novel is ostensibly set in London the townscape is unmistakably that of Deacon Brodie's Edinburgh while Henry Jekyll himself is, like the Deacon, a dangerously divided personality: 'I concealed my pleasures,' he says; 'I regarded and hid them with an almost morbid sense of shame. Though so profound a double-dealer, I was in no sense a hypocrite; both sides of me were in dead earnest.'

LIZA KALITINA
Ivan Turgenev, *Liza* (1859)

Countess Lambert (1821–83)

Russians responded enthusiastically to the spiritually pure heroine of Ivan Turgenev's *Liza* (also known as *A Nest of Gentlefolk*). Liza Kalitina seemed to symbolize all that was noble in the Russian character and she was promoted as an example to all Russian women. In the novel Liza Kalitina falls in love with Lavretsky but sacrifices her own happiness because he is a married man. Rather than impinge further on his life she retreats to a convent in one of the most remote districts of Russia. Liza's religious zeal is noted by Lavretsky at a critical stage in the story for he sees her at morning service: 'She prayed fervently; her eyes shone with a quiet light; quietly she bowed and lifted her head. . . . Her face seemed to him to be joyous, and once more he felt softened, and he asked, for another's soul, rest – for his own, pardon.'

Turgenev based the character on his friend Countess Elizaveta Egorovna Lambert, three years his junior. She was the daughter of Count Kankrin, Nicholas I's finance minister, and the wife of Alexander II's aide-de-camp. A deeply religious woman, Countess Lambert used her exalted position and aristocratic connections to do charitable work. From 1856 to 1867 Turgenev corresponded with Countess Lambert and he was deeply impressed by her warm personality and the clarity of her religious convictions. She was delighted by *Liza* and wrote to tell Turgenev that the novel 'is the visionary work of the pagan who has not renounced the worship of Venus, but who already understands a stricter form of worship towards which the strivings of his sick and relenting soul are bearing him a little against his will.' In an epilogue to the novel Turgenev imagines a last meeting between the autobiographical Lavretsky and Liza who 'passed onwards steadily, with the quick but silent step of a nun, and did not look at him. Only an almost imperceptible tremor was seen to move the eyelashes of the eye which was visible to him.'

CHARLES FOSTER KANE

Film, *Citizen Kane* (1941, directed by Orson Welles)

William Randolph Hearst (1863–1951)

Citizen Kane is often cited as among the best ten films ever made, sometimes described as a cinematic box of tricks. Written by Herman J. Mankiewicz, it charts the extraordinary career of an American millionaire, who runs newspapers and radio stations, runs for high office but fails at the polls because a rival exposes his secret love-nest with a singer, and who dies wealthy and surrounded by ostentation but in his heart believing he is unloved. The leading theme of the story is the old truth that money cannot buy happiness, but along the way other social and political evils are explored. The narrative is framed within the context of journalists trying to piece together the important elements in Kane's life after he has died, and *Citizen Kane* is very much concerned with the manner in which the realities of the world are presented for consumption by the mass media. At one point a correspondent cables Kane from Cuba: 'Food marvellous-girls delightful-stop-could send you prose poems about scenery but don't feel right spending your money-stop-there's no war in Cuba.' Kane cables back: 'You provide the prose poems – I'll provide the war.'

Kane was quite closely based on the life and times of William Randolph Hearst. He was born in San Francisco and educated at Harvard and inherited the *Examiner* from his father. (Kane's paper is the *Enquirer*.) He jazzed up the paper with yellow journalism and brilliant picture journalism, specializing in sensation, violence and scandal. After this success on the West Coast, he invaded New York in 1895, purchasing the ailing *Morning Journal* and turning it into a success. He tried to enter high office, twice failing to become mayor of New York (Kane tries for the state governorship) and serving two terms in the US House of Representatives. He was unsuccessful in winning nomination for US president. Like Kane he built exotic and expensive castles – Hearst built San Simeon in California – Kane had Xanadu. He had a long-standing love affair with Marion Davies, whom he tried to promote to film stardom, which parallels Kane's attempts to turn Susan Alexander into an opera singer. From Havana, Frederick Remington sent Hearst a cable: 'Everything is quiet. There is no trouble here. There will be no war. I wish to return.' Hearst cabled this answer: 'Please remain. You furnish the pictures and I'll furnish the war.'

Ivan Turgenev (1818–83)

Dostoevsky's *The Devils* – also known as *The Possessed* – contains a bitter attack on his great Russian literary contemporary Ivan Turgenev. In the course of the novel the radical Peter Verkhovensky meets Karmazinov whose interest in political unrest is consistent with his virulently anti-Russian character. Like Turgenev, Karmazinov is a literary celebrity; when he receives Peter, he is wearing 'a kind of indoor wadded jacket with little mother-of-pearl buttons, but it was very short which was not becoming to his rather prominent belly and his firmly rounded thighs'. With aristocratic air and 'shrill voice' he announces his atheism to Peter and adds 'Russia, as she is now, has no future. I've become a German and I'm proud of it.' Dostoevsky had personal as well as political reasons for his dislike of Turgenev though he had admired him enormously when the two first met in 1845. Subsequently Dostoevsky turned to Turgenev in 1865 when he had lost all his money at the Wiesbaden roulette tables; he asked Turgenev for one hundred thalers and was given fifty thalers (which he paid back eleven years later). In 1867 Dostoevsky was in Germany again, still losing money through his gambling, and decided to call on Turgenev in Baden-Baden. Dostoevsky was determined to have an emotional showdown with his fellow author whose moral outlook he despised and whose work he now distrusted. Dostoevsky's verbal assault on Turgenev – for living outside Russia and thus attacking the homeland, in *Smoke* (1867), from a safe distance – provoked Turgenev into declaring that he felt 'more a German than a Russian'. This attitude was anathema to Dostoevsky who then pilloried Turgenev as the superficial and self-seeking Karmazinov. Turgenev did not take Dostoevsky's portrait seriously, regarding him as 'non compos mentis' and 'a madman'.

ALROY KEAR
W. Somerset Maugham, *Cakes and Ale* (1930)

Hugh Walpole (1884–1941)

The character Alroy Kear, in Somerset Maugham's *Cakes and Ale*, has come to epitomize the literary opportunist. Kear is intent on succeeding Edward Driffield (actually Thomas Hardy) as the Grand Old Man of English letters and intends, with the blessing of the second Mrs Driffield, to write the definitive life of the dead novelist by way of furthering his own career. Early in the novel Maugham takes Kear to task: 'His career might well have served as a model for any young man entering upon the pursuit of literature. I could think of no one among my contemporaries who had achieved so considerable a position on so little talent. . . . It sounds a little brutal to say that when he had got all he could get from people he dropped them. . . . He could use a man very shabbily without afterward bearing him the slightest ill-will.'

Before publication, *Cakes and Ale* was submitted to the Book Society and duly seen by Hugh Walpole, chairman of the selection committee. He instantly realized that Kear was a vicious portrait of himself and attempted, unsuccessfully, to stop publication of the book. He also wrote a letter of protest to Maugham who replied 'I certainly never intended Alroy Kear to be a portrait of you.' Walpole was distraught; Virginia Woolf notes, in her diary for November 1930, that she had seen Walpole writhing under Maugham's 'wincing & ridiculous & flaying alive story'. Walpole's bubble was effectively burst and he was never able to lord it over English letters again. Maugham's malice provoked sòme counterattacks: in 1931 the American writer Elinor Mordaunt published (under the pseudonym A. Riposte) *Gin and Bitters* in which Leverson Hurle (i.e. Maugham) is likened to 'a sick monkey'; and Walpole himself included a Maughamish novelist, Somerset Ball, in his *Captain Nicholas: A Modern Comedy* (1934).

JACK KETCH

'Punch and Judy' traditional British puppet entertainment

Jack Ketch (died 1686)

Ketch became a generic name for the public hangman and appeared in *Punch and Judy* in the opening years of the 18th century. In this play he is fooled by Mr Punch, who claims he does not know how to put his head in the noose. When Ketch demonstrates the method, Punch hangs him instead.

John Ketch was appointed public executioner in 1663 and first appears in print in a broadside of December 1672, *The Plotters Ballad: Being Jack Ketch's Incomparable Receipt for the Cure of Traytorous Recusants and Wholesome Physick for a Popish Contagion.* Among his most famous victims were William, Lord Russell, executed for his alleged part in the Rye House Plot in 1683, and the Duke of Monmouth, executed after his part in the 'Monmouth rebellion' against James II in 1685. Ketch's beheading of Russell was typically clumsy and in a pamphlet published after the event, Ketch asserted that the victim did not 'dispose himself as was most suitable' and that he was in consequence interrupted in taking proper aim with his axe. When Monmouth was about to be executed he handed Ketch money and said: 'Here are six guineas for you. Do not hack me as you did my Lord Russell.' Monmouth felt the axe and said it was not sharp enough. Evidently unnerved by this, Ketch's first blow inflicted only a slight wound. Monmouth struggled to his feet, looked reproachfully at Ketch, and put his head on the block once more. Several subsequent strokes of the axe were badly aimed and the crowd began to shout angrily at Ketch, who threw down his axe, claiming: 'I cannot do it! My heart fails me!' The Sheriff said: 'Take up the axe, man!' and the crowd called: 'Fling him over the rails!' Ketch finished the job with two further strokes, but even so a knife had to be used finally to sever the head. The crowd was so angry that Ketch had to leave the scene strongly guarded. A year later he was turned out of his office for insulting one of the sheriffs and succeeded by a butcher named Rose. When Rose himself was hanged at Tyburn, Ketch regained his job. He died in 1686.

KING OF SIAM

Operetta, *The King and I* (1956, by Richard Rodgers and Oscar
Hammerstein)

Mongkut (1804–68)

In 1862 an extraordinary English woman, Anna Leonowens,
arrived in Bangkok. She had come to teach the sixty-seven
children of the King of Siam. It is one of the accidents of history
that she was also to teach the King himself some of the
fundamental principles of civilization, as far as it may be
understood that the Western world is 'civilized'. She wrote a
fascinating autobiography which, in its turn, was to teach the
West a great deal about what was then a little-known and even
less understood part of the world. It was made into a successful
film in 1946, with Rex Harrison as the King of Siam and Irene
Dunne as Anna. It was turned into a stage musical and later
filmed with Yul Brynner and Deborah Kerr in 1956.

Rarely can an Eastern potentate have become so widely known
to the Western world, and rarely must the history of a public
figure have become so distorted in its transformations – book,
film and musical entertainment. Mongkut was even more
extraordinary a character than the role associated with Yul
Brynner has suggested. He was one of several royal children of
the Siamese King. He married young and had two children. It
was the tradition that at the age of twenty he became a Bhuddist
monk, which meant he was to live a celibate life. His father
died and his elder brother became King. When he was forty-
six his brother died, and so in 1851 Mongkut became King of
Siam. As a King he had a harem, estimated to number some
three thousand women. He reigned seventeen years and fathered eighty-two children, sixty-six of whom survived him
when he died in 1868. One of his most far-reaching reforms
was his allowing his concubines to return to their families if
they wished, even to marry other men if they wanted. This
did not apply to the mothers of his children.

Anton Rubinstein (1829–94)

The Jewish theme, so important to George Eliot's last novel *Daniel Deronda*, is initially orchestrated into the plot through the person of the musician Julius Klesmer: '"Ah, here comes Herr Klesmer," said Mrs Arrowpoint, rising: and presently bringing him to Gwendolen, she left them to a dialogue which was agreeable on both sides, Herr Klesmer being a felicitous combination of the German, the Slave and the Semite, with grand features, brown hair floating in artistic fashion, and brown eyes in spectacles.' Klesmer, who facetiously refers to himself as the Wandering Jew, has a devastating impact on all women who encounter him: his pupil Catherine Arrowpoint falls in love with him and Gwendolen Harleth, the self-assured heroine, confesses 'I feel crushed in his presence; my courage all oozes from me.'

The portrayal of the larger-than-life artistic temperament was inspired by Anton Rubinstein, the Russian pianist and composer. George Eliot was in Weimar in 1854 when Franz Liszt introduced her to Rubinstein whose opera *The Siberian Huntsmen* was about to be produced at the Court Theatre. Rubinstein, like Klesmer, rose from poverty to virtuosity and was supremely self-confident of his genius. When he came to London in May 1876 Mary Ann Evans (George Eliot) was in poor health and indisposed to interrupt her work on *Daniel Deronda* yet she accepted an invitation to have lunch with him. As her companion George Henry Lewes said, 'We shall so like to renew our acquaintance with Klesmer, whom we met at Weimar in '54.' On Rubinstein's return visit to London, the following year, Mary Ann was too ill to meet him but Lewes went to see him present duets from his opera *The Maccabees*.

LARA

Lord Byron, *Lara, A Tale* (1814)

Lord Byron (1788–1824)

At the end of Byron's *The Corsair* Conrad disappears. He reappears in *Lara*, but he is disguised. He returns to the home of his ancestors in Spain, which he had left as a young man. His companion is a youthful page, Kaled, who is in reality the faithful Gulnare. Lara is usually taken as a portrait of a typically 'Byronic' hero – brooding, withdrawn and gloomy: "'tis quickly seen,/Whate'er he be, 'twas not what he had been:/ That brow in furrow'd lines had fix'd at last,/And spake of passions, but of passions past:/The pride, but not the fire, of early days,/Coldness of mien, and carelessness of praise;/A high demeanour, and a glance that took/Their thoughts from others by a single look; And sarcastic levity of tongue,/The stinging of a heart the world hath stung.' He avoids contact with companions and neighbours, but is eventually caught up in a feud. He is killed and dies in the loyal Gulnare's arms.

Byron's sense that he has been abandoned by his father, Captain John Byron, a dissolute fortune-seeker, comes through very strongly in *Lara*: 'The chief of Lara is returned again:/And why had Lara cross'd the bounding main?/Left by his sire, too young such loss to know,/Lord of himself.' Lady Byron recounted that Byron once told her that Lara was based on a self portrait: 'There's more of me in that than any of them.' As he said this he shuddered and could not look her in the eye. He told Lady Blessington: 'I am so changeable, being everything by turns and nothing long – I am such a strange *mélange* of good and evil, that it would be difficult to describe me.' Reading his *Letters and Journals* after the poet died, Mary Shelley described the mercurial changes of character characteristic of Byron: 'the fascinating – faulty – childish – philosophical being – daring the world – docile to a private circle – impetuous and indolent – gloomy and yet more gay than any other'. As Byron wrote in *Lara*: 'they who saw him did not see in vain,/And once beheld, would ask of him again:/And those to whom he spoke remembered well,/And on the words, however light, would dwell:/None knew, nor how, nor why, but he entwined/Himself perforce around the hearer's mind.' (See also DON JUAN.)

Olga Ivinskaia (born 1912)

In one of the poems appended to Boris Pasternak's novel *Doctor Zhivago* Zhivago reminds his beloved Lara 'You had come from Kursk to be a student': Olga Ivinskaia, daughter of a schoolteacher, spent her childhood in Kursk hence the reference.

Pasternak began to write his novel in 1945, a year before he knew Ivinskaia, but the creation of the character of Lara was a loving tribute to her. When Pasternak first met Ivinskaia, in the autumn of 1946, she ran the new-authors' section of the Soviet periodical *Novyi mir* (New World). Like Pasternak, whose poetry she had worshipped for years, she had been married twice: her first husband had hanged himself in 1939, her second was killed in action in 1943 and she lived with her daughter Irina in a Moscow apartment. In 1949 Ivinskaia was arrested, confined in KGB headquarters (the Lubianka) and interrogated about Pasternak's alleged anti-Soviet activities. After a year in the Lubianka, during which time she refused to incriminate Pasternak, she was sent to a concentration camp.

Pasternak's reaction was to compose the description of Lara's disappearance in *Doctor Zhivago*: 'She vanished without a trace and probably died ... in one of the innumerable mixed or women's concentration camps in the north.' Her misfortune was a form of torture for Pasternak who had heart attacks in 1950 and 1952. After the death of Stalin in 1953, Ivinskaia was released. Two months after Pasternak's death on 30 May 1960, however, Ivinskaia was arrested again and charged with currency offences relating to royalties from *Doctor Zhivago*, a novel banned in the Soviet Union. She was sentenced to eight years' imprisonment in Siberia but was released in 1964 whereupon she returned to Moscow to work as a translator.

SIR HUGO LATYMER
Noel Coward, *A Song at Twilight* (1966)

W. Somerset Maugham (1874–1965)

Noel Coward's *A Song at Twilight* is the first in a trilogy of plays set in a Swiss hotel. Although he was sixty-seven and unwell at the time of the first production, Coward defied his doctors by himself taking the leading role of Sir Hugo Latymer. Described in the stage directions as 'an elderly writer of considerable eminence' Sir Hugo has kept a secret from his public. For twenty years he has played the part of the happily married man in order to conceal his homosexuality. The tension in the play is provided by the return of Sir Hugo's first female lover Carlotta who arrives unexpectedly to go over their early years together. Reminding him of the way he treated her as an experiment in heterosexuality, she reveals that she is in possession of homosexually incriminating letters written by Sir Hugo to the real love of his life.

When playing the part of Sir Hugo, Noel Coward made up to look like Somerset Maugham whose homosexuality was hidden from the public throughout his successful career. Maugham treated his wife Syrie abominably and had a well-deserved reputation for verbal cruelty and bitchiness. He admitted (to his cousin Robin) that his greatest mistake was that 'I tried to persuade myself that I was three-quarters normal and that only a quarter of me was queer – whereas really it was the other way round.' Nevertheless Maugham kept up the pretence of his heterosexuality and in his autobiographical writing referred in passing to his lover Gerald Haxton as 'a very useful companion'. Like Sir Hugo's lover in Coward's play, Gerald was an alcoholic; unlike Sir Hugo, though, Maugham did not abandon his lover but built his emotional life around Gerald. After Gerald's death, in 1944, Maugham was devastated. When Coward saw Maugham in 1965 he found him 'living out his last days in a desperate nightmare, poor beast. He rarely makes sense and, of course, he *knows* his mind has gone.'

Alfred de Musset (1810–57)

George Sand's novel *Elle et Lui* is a classic study of the complex of personality failures which contribute to the strained relationship between a bohemian couple, Laurent and Thérèse. Laurent is a colourful, dandified, changeable young man, with a fatal weakness for drink, which takes the form of serious but periodic lapses. He suffers inner guilt from this inability to restrain himself. What seems on the surface an attractive and carefree quality, is – in contrast to Thérèse – in truth utter irresponsibility. Thérèse is a painter who works studiously at her canvasses as a means of bringing money into the house.

Laurent is a far-from-flattering portrayal of the French poet and dramatist Alfred de Musset, who met George Sand in 1833. The couple then proceeded to 'enjoy' what might with some considerable justice be described as a tempestuous relationship. He was born in Paris, studied law and medicine and finally discovered himself as a writer. He translated De Quincy's *Opium Eater* and achieved recognition with his first collection of poems, which were approved by Victor Hugo among others, in 1830. He tried stage plays and then wrote dramas for reading only. His output was considerable and his plays remarkable for character insight and the portrayal of love between the sexes with wit and sensitivity.

George Sand and Alfred de Musset set out to winter in Venice but split up and Alfred returned alone. He was beginning to take to drink in a big way, using a mixture of beer, brandy and absinthe. *Confessions d'un infant du siecle* (1835) is one of the key works of its time, a study of personal and political disillusionment. He continued to write extensively, was appointed Home Office Librarian in 1838, and was elected to the Academy in 1852. He died of heart failure, certainly hastened by drink.

His brother Paul de Musset was so angered by George Sand's *Elle et Lui* that he wrote a version of the story to defend Alfred, *Lui et Elle,* in which George Sand appears as Olympe, a vain but untalented songstress, and Alfred is a composer of genius named Edouard de Falconey. Louise Colet (see EMMA BOVARY) a later mistress of Alfred's, wrote yet a third version of the story, *Lui.* (See THÉRÈSE.)

Virginia Poe (1822–47)

Edgar Allan Poe's poem 'Annabel Lee' celebrates the author's love for a girl taken from him by death. 'She was a child and I was a child,/In this kingdom by the sea.' When Poe first met his cousin Virginia Eliza Clemm, in Baltimore in 1829, he was twenty and she was seven. At the time Poe was in need of some emotional stability and felt he had found it when he came to live with his widowed aunt Muddy (Maria Poet Clemm) and her two children Henry and Virginia. Little Virginia doted on her cousin Eddy and he not only treated her as a sister but called her 'Sis'. However in 1835, in a secret ceremony, Poe married the thirteen-year-old Virginia and then brought her and aunt Muddy to stay with him in Richmond where he worked on the *Messenger*. On 16 May 1836 a second, open, marriage was conducted in Richmond, the marriage bond recording the falsehood that Virginia was 'of the full age of twenty-one years'. Poe writes in 'Annabel Lee' that 'this maiden she lived with no other thought/Than to love and be loved by me'. It is unlikely that the marriage was ever consummated for Poe was fascinated by the notion of the eternally young female who was claimed by death.

He wrote, in *The Philosophy of Composition,* that 'the death, then, of a beautiful woman is, unquestionably, the most poetical topic in the world'; by 1841 Poe knew that Virginia was dying and by 1846 he had seen her coughing blood over her habitually white dress. Virginia's tubercular condition deteriorated and Poe wrote on 29 January 1847, the day before her death, 'My poor Virginia still lives, although failing fast and now suffering much pain.' She was buried in the graveyard of Fordham Dutch Reformed Church. When this cemetry was destroyed in 1875 Poe's biographer William F. Gill rescued the bones and eventually brought them to Baltimore where they were buried beside Poe: 'And so, all the night-tide, I lie down by the side/Of my darling – my darling – my life and my bride.'

ADRIAN LEVERKÜHN
Thomas Mann, *Doctor Faustus* (1947)

Arnold Schoenberg (1874–1951)

'Leverkühn was not the first composer,' writes Thomas Mann in *Doctor Faustus*, 'who loved to put mysteries, magic formulas, and charms into his works.' Serenus Zeitblom, who narrates the novel, is friend and confidant to Adrian Leverkühn; when he becomes aware of the composer's 'intellectual passion for austere order' he begins to understand 'the idea of the dae-monic'. Leverkühn's Faustian fantasy encourages him rigidly to systematize the principles of musical composition: 'you have four modes, each of which can be transposed to all the twelve notes of the chromatic scale, so that forty-eight different versions of the basic series may be used in a composition and whatever other variational diversions may present themselves'. Leverkühn sacrifices everything to his musical ambitions which are summed up in his last work, a symphonic cantata *The Lamentation of Dr Faustus* which the narrator calls 'the most frightful lament ever set up on this earth'.

Even before he had read the novel Arnold Schoenberg was furious that Mann had attributed to the fictional composer Leverkühn his own technical innovation – the twelve-note method of composition. Schoenberg even wrote to Mann with fabricated evidence suggesting that musicologists might credit Mann with the creation of the twelve-note technique. Mann replied, on 17 February 1948, 'In a novel that attempts to give a picture of an epoch as a whole, I have taken an enormously characteristic cultural phenomenon of the epoch and transferred it from its real author to a fictional artist, a representative martyr of the age.' He also appended a note to the novel acknowledging the twelve-note system to be 'the intellectual property' of Schoenberg.

LILY OF KILLARNEY, THE COLLEEN BAWN

Gerald Griffin, *The Collegians* (1829)

Ellen Hanley (1803–19)

The Collegians is set in Killarney. Hardress Cregan, a young man of good family, is in love with a beautiful young girl, named Eily O'Connor, who comes from lower down the social scale. He is loved by a female of his own class. The Cregan family are hard up and Hardess's mother tries to pursuade him to marry the richer of his two loves. Eventually his mother connives at the murder of Eily, whom he has secretly married, so that he is free to marry the daughter of the wealthy landowner.

Griffin's novel was based on a real murder case, one of the sensations of its day – the murder of the pretty little sixteen-year-old peasant girl, Ellen Hanley. Ellen's body was found by the River Shannon at Limerick. She had been orphaned at the age of six and brought up by her uncle, a shoemaker. Her striking beauty had caught the eye of raffish Lieutenant John Scanlan, from Ballycahane Castle nearby. He promised to marry her and got her to run away from her uncle's house. With his boatman, Stephen Sullivan, dressed as a priest, a bogus marriage ceremony took place. Scanlan eventually tired of Ellen and resolved to rid himself of her encumbrance. She was last seen alive in the company of Scanlan and Sullivan at a farmhouse near the Shannon estuary. Her body was washed ashore weeks later. Scanlan and Sullivan seemed to vanish into thin air, but their crime assumed considerable political and social significance as it was perceived as an example of the brutal treatment of the Irish by the oppressive British. The Lieutenant was eventually discovered hiding in a pile of straw in his own castle. He was tried at Limerick, found guilty and hanged. Sullivan was found later, already in jail at Tralee, charged with uttering false banknotes. He confessed that he had murdered Ellen at Scanlan's request by beating her to death in his boat in the middle of the river. The trial at Limerick was attended by Griffin while he was a reporter for a local paper.

The novel was adapted for the stage by Dion Boucicault in 1860 and played to capacity audiences. His version, *Lily of Killarney*, has a happy ending – the attempted murder of Eily fails. This version of Ellen's story was used as the basis of the opera *Lily of Killarney*, music by Sir Julius Benedict and libretto by John Oxenham (1862), which contains the celebrated numbers 'The Moon has Raised her Lamp Above' and 'Eileen Mavourneen'.

LITTLE MISS MUFFET
Nursery rhyme, 'Little Miss Muffet'

Patience Muffet, daughter of
Dr Thomas Muffet (1553–1604)

Little Miss Muffet is one of the most popular of all traditional English nursery rhymes: 'Little Miss Muffet/Sat on a tuffet,/Eating her curds and whey;/There came a big spider,/Who sat down beside her/And frightened Miss Muffet away.' Dr Thomas Muffet (or Moffet) was one of the most distinguished entomologists of his day, educated at Merchant Taylor's School and Trinity College, Cambridge. He studied at Basle and visited Italy, Spain and Germany 1579–82. He practised medicine at Ipswich and London, and published numerous works, including a lively one in verse: *The Silkworms and Their Flies* in 1599. He was patronized by Henry Herbert, Second Earl of Pembroke, who encouraged him to settle at Wilton in Wiltshire, for which constituency he was MP in 1597. Scientific works by Muffet were published several years after his death, an indication of his authority in his field.

It has been said that his 'admiration for spiders has never been surpassed' and even though no published record of the *Little Miss Muffet* verse earlier than 1805 has been located, his established interest in insects, his known exploitation of verse forms, and the fact that he had a daughter, Patience, as well as the well-attested durable oral traditions which exist in nursery and folk rhymes, would suggest Patience Muffet as an extremely likely original for the nursery rhyme. Other variants – *Little Mary Esther Sat upon a Tester* – *Little Miss Mopsey, Sat in the Shopsey* – and the similarities with such rhymes as *Little Tommy Tacket, Little Jack Horner*, as well as with singing games such as *Little Polly Sanders, Little Alice Sander,* all supply evidence of the long-standing existence and durable life of such tales. Miss Muffet probably originally sat on a grassy hillock, but tuffet has been glossed as a three-legged stool. Some versions have her sitting on a buffet, which is also a stool, especially in the North of England. The story may be associated ultimately with the cushion-dance custom, a May-Day ritual linked with mating and marriage, dating from pre-Christian times, which has someone sitting and waiting for something to happen – the appearance of the spider being a jocular parody of what should occur at the right moment.

LITTLE NELL
Charles Dickens, *The Old Curiosity Shop* (1841)

Mary Scott Hogarth (1819–37)

The Old Curiosity Shop is one of Dickens's most effective studies of the theme of inverted parent/child relationships. Grandfather Trent is determined that his daughter's child, Nell, should be brought up as a lady. To this end he spends all his money in gambling trying to win a fortune so that Little Nell shall want for nothing. To keep up his investment – for, like all compulsive gamblers, he believes it is only a matter of time before his luck will turn – he has to borrow large sums from Daniel Quilp, the dwarf. Nell tries to protect grandfather like a mother protecting her son, but in the end the two have to leave their house and flee from Quilp. Nell eventually succumbs to the strain, and dies. Old Trent goes mad with grief. Little Nell is one of Dickens's most pathetic divine children: 'For she was dead. There, upon her little bed, she lay at rest. . . . No sleep so beautiful and calm, so free from trace of pain, so fair to look upon. She seemed a creature fresh from the hand of God, and waiting for the breath of life; not one who had lived and suffered death.'

Nell was based on the character of Mary, the younger sister of Dickens's wife, Catherine. She was a very pretty and lively girl and the novelist was deeply fond of her. She joined him and his wife when they set up home in 1836. One evening in May 1837 they had gone to the theatre. Mary was suddenly taken ill and died in Dickens's arms: 'sank under the attack and died – died in such a calm and gentle sleep, that though I had held her in my arms for sometime before, when she was certainly living . . . I continued to support her lifeless form, long after her soul had fled to Heaven', he wrote in a letter. He told her grandfather: 'Since our marriage she has been the grace and life of our home – the admired of all, for her beauty and excellence.' He took her ring from her finger and wore it himself for the rest of his life. He paid for her funeral at Kensal Green and hoped to be buried next to her himself one day. The tombstone bore an inscription which he composed: 'Mary Scott Hogarth. Died 7th May 1837. Young, beautiful and good, God in His Mercy Numbered her with his Angels at the early age of Seventeen.' He described her as: 'the dearest friend I ever had. Words cannot describe the pride I felt in her, and the devoted attachment I bore her. . . . She had not a single fault.'

SOMERSET LLOYD-JAMES

Simon Raven, *Alms for Oblivion* (ten volumes, 1959–74)

Sir William Rees-Mogg (born 1928)

'Bristling with intellectual frills,' is how Somerset Lloyd-James is seen by the political powers-that-be in *Friends in Low Places* (1956), chronologically the fifth stage of Simon Raven's *Alms for Oblivion* sequence. Lloyd-James, who has been at the same school as Fielding Gray (the novelist based on Raven himself) is, by 1955, editor of the economic journal *Strix* and in a position to help old friends. He is enigmatic in appearance for 'As someone had once observed of Somerset, he derived much of his massive self-confidence from a poker-face which he thought he possessed but didn't. When Somerset was bluffing his eyes glazed over.' As one of his contributors tells him, when he declares his parliamentary ambitions, 'You are now a successful, even a powerful man, who need depend only on his own undoubted abilities. What can you possibly want in Parliament? Your abilities will go for nothing there.' Nevertheless Lloyd-James pursues his political career and is, by 1962, an MP; ten years later he is Parliamentary Under-Secretary of State at the Ministry of Commerce.

According to Simon Raven he originally modelled the character, in appearance and professional skill, on Sir William Rees-Mogg, editor of *The Times* from 1967 to 1981. Like Lloyd-James, Rees-Mogg was at school (Charterhouse) with Raven; like Lloyd-James he combined a brilliant career in journalism with parliamentary aspirations. He stood, unsuccessfully, as a Conservative in a by-election of 1956 and the general election of 1959.

There fact departs from fiction, for in Raven's series of novels Lloyd-James develops into an unscrupulous character who eventually – in *Bring Forth the Body* (1974) – kills himself when confronted by living proof of his disreputable past. When asked if he thought Sir William Rees-Mogg might be annoyed at having suggested such a character Raven replied 'I doubt if he's bothered to read it: I'm sure he's got better things to do.'

LORD JIM
Joseph Conrad, *Lord Jim* (1900)

Captain Clark of the *Jeddah*, Singapore (1880) and **Jim Lingard** (died 1917)

Jim is given no surname by Conrad. He trains as a seaman and becomes mate on the steamship *Patna*. The *Patna* puts out from an eastern port carrying eight hundred pilgrims to Mecca when it strikes a submerged object. The Europeans in charge of the ship believe it is doomed and decide to abandon ship. There are only seven lifeboats and the pilgrims are left to sink – as they suppose – on the *Patna*. When they are returned to shore Jim and the others learn that the *Patna* survived and reached Aden. Jim has to live with the terrible guilt that he did not live up to his responsibilities. He loses his certification and takes a succession of shore jobs. He becomes an agent at a trading post and is gradually accepted by the natives as a kind of ruler – Tuan Jim (Lord Jim). As the result of the intrigue of one Gentleman Brown, a pirate and freebooter, the leading native is killed and Jim is seen as morally responsible. His body is brought to his father and Jim says: 'I am come in sorrow. . . . I come ready and unarmed.' The boy's father shoots Jim. Conrad writes: 'the white sent right and left . . . a proud and unflinching glance. Then with his hand over his lips he fell forward, dead.'

Conrad used a variety of sources for this story of a man in search of his own moral integrity. The *Patna* episode was based on the history of the steamer *Jeddah,* which left Singapore in the summer of 1888 bound for Mecca, met foul weather and was in danger of going down. Captain Clark abandoned the *Jeddah* off Cape Gardafui. He announced the *Jeddah*'s total loss at sea, only to learn later that she had reached Aden. The court of enquiry resulted in the loss of his certificate.

The episode of Jim's becoming a great white chief and marrying a native girl was based on the story of Jim Lingard, who was known as Tuan Jim and lived as a trader at Tandjong Redeb on the Berouw River. He died in 1917. Also Conrad may have used the story of Sir James Brooke (1803–68) who became Raja of Sarawak and put down piracy among Malays, Dayaks and other tribes in Bornean seas, and was adored by the natives.

EILERT LØVBORG
Henrik Ibsen, *Hedda Gabler* (1890)

Julius Hoffory (1855–97)

Eilert Løvborg is first mentioned in Ibsen's *Hedda Gabler* as a man whose disreputable past has been eclipsed by his current celebrity as the author of a sensationally successful outline of civilization. He has been reformed, it seems, by Thea Elvsted whose children he tutors. When he arrives, in the second act, he is described as 'slim and lean. The same age as Tesman, he looks older, as though worn out by life.' He has brought with him the manuscript of his new work, a sequel to his outline, and come full of nostalgia for his time with Hedda – 'my days and nights of passion and frenzy, of drinking and madness'. Under the influence of Hedda he reverts to type and makes a dreadful exhibition of himself at a party. Hedda destroys his manuscript and encourages him to kill himself though she is devastated by the squalid manner of his death.

Julius Hoffory, the Dane who translated Ibsen into German, was delighted that Ibsen had modelled Løvborg on him. As Professor of Scandinavian Philology and Phonetics in Berlin he was respected as a scholar; in his private life he enjoyed wine and women and once lost a manuscript during a wild night of passion. When *Hedda Gabler* appeared Hoffory drew attention to himself as the original by adopting 'Løvborg' as his pseudonym. His own condition, however, increasingly alarmed Ibsen. Hoffory came to see Ibsen in 1890 and acted so erratically – forgetting names and finding difficulty with words – that he had to enter a sanitorium. Though he was released he never recovered and Ibsen noted: 'I am afraid he must be regarded as incurable. . . . He continually sends me old, paid hotel bills, private letters and the like, with no indication of what he expects me to do with them.' Ibsen henceforth tried to avoid Hoffory who eventually died insane at an early age.

TERTIUS LYDGATE
George Eliot, *Middlemarch* (1872)

Edward Clarke (died 1852)

Tertius Lydgate is an ambitious provincial physician, whose future is animated by dreams supported by his faith in the march of science and medical reform. He is in several important respects the 'hero' of the novel. The breadth of his vision is severely restricted by his marriage to the selfish Rosamond Vincy. George Eliot sums him up: 'He was but seven and twenty, an age at which many men are not quite common – at which they are hopeful of achievement, resolute in avoidance, thinking that Mammon shall never put a bit in their mouths and get astride their backs, but rather that Mammon, if they have anything to do with him, shall draw their chariot.' Of his faith in the future of his profession she wrote: 'He carried his studies in London, Edinburgh, and Paris, the conviction that the medical profession as it might be was the finest in the world; presenting the most perfect interchange between science and art; offering the most direct alliance between intellectual conquest and the social good.' His wife's materialism is the destruction of his hopes.

Tertius is based on Edward Clarke, who married George Eliot's sister Chrissey, in 1837. Edward was the fifth son of Robert Clarke, of Brooksby Hall, Leicestershire. Edward's earnings as a physician in the country were never enough to run his family. He was helped by various members of the Eliot family; his wife's father bought from him a house at Attleborough that had been left by an uncle to Chrissey. He paid £250 for it. He later sent him a further £800. It was agreed that if the sum could not be repaid, it would be in order to take the debt from the estate he would inherit from his wife's family. However Edward went bankrupt in 1845. He had six children, and died suddenly in December 1852.

Tertius was always willing to show he was better born than most country doctors. He goes bankrupt with debts of £1,000.

M

Ian Fleming, *Casino Royale* (1953), *Live and Let Die* (1954),
Moonraker (1955), *Diamonds Are Forever* (1956), *From Russia
with Love* (1957), *Doctor No* (1958), *Goldfinger* (1959), *For
Your Eyes Only* (1960), *Thunderball* (1961), *The Spy Who
Loved Me* (1962), *On Her Majesty's Secret Service* (1963), *You
Only Live Twice* (1964), *The Man With the Golden Gun* (1965),
Octopussy and the Living Daylights (1966)

Mrs Valentine Fleming (1885–1964)

In the James Bond novels, secret agent 007 is always activated
by M, Head of the British Secret Service. Behind his desk at
the room at the end of a corridor in a 'gloomy building
overlooking Regent's Park' M supervises Bond who knows, as
early as *Casino Royale* (1953), that 'one didn't argue with M'.
Although M has been identified with Ian Fleming's Naval
Intelligence boss Admiral John Godfrey and with Sir Stewart
Menzies, once head of MI6, the most plausible theory is put
forward in John Pearson's *The Life of Ian Fleming* (1966).

As a child Fleming called his mother 'M' and the fictional M,
Pearson argues, is based on Fleming's mother Mrs Valentine
Fleming. Born Evelyn St Croix Rose, she married Valentine
Fleming in 1906 and assumed command of the four Fleming
boys when, as Captain Fleming, their father went to fight in
France in 1914 and was killed in action in 1917. Ian was nine
when Mrs Val became acting head of the family and reigned
supreme at home. She sent Ian away from home, to Eton and
Sandhurst, and was disappointed at his lack of discipline and
wayward nature. Her attitude to Fleming was to treat him as
a gifted but spoilt child; exactly the way M treats Bond.
Pearson writes: 'While Fleming was young, his mother was
certainly one of the few people he was frightened of, and her
sternness towards him, her unexplained demands, and her
remorseless insistence on success finds a curious and constant
echo in the way M handles that hard-ridden, hard-killing
agent, 007. Never has a man who slaughtered so mercilessly
taken orders so meekly.' The point, made in all the Bond books,
is that 007 adores M, as is obvious in this extract from *Doctor
No* (1958): 'Sitting here in this room opposite M was the
symbol of normality he had longed for. He looked across
through the smoke clouds into the shrewd grey eyes. They
were watching him.'

MACBETH
William Shakespeare, *Macbeth* (1606)

Macbeth (1005–57)

Shakespeare's tragedy *Macbeth,* based on Holinshed's *Chronicle of Scottish History,* is great drama but bad history. In the play Macbeth is a madly ambitious man who, with the blessing of his bloodthirsty wife, murders his way to the crown of Scotland: 'I am in blood/Stepp'd in so far that, should I wade no more,/Returning were as tedious as go o'er.'

Duncan I (1001–40), the victim of Macbeth's regicide in the play, was founder of the royal House of Dunkeld and first monarch of a united Scotland. His marriage to a sister of the Danish earl Siward of Northumbria produced two sons, Malcolm Canmore and Donald Ban, whose hereditary right to the throne was threatened when Macbeth claimed the kingdom on the grounds of tanistry – succession by a previously elected member of the royal family. Like Duncan, Macbeth was a grandson of Malcolm II; his wife Gruoch – Shakespeare's Lady Macbeth – was granddaughter of Kenneth III. Macbeth was a formidable warrior and on 14 August 1040 defeated and killed his cousin Duncan I in battle. Five years later Duncan I's father Crinana challenged Macbeth in battle but he too was defeated and killed. Macbeth ruled Scotland for seventeen years with a good measure of success; he strengthened the position of the Church and was confident enough to leave Scotland in 1050 and go on a pilgrimage to Rome. Macbeth had no children but Gruoch had a son, Lulach, by a previous marriage and he was regarded as the rightful successor. Yet Malcolm Canmore, Duncan I's son, was determined to destroy Macbeth and in 1054 he defeated the King at Scone. Three years later Malcolm avenged the death of his father when he defeated and killed Macbeth at Lumphanan on 15 August 1057. Malcolm III ruled Scotland until 1093.

DENRY MACHIN
Arnold Bennett, *The Card* (1911)

H. K. Hales

The Card is a comic novel which details the career of a local
lad who makes good. Edward Henry Machin – his mother
calls him Denry for short – progresses from board school to
become Bursley's youngest mayor. He 'wins' a scholarship by
fiddling the results, loses his job as a solicitor's clerk after
inviting himself to a municipal ball where he dances with the
Countess of Chell (see COUNTESS OF CHELL) whose ball it was,
becomes rent collector, estate agent, salvages sovereigns from
a wreck, takes the Countess to the official opening of the
Policemen's Institute she has donated in his mule-cart (after he
has put her carriage out of action), and starts the Five Towns
Universal Thrift Club. He earns considerable income, becomes
a newspaper magnate, marries well, and rescues the local
football team from financial ruin by buying them 'the greatest
centre forward in England'. He is a complete joker, carrying
into real life the classic attitudes and activities of the comedian
– leg-pulling, trickery, double dealing, grabbing every oppor-
tunity which presents itself – and getting the applause of the
world for his efforts.

Several incidents are based on Bennett's own life and experiences, such as his days of collecting rent for his father, and his
father's experiences of newspaper rivalry. Denry is witty, quick
on the draw, an exhibitionist with a real affection for his
mother. The rise from obscurity to success and public acclaim
Bennett took from his school friend H.K. Hales, who published
The Autobiography of 'The Card', and did enjoy a very successful
career himself. He challenged Bennett with having based
Denry on him, and demanded a share of the royalties! Bennett
replied that the debt was paid as he had given Hales so much
free publicity.

Bennett also used the character of Hales for Dick Povey in *The
Old Wives' Tale*. Hales, like Povey, was a motor-car and cycle
enthusiast and dealer, and made a successful balloon ascent – a
feature of *The Old Wives' Tale*.

REGAN MACNEIL
William Peter Blatty, *The Exorcist* (1972)

A boy from Mount Rainier

Demonic possession dominates William Peter Blatty's novel *The Exorcist* and the screenplay he wrote for the William Friedkin film of 1973. The story describes the hideous transformation of eleven-year-old Regan MacNeil from a charming all-American girl in Washington, DC, to a murderous foul-mouthed monster. Ironically, Regan's mother, Chris MacNeil, is an atheist who eventually requests an exorcism from a priest, Father Karras, who has lost his faith.

Blatty was educated by Jesuits and at one time considered training for the priesthood. When he was a student at Georgetown University in Washington, DC, he read, in the *Washington Post* of 20 August 1949, a chilling account of exorcism concerning a fourteen-year-old Mount Rainier boy: 'Only after twenty to thirty performances of the ancient ritual of exorcism, here and in St Louis, was the devil finally cast out of the boy.' Fascinated by the case Blatty was able to read the exorcist's diary and collect details of levitation, rappings, telekinesis, paranormal strength, change of voice and brandings of words on the victim's flesh. To this situation Blatty added a plot involving murder (though there were no murders or deaths in the case of the Mount Rainier boy) and 'changed the boy in my story to a girl, although more to ease the exorcist's anxiety than from fear of doing any real harm to the boy'.

In a 1974 book about the making of the film of *The Exorcist*, Blatty mentions that the exorcist asked him never to reveal the boy's identity. Blatty also points out that he modelled the character of Regan's mother, Chris MacNeil, on actress Shirley MacLaine; and based Father Merrin, the exorcist, on Pierre Teilhard de Chardin (1881–1955), the Jesuit philosopher.

Marilyn Monroe (1926–62)

The action of Arthur Miller's *After the Fall* 'takes place in the mind, thought, and memory of Quentin'. A lawyer, Quentin addresses the audience and confesses the sins and sensations of his life. Though he has married three times it is his second wife, Maggie, who brings out the best and worst in him. When he first meets her he is astonished by her beauty and aura of innocent sensuality. Later she becomes a famous singer noted for her sexually exciting interpretation of popular lyrics though Maggie insists 'it's not I say to myself, "I'm going to sound sexy", I just try to come *through* – like in love'. Quentin sees that success has not brought her security and reflects how 'she was chewed and spat out by a long line of grinning men! Her name floating in the stench of locker rooms and parlour-car cigar smoke.' When he marries her he realizes that her great gifts include a talent for self-destruction and that she is too fragile to survive in a brutal world. Though Miller tried to focus attention on the play's issues, rather than the character of Maggie, the public responded to the drama for its insight into the nature of Marilyn Monroe.

Arthur Miller married Marilyn in 1956. He had won the Pulitzer Prize for *Death of a Salesman* but had never experienced anything like the public attention directed towards his wife. With the release in 1953 of *Gentlemen Prefer Blondes* and *How to Marry a Millionaire* she became America's greatest sex symbol; every detail of her life was devoured by the public and the strain affected the marriage. After Miller and Marilyn separated in 1960 she became less reliable as a person and performer though she turned in a fine performance in her last film – *The Misfits* (1961), scripted by Miller. She died in mysterious circumstances, from an overdose of pills, and was (as Miller said of Maggie in an article) 'a victim ... of her exploitation as an entertainer'.

NORMAN MAINE

Film, *A Star is Born* (written by Dorothy Parker, Alan Campbell, Robert Carson and Moss Hart; directed by George Cukor in 1945)

John Gilbert (1895–1936)

A Star is Born is one of the most durable Hollywood narratives, it was filmed in 1937 with Frederick March and Janet Gaynor, in 1954 with James Mason and Judy Garland, and again in 1979 with Chris Kristopherson and Barbara Streisand. In some ways it may well trace its origins back to the 1932 film *What Price Hollywood*. The story of *A Star is Born* is simple and direct – a study of the collapsing marriage between two film stars, one on the way down (Norman Maine) the other on the way up (Vicki Lester). As the young star's career ascends and she earns public and professional acclaim, her husband descends into alcoholism and suicide by drowning.

It is based on the real life career and professional eclipse of John Gilbert. He was the son of a theatrical family in Logan, Utah. Family connections made his entry into films a simple matter and by 1919 he was playing romantic leads with Mary Pickford. In the early 1920s he very nearly rivalled Valentino at the box office with a series of smash hits – *Monte Cristo, Arabian Love, Cameo Kirby, He Who Gets Slapped, The Merry Widow, The Big Parade* and *Bardlays the Magnificent*. He starred with Greta Garbo in *Flesh and the Devil* (based on *Anna Karenina*) and *A Woman of Affairs*. There was talk of an off-screen romance, which Garbo always denied. By 1928 he was the highest-paid star in the business.

His eclipse was almost instantaneous. At his height he was earning $10,000 a week, and married the star Ina Claire in 1929. Returning from his honeymoon he found he had lost a fortune in investments. Then came the talkies. He made *His Glorious Night,* his first talkie, but unfortunately his voice was rather prissy and contrasted so much with his established screen character of passionate romance that he was no longer to be taken seriously. At the same time as he fell out of fashion, Ina Claire made a great hit in *Talkie Heaven*, with her quality Boston tones. He took to drink in a big way, and died of a heart attack in 1936. The suicide by drowning was taken from the death of another failed actor, John Bowers, who walked into the waves at Malibu in 1936.

Sir William Knollys, Earl of Banbury
(1547–1632)

Malvolio is Olivia's steward. He is a pompous, puritanical prating ass, without a shred of humour. This makes him the butt of endless comicality from other characters. He fancies himself in love with Olivia, and her uncle, Sir Toby Belch and Maria, maid to Olivia, hatch a plot to make Malvolio think that Olivia loves him. The plot involves a forged letter, which Malvolio believes, and gulling him into wearing outlandish clothes which he thinks will impress the object of his passion. When he appears before Olivia smiling, wearing yellow cross-garters, quoting sections from the letter, she thinks he is mad. He has always taken delight in spoiling the fun and amusement of others so his ultimate exposure to such public ridicule seems justified. He accuses Toby and his companion Sir Andrew of turning Olivia's house into an ale-house: 'Is there no respect of place, persons, nor time, in you?' he demands. Sir Toby's retort is famous: 'Dost thou think, because thou art virtuous, there shall be no more cakes and ale?'

Shakespeare's portrait of Malvolio, Leslie Hotson believes (*The First Night of Twelfth Night*, 1954) is based on that of Sir William Knollys, comptroller of Queen Elizabeth's household. He had several of Malvolio's characteristics – he was strongly puritan in his sympathies, and was known to have interrupted revellers clad in his nightshirt. He was a supporter of Essex and declared a 'time-server' – which phrase is used by Maria to describe Malvolio. Knollys also pictured himself as a woman-slayer, and notoriously attempted the seduction of his ward, Mary Fitton (1578–1647) who was one of the Queen's maids of honour. Knollys began to take what at first seemed a fatherly interest in her, but his passion for Mary became one of the scandals of the day. Early in 1601 she began to associate with William Herbert, Third Earl of Pembroke, by whom she had a stillborn child. William Kempe, the comic actor who was a member of Shakespeare's company, dedicated his *Nine Days Wonder* (1600) to Mistress Anne Fitton 'Mayde of Honour to the Mayde Royal'. This must be intended for Mary, as she alone, and not her sister Anne, was maid of honour.

MANDERLEY
Daphne du Maurier, *Rebecca* (1938)

Menabilly

Rebecca is narrated by a heroine who is haunted by a house: Manderley, the de Winter family home, is strangely 'secretive and silent'. Daphne du Maurier first saw such a house in 1924, when she was seventeen and had come to Cornwall from London. First she read, in a guidebook, about an Elizabethan house three miles from the harbour at Fowey. The she asked the locals for information about the house and was told it was shut up and abandoned by an owner who lived in Devon. Intent on exploring it Daphne du Maurier rose one morning at 5 am and approached with a sense of expectancy which she records in *The Rebecca Notebook* (1981): 'I edged my way on to the lawn, and there she stood. My house of secrets. My elusive Menabilly. . . . She was, or so it seemed to me, bathed in a strange mystery. She held a secret – not one, not two, but many – that she withheld from many people but would give to one who loved her well.'

In 1937 du Maurier found herself in Alexandria with her soldier husband; she was homesick for Cornwall and thought lovingly of Menabilly. Recalling a rumour that the owner 'had been married first to a very beautiful wife, whom he had divorced, and had married again a much younger woman', du Maurier began to write her novel. Five years after the publication of *Rebecca*, Daphne du Maurier learned that Menabilly was available for rent. At last it was to be lived in: 'I took a bold step and moved house on my own, with a nanny and three young children. I rented the old manor house Menabilly that I had written about in *Rebecca*, which had no electricity and no hot-water system, and was full of dry rot. My husband, in far-off Tunis, told his brother officers, "I am afraid Daphne has gone mad".' She lived in her 'house of secrets' for twenty-six years.

Count Giralama Mattioli (1640–1703)

The man in the iron mask has always aroused romantic curiosity, even in his own lifetime. Several solutions have been offered as to the identity of the mysterious prisoner of the reign of Louis XIV who always wore an iron mask when being moved from one prison to another. He spent most of his time at Pignerol, but sojourned in other French prisons, dying finally at the Bastille on 19 November 1703.

The explanation given the most wide circulation, and which has certainly fanned popular interest in this figure, was that which Alexandre Dumas included in *Vicomte de Bragelonne*, that the 'Mask' was in reality the bastard elder brother of Louis XIV, the son of Anne of Austria (1601–66), wife of Louis XIII, and her minister, Cardinal Jules Mazarin (1602–61). When the prisoner was buried his name was given as 'Marchiali'. One widely accepted solution was that the 'Mask' was General du Bulonde, who was imprisoned for raising the siege of Cuneo in 1691 contrary to orders of Nicolas Catinat, Marshall of France. This may be discounted as evidence indicates that the 'Mask' was imprisoned at Pignerol by 1666, and some twenty years later was transferred to the island of St Marguerite. This evidence predates the siege of Cuneo. Another candidate is the Duke de Vermandois, illegitimate son of Louis XIV and his mistress, Louise Francoise de Labaume Leblanc, Duchess de la Vallière (1644–1710). The Duke was imprisoned for life for giving the Dauphin a box on the ears. It has even been suggested that 'Mask' was the Duke of Monmouth, who supposedly escaped beheading in 1685 after the failure of the Monmouth Rebellion against James II. Another candidate is Nicolas Fouquet, Vicomte de Melun et de Vaux and Marquis de Belle-Isle (1615–80), who had attempted to gain political power after the death of Mazarin, but who was conspired against by Colbert and arrested in 1661. His trials took three years and he was imprisoned for life at the fortress of Pignerol, where he died. Working on the private papers of Louis XIV and his ministers including Francois Michel le Tellier, Marquis de Louvois (1641–91), Franz Funk-Brentano has put forward the convincing explanation that the 'Mask' was in fact Count Giralamo Mattioli, leading minister to the Duke of Mantua. He acted treacherously to Louis XIV in 1678 as he had agreed by treaty to surrender to Louis the Fortress of Casale, the key to Italy, but later went back on his word. He was tricked into coming to France and there was imprisoned at Pignerol.

MANON

Antoine-Francois Prévost, *Manon Lescaut* (1731)

Manon Porcher

Manon's is one of the great love stories of the world. A simple and moving narrative, harsh in its realities, but coloured with poignant and moving qualities which are moving, often in spite of the resistance of sophisticated taste. André Gide, for example, placed it in his list of the ten best French novels. The Chevalier des Grieux is seventeen years old and is studying for the priesthood. He meets Manon Lescaut in a tavern and he believes her to be a girl who is being forced against her own wishes into entering a convent. She is fourteen years old but they fall passionately in love. He is conscious of the fact that although she is younger than he is, in many ways she seemed more mature: 'Love had already so enlightened me . . . I spoke to her in a way that made her understand my feelings; for she was far more experienced than I.' The only solution to the problems of their lives seem to them to lie in flight. With little money, they attempt a life together. But Manon constantly betrays him. She seeks a life of excitement and amusement, but each time – after abandoning him – she returns to be forgiven. He tries to put her out of his mind and to return to his studies, but she returns and captures him again. In their attempts to raise money he takes to gambling and she becomes a prostitute. Eventually she is deported to America but des Grieux determines to go with her to Louisiana. Here they hope to marry, but the son of the governor of Louisiana has fallen in love with her and he prevents the marriage. While trying to escape from Louisiana, Manon dies: 'I remained for more than twenty four hours with my lips pressed to the face and hands of my dear Manon . . . I formed the resolution to bury her and to wait for death on her grave.' He is discovered and tried for her murder, but is acquitted, and learns soon after that his father has died. He blames himself for this tragedy. The implication is that des Grieux is now a sadder but a wiser man.

Prévost based the novel on the true-life adventures of Manon Porcher who had been hounded by the French authorities for debauchery and prostitution and deported to the convict settlement in Louisiana where she was followed by her aristocratic young lover, Avril de la Varenne. They were married. The story has been the subject of several operas – by Auber, Massanet and Puccini.

THE DUKE OF MANTUA

Opera, *Rigoletto* (1851, music by Verdi, libretto by Piave)

Francis I (1494–1547)

'La donna è mobile/qual piume al vento,/muta d'accento/e di pensiero.' Woman is changeable, like a feather in the breeze, sings the Duke in Verdi's tragic opera *Rigoletto*. She changes her tune and her mind. We are always deceived as much by a pretty face, in tears or full of laughter. It is one of the most celebrated moments in 19th-century opera. It was one of Caruso's greatest roles. Among modern exponents of the part are Placido Domingo and Luciano Pavarotti. The Duke is master of a licentious court, and takes his pleasures where he wishes. Rigoletto, his jester, has a beautiful daughter, Gilda, whom he attempts to protect in purity by keeping her in secret. The Duke hears rumours of Rigoletto's 'secret' and believes the old man is keeping a mistress. He resolves to abduct her and unwittingly Rigoletto aids the conspiracy against his own daughter.

Rigoletto plots his revenge for the loss of Gilda's honour, intending to have the Duke murdered at an inn. Maddalena, the assassin's sister, smitten with the Duke herself, persuades the murderer to spare the Duke's life and to kill any man who may arrive and present the body in a sack to the waiting Rigoletto. Gilda overhears this plot and resolves to sacrifice herself for the Duke, whom she loves, and enters disguised as a man, to be stabbed to death. As Rigoletto gloats over what he supposes to be the body of the hated Duke, he hears his voice sing 'La donna è mobile' and tears open the sack to find the body of his own daughter.

Verdi and his librettist, Piave, based their opera on Victor Hugo's drama *La Roi d'amuse* (1832) and changed the names of the leading characters in accordance with the Austrian censorship in Italy at the time. Hugo's protagonist was based on Francis I of France, who was born at Cognac, the son of Charles, Comte d'Angoulème. In 1514 he married Claude, daughter of Louis XII, whom he succeeded that year. In war and foreign diplomacy he pursued vigorous policies, recapturing Milan and signing a concordat with the Pope. When the emperor Maximilian died in 1519, Francis challenged Charles of Spain for the Austrian imperial crown. Charles V was elected and in the ensuing war the French were driven out of Italy, eventually surrendering all Francis I's Italian possessions. He fostered arts and scholarship, maintained a lavish court, but Hugo's portrait of his licentiousness, followed in *Rigoletto*, has considerable basis in historical fact.

THE MAN WHO LOVED ISLANDS
D. H. Lawrence, *The Woman Who Rode Away* (1928)

Sir Compton Mackenzie (1883–1972)

While living on Capri in 1919, D. H. Lawrence became friendly with fellow writer Compton Mackenzie, a man – so Lawrence said – 'one can trust and like'. Mackenzie suggested that Lawrence consider coming with him on a writing trip to the South Sea islands but nothing came of the plan. Instead Mackenzie, at the suggestion of his publisher, went to the Channel island of Jethou which he leased from the British government at a cost of £1,000 a year. To Lawrence this insular passion was unwholesome so he satirized Mackenzie as 'The Man Who Loved Islands', a story included in the American, but not the British, edition of *The Woman Who Rode Away* (1928).

Mackenzie's search for absolute isolation is traced in a parable of antisocial escapism: 'There was a man who loved islands. He was born on one, but it didn't suit him, as there were too many other people on it, besides himself. He wanted an island all of his own: not necessarily to be alone on it, but to make it a world of his own.' Although the protagonist of the story has spiritual ideals, his pursuit of peace is achieved at the expense of others; each island he adopts is contaminated by human contact and so he moves on. Eventually he ends up on an island with only sheep for company: 'He was glad. He didn't want trees or bushes. They stood up like people, too assertive. His bare, low-pitched island in the pale blue sea was all he wanted.'

Mackenzie's own life was frequently a testing-ground for his fiction. After the success of *Sinister Street* (1913) he had a spectacular war career in the British Aegean Intelligence Service. After the First World War he lived on Capri, then Jethou and eventually settled on the little Hebridean island of Barra. There he wrote prolifically and conducted a campaign aimed at restoring political independence to Scotland. Towards the end of his life he divided his time between Edinburgh and the South of France.

MARIA

Ernest Hemingway, *For Whom the Bell Tolls* (1941)

Maria

For Whom the Bell Tolls, Ernest Hemingway's celebrated novel of the Spanish Civil War, brings the hero Robert Jordan into contact with a beautiful and vulnerable Spanish girl Maria. She tells Jordan that she has been in prison at Valladolid and explains that her father was shot as a Republican. Jordan tells Maria that his father (like Hemingway's) shot himself and she feels that this brings them closer together. Later Maria comes to Jordon in the night. Jordan asks her if she has loved others and she replies 'Never. . . . But things were done to me. . . . Where things were done to me I fought until I could not see. I fought until – until – until one sat upon my head – and I bit him – and then they tied my mouth and held my arms behind my head – and others did things to me.'

During the Spanish Civil War, Hemingway visited Spain four times. On one of his visits, in the spring of 1938, he went to see a friend who was recovering from wounds at hospital in Mataró, north of Barcelona. There, in Mataró hospital, Hemingway met the nurse Maria who told Hemingway of her experiences of the war; she had been raped by Fascist soldiers and yet all those she nursed thought of her as the 'soul of serenity'. Hemingway used Maria's harrowing past and quietly courageous character as the basis for the Maria of his novel. He changed her appearance, however, to that of Martha Gellhorn, the woman who was to become his third wife and to whom *For Whom the Bell Tolls* is dedicated: 'She had high cheekbones, merry eyes and a straight mouth with full lips. Her hair was the golden brown of a grain field that has been burned dark in the sun.' Hemingway found the title of his novel, via *The Oxford Book of English Prose*, in a passage by John Donne.

MISS MARPLE

Agatha Christie, *Murder at the Vicarage* (1930), *The Thirteen Problems* (1932), *The Regatta Mystery* (1939), *The Body in the Library* (1942), *The Moving Finger* (1943), *A Murder is Announced* (1950), *Three Blind Mice* (1950), *They Do It With Mirrors* (1952), *A Pocket Full of Rye* (1953), *4.50 from Paddington* (1957), *The Adventure of the Christmas Pudding* (1960), *Double Sin* (1961), *The Mirror Crack'd from Side to Side* (1962), *A Caribbean Mystery* (1964), *At Bertram's Hotel* (1965), *Sleeping Murder* (1976)

Mrs Miller

In *The Murder of Roger Ackroyd* (1926) Agatha Christie took considerable care over the presentation of Dr Sheppard's sister Caroline, a lady she described in *An Autobiography* (1977) as 'an acidulated spinster, full of curiosity, knowing everything, hearing everything: the complete detective service in the home'. When the novel was adapted (by Michael Morton) as the play *Alibi*, Caroline was dropped and substituted by a much younger woman who could provide Hercule Poirot with a romantic interest. 'At that moment, in St Mary Mead,' Christie remembered, 'though I did not yet know it, Miss Marple was born.'

Miss Jane Marple, village gossip and amateur sleuth, first appeared in 1930 in the novel *Murder at the Vicarage* and the character was evidently inspired by Christie's grandmother, Mrs Miller, who brought up the author's mother at her home in Ealing. The main quality Mrs Miller had in common with Miss Marple was, Agatha Christie noted, a fatalistic outlook: 'though a cheerful person, she always expected the worst of everyone and everything, and was, with almost frightening accuracy, usually proved right'. Although her prophecies were of a mundane rather than a criminal nature they were taken very seriously indeed. Once she accurately predicted the escape, up the chimney, of a tame squirrel adopted by Agatha's brother and sister; on another occasion she warned that a disturbance would bring down a jar on a shelf over the drawing-room door and, sure enough, there was a thunderstorm that banged the door and brought down the jar. 'Anyway,' Agatha Christie remembered, 'I endowed my Miss Marple with something of Grànnie's powers of prophecy. There was no unkindness in Miss Marple, she just did not trust people. Though she expected the worst, she often accepted people kindly in spite of what they were.'

MARTINET

Traditional term for one who practises a strictly disciplined
adherance to rules and regulations – current from early 18th
century

General Jean Martinet (died 1672)

General Martinet's name has now passed into the language. At
one time it was associated with the particular system of drill
which he invented. In Wycherley's play *The Plain Dealer* a
character exclaims: 'What! Do you find fault with Martinet?
'Tis the best exercise in the world!' So his name was associated
with military drill as early as only four years after his death.
Gradually the word is used in a more general sense for a
military or naval officer who is a stickler for precision and
discipline. In France it was the name given to an instrument
used in schools as a means of corporal punishment. Paul du
Chaillu, writing in *Land of the Midnight Sun* in 1881 says: 'I
saw what resembled a policeman's club, at the end of which
was a thick piece of leather, the whole reminding one of a
martinet.'

The term seems to have originated from the manner in which
General Martinet habitually exercised his military duties and
responsibilities during the middle years of the reign of Louis
XIV. Jean Martinet was lieutenant-colonel of the King's Regiment of Foot and Inspector General of Infantry. He drilled
and trained foot soldiers in the new model army of professional
fighting men which was created by Louis and Francois Michel
le Tellier, Marquis de Louvois (1641–91). Martinet won
renown as a military engineer and pioneer tactician, devising
forms of battle manoeuvre, pontoon bridges and a new type
of assault boat with a copper bottom (used in Louis XIV's
Dutch campaign), in the years 1660–70. Martinet played a
significant role in making the French army the first and the
best regular army in Europe. The key achievement of Martinet
and his colleagues – Turenne, Condé, Luxemburg – was the
introduction of a uniform system of drill and training. This
was the period when the soldier of fortune, the man who
joined a regiment with his own arms and equipment, and had
learned his trade from his own (often varied) experience, began
to be replaced by the professional, enlisted, full-time career
soldier, recruited into permanent regiments which were
trained by their own officers. Martinet, who had in large part
made this possible, was ironically shot by accident by his own
men when he led the infantry assault at the siege of Duisburg
in 1672.

Nelson Doubleday (1889–1949)

In 1940 Somerset Maugham arrived in America for a speaking tour that would advocate American involvement in the Second World War. He was welcomed in New York by his American publisher Nelson Doubleday who had taken over the family firm in 1929 with spectacular success. Maugham liked Doubleday and appreciated all his efforts to further his reputation in the USA. When Maugham mentioned that he wanted to find somewhere to complete his new novel, Doubleday offered to build him a house, with a separate cottage for writing, on his South Carolina plantation. Accepting the offer, and gladly agreeing to contribute to the cost from future royalties, Maugham moved into Parker's Ferry, Yemassee, South Carolina in December 1940.

As he worked on *The Razor's Edge* he saw Nelson Doubleday regularly as he used the plantation as a holiday home; inevitably Nelson appeared in the novel, as Gray Maturin. Gray is a big easygoing man: 'Though built on so large a scale he was finely proportioned, and stripped he must have been a fine figure of a man. He was obviously very powerful. His virility was impressive. He made Larry who was sitting next to him, though only three or four inches shorter, look puny.' Isabel the heroine of the novel, is in love with the spiritual Larry Darrell but marries the dependable Gray who 'was so kindly, so unselfish, so upright, so reliable, so unassuming that it was impossible not to like him'.

When Maugham heard that Doubleday was dying, in 1949, he came to New York to see him and spent weekends at his home in Oyster Bay. At Doubleday's funeral Maugham said 'It was touching to see the thoughtful tact with which the great big man sought for ways in which he could give pleasure to his friends. . . . For thirty years Nelson Doubleday gave me his constant and affectionate friendship. The recollection of it is a treasure that can never be taken away from me.'

Ivan Stepanovich Mazepa-Koledinsky
(1644–1709)

After the battle of Pultowa, a Ukrainian cavalry commander in the service of Charles II of Sweden is near to death. The King asks him to tell his story: 'Of all our band, Though firm of heart and strong of hand,/In skirmish, march, or forage, none/Can less have said, or more have done/Than thee, Mazeppa!' The old warrior obliges with the narrative of seventy years' adventurous life, and tells his companions of his early life as page to Casimir V, King of Poland. He was discovered in his liaison with the wife of a local magnate and punished by being bound naked on the back of a wild horse. The horse was then whipped into madness and let loose. Mazeppa was carried on wild chase through forest and woodlands, through streams and finally to the plains of the Ukraine, where the horse drops dead. Mazeppa was released by peasants and brought back to health by the Cossacks.

Byron based this adventure on part of the life story of Mazepa-Koledinsky. He was educated at the court of the King of Poland, Casimir, and was punished for an intrigue with the wife of a Polish nobleman by being strapped on the back of a wild horse and sent into the steppe. The Dnieperian Cossacks rescued him and he became a Cossack leader. In 1687 he was made commander of the Cossacks and served under Peter the Great and was sufficiently honoured as to sit at the Tsar's own table. He changed to the service of Charles II of Sweden because he believed that Charles would defeat the Tsar. He was in touch with Charles's ministers when Peter ordered him to cooperate with his forces then mobilized in the Ukraine. This was in October 1708, and he had agreed with the Swedes to close the Ukraine to the Russians. Peter's wrath at Mazepa's treason was immense, and his effigy was burnt by the hangman and he was excommunicated. After the terrible defeat at Pultowa he went with Charles to Turkey with the remaining 1,500 horses of their original 80,000 cavalry and the Sultan refused to hand them over to Peter the Great, in spite of an offered ransom of 300,000 ducats. Mazepa died at Bender on 22 August 1709.

MR MERDLE
Charles Dickens, *Little Dorrit* (1857)

John Sadleir (1814–56)

Mr Merdle MP is a swindler, banker, forger and thief whose enterprises flourish at a time when company law was in its infancy. His financial manipulations form the basis of the plot mechanism of the novel, and ruin Clennam, the Dorrits and others. 'Immensely rich; a man of prodigious enterprise; a Midas without the ears, who turned all he touched to gold. He was in everything good, from banking to building.... His desire was to the utmost to satisfy Society . . . and take up all its drafts upon him for tribute. He did not shine in company; he had not very much to say for himself; he was a reserved man, with a broad, overhanging, watchful head, that particular kind of dull red colour in his cheeks which is rather stale than fresh, and a somewhat uneasy expression about his coat-cuffs, as if they were in his confidence, and had reasons for being anxious to hide his hands.'

Dickens based Merdle on the Irish politician and swindler, Sadleir. He was educated at Clongowes College and became a solicitor in Dublin. He was a director of the Tipperary Joint Stock Bank, and chairman of the London and County Joint Stock Bank in 1848. He was MP for Carlow and for Sligo in 1853 and was made junior lord of the treasury in 1853. He committed suicide in 1856 on the failure of the Tipperary Bank, then managed by his brother James, which had been brought about by his fraudulent practices. Dickens had a long-standing interest in financial speculation and chicanery – with the exception only of *Barnaby Rudge* and *A Tale of Two Cities*, all his novels contain significant treatment of swindling and financial manipulation – but he confessed to his biographer, John Forster, that he shaped Mr Merdle himself out of the 'precious rascality' of John Sadleir, as early as the sixth episode of *Little Dorrit* (May 1856). It is the case that some aspects of the Merdle story are reminiscent of the escapades of George Henry Hudson, the Railway King, who fled to France in the financial panic of 1847–48, but Dickens says in the 'Preface' to *Dorrit*, 'If I might make so bold as to defend that extravagant conception, Mr Merdle, I would hint that it originated after the railroad-share epoch, in the times of a certain Irish bank.' Sadleir slit his throat on Hampstead Heath as his empire crashed in 1856.

DIANA MERION

George Meredith, *Diana of the Crossways* (1885)

Caroline Norton (1808–77)

Diana Merion, heroine of Meredith's novel, is the witty and lively daughter of a good Irish family. She marries the dull Warwick, who does not understand her or appreciate her true qualities. In a fit of jealousy he brings an action for divorce against her, in which he cites Lord Dannisburgh. Warwick loses his case. An ambitious young politician, Dacier, who is in love with her, finds that some important political confidences he has given her have been passed on to a national newspaper. Diana has done this because she was pressed for money. It leads to the end of the relationship between Dacier and Diana. Warwick dies, and Diana finally marries Redworth, a loyal admirer.

Meredith based Diana on the beautiful Caroline Norton, daughter of Thomas Sheridan (1775–1817), a colonial administrator, who was the son of Sheridan the playwright. Caroline married the Hon George Chapple Norton in 1827, and enjoyed a literary career – *The Sorrows of Rosalie, With Other Poems* (1829), *A Voice From the Factories* (1836) – as well as miscellaneous pieces for journals. In 1836 her husband brought an action for divorce against her in which he cited William Temple, Lord Melbourne, the Prime Minister. The evidence was insubstantial, and many believed at the time that the action was brought to discredit Melbourne. Her husband died in 1875 and she married Sir William Stirling-Maxwell. Caroline was accused of obtaining a Cabinet secret from her lover and selling it to *The Times*.

Meredith knew her well and admitted to Robert Louis Stevenson that he had used her character and incidents from her life in composing *Diana of the Crossways*. After its publication several of Caroline's relatives expressed their shock and anger, and fearing legal action Meredith published the 'Apology' reprinted in all subsequent editions: 'A lady of high distinction for wit and beauty, the daughter of an illustrious Irish house, came under the shadow of a calumny. It has latterly been examined and exposed as baseless. The story of *Diana of the Crossways* is to be read as fiction.'

Jean Gordon (1670–1746)

Meg Merrilies, the gypsy queen whose 'eye had a wild roll that indicated something like real or affected insanity', is vividly present in Sir Walter Scott's *Guy Mannering* on account of her extraordinary appearance – six feet tall with 'dark elf-locks [that] shot out like the snakes of the gorgon' – and her ability to help Harry Bertram to recover his estate. Poignantly, Meg tells the hero: 'I've held you on my knee, Henry Bertram, and sung ye sangs of the auld barons and their bloody wars . . . and Meg Merrilies will never sing sangs mair, be they blithe or sad. But ye'll no forget her. . . . For if ever the dead came back among the living, I'll be seen in this glen mony a night after these crazed banes are in the mould.'

Jean Gordon, Scott's prototype, was born in Kirk-Yetholm on the Scottish border and married Patrick Faa who was transported to the American Plantations after being found guilty of fire-raising. Misfortune ran in the family for one of Jean's sons was murdered and three were hanged for sheep-stealing at Jedburgh. She herself presented a petition, at Jedburgh in 1732, expressing her willingness to leave Scotland after being indicted as an Egyptian and common vagabond. When she entered England she embarked on a career of begging and petty crime but her character was still strong enough to cause trouble. After the failure of the 1745 uprising Jean, passing through Carlisle, was horrified to see the heads of Jacobite rebels on the Scotchgate. True to her Jacobite sympathies she protested so loudly that the mob decided to duck her to death in the Eden. She was stoned and ducked, yet every time she managed to get her head above water shouted 'Up wi' Chairlie yet!' She managed to drag herself out of the water but was found dead, the next day, from exposure.

Pierre Galindo

Albert Camus's first novel *The Outsider* was received with
international acclaim on account of its evocation of an absurd
universe; its resistance to authority made it popular with the
forces of the French Resistance and it circulated among inmates
of Nazi concentration camps. It is narrated by Meursault, a
French Algerian, who hears of his mother's death, buries her,
befriends the loutish Raymond, then goes to the beach where
he shoots an Arab who has quarrelled with Raymond. During
his trial Meursault remains indifferent to the rule of law and
to moralistic pressure. He ends by welcoming his imminent
death: 'For all to be accomplished, for me to feel less lonely, all
that remained was to hope that on the day of my execution
there should be a huge crowd of spectators and that they should
greet me with howls of execration.'

The character was based on Pierre Galindo whose sister Chris-
tiane was one of Camus's girlfriends. In 1938 Pierre came to
Algiers for his summer holiday; his muscular appearance and
terse talk greatly impressed Camus who warmed to Pierre as a
complete contrast to his own introverted intellectuality. As
well as being a pied-noir (Algerian-born Frenchman) who
embodied Camus's ideal of proletarian toughness, Pierre had
first-hand knowledge of the life that had eluded Camus. As an
employee of an export firm he knew the sleazy areas of Oran
and he also told Camus that he had been in a fight with some
Arabs on the beach at Oran. Pierre's bravado and his anecdote
about the encounter with Arabs provided Camus with enough
material for *The Outsider*. When the novel was published
Pierre was delighted, according to Patrick McCarthy's *Camus*:
'he recognised himself with enormous pride and he began
acting the role of Meursault. Having become a character in a
famous novel he transformed the novel into real life.'

WILKINS MICAWBER

Charles Dickens, *David Copperfield* (1850)

John Dickens (1785–1851)

Micawber is improvidence personified. He is an agent for the firm of Murdstone and Grinby, and David lodges with him while he works there. He is pompous, long-winded and with genteel pretensions, and although he lives permanently beyond his income, he is buoyed up by an unquenchable optimism. He moves from debt to debt and job to job and spends some time in the Marshalsea prison for debt. He is a great friend to David, and finally unmasks the villainy of Uriah Heep ('You heap of infamy!') He is repaid by Betsy Trotwood who makes good his debts and he and his family sail for Australia. He is described in the novel: 'A stoutish, middle-aged person, in a brown surtout and black tights and shoes, with no more hair upon his head . . . than there is upon an egg, and with a very extensive face. . . . His clothes were shabby, but he had an imposing shirtcollar on. He carried a jaunty sort of a stick, with a large pair of rusty tassels to it.' His method of expressing himself is equally unique: 'My dear . . . your papa was very well in his way and heaven forbid that I should disparage him. Take him for all in all, we ne'er shall – in short, make the acquaintance probably, of anybody else possessing, at his time of life, the same legs for gaiters, and able to read the same description of print, without spectacles.'

John Dickens, the novelist's father, was a clerk in the Navy Pay Office at Portsmouth, where he married Elizabeth Barrow (see MRS NICKLEBY) and was later employed in similar circumstances at London, Chatham and later at Somerset House. He was arrested for debt in 1824. He later became parliamentary reporter for the *Morning Herald* and the *Mirror of Parliament*. His ability constantly to live beyond his means was a permanent source of concern to Charles Dickens, who nevertheless loved and admired his father dearly. Robert Langton, who knew John Dickens, described him as 'a chatty, pleasant companion . . . possessing a varied fund of anecdotes and a genuine vein of humour. He was a well built man, rather stout . . . a little pompous. . . . He dressed well, and wore a goodly bunch of seals suspended across his waistcoat.' His verbal prolixity was notorious. 'I do not think he will live long' from his lips became 'I must express my tendency to believe that his longevity is (to say the least of it) extremely problematical.'

DR MIDDLETON
George Meredith, *The Egoist* (1879)

Thomas Love Peacock (1785–1866)

George Meredith married Mary Ellen Nicolls, a widow seven years his senior, in 1849 and for some time was financially obliged to her father Thomas Love Peacock. The established author (of, for example, *Nightmare Abbey*) and the aspiring writer did not have a harmonious relationship; Meredith disapproved of his father-in-law's politics and Peacock disliked Meredith's flamboyant personality and habit of smoking incessantly. Meredith's marriage was a difficult one and Mary Ellen left him in 1857 to live with the pre-Raphaelite painter Henry Wallis. When she eventually desired to return to her husband, Meredith rejected her. After her death, in 1861, he agonized over his inflexibility.

In *The Egoist* Meredith recalled his married life by portraying his father-in-law in the person of Dr Middleton, the rigidly reactionary father of his heroine Clara Middleton. Preposterously, Dr Middleton encourages the Egoist's courting of Clara on account of his social standing and the quality of his wine cellar. For Dr Middleton has a passion for port: 'Port is deep-sea deep. It is in its flavour deep. . . . It is like a classic tragedy, organic in conception.' Meredith's description of the prejudiced classical scholar is unmistakably Peacockian: 'The Rev Doctor was a fine old picture; a specimen of art peculiarly English; combining in himself piety and epicurism, learning and gentlemanliness, with good room for each and a seat at one another's table: for the rest, a strong man, an athlete in his youth, a keen reader of facts and no reader of persons, genial, a giant at a task, a steady worker besides, but easily discomposed. He loved his daughter and he feared her. However much he liked her character, the dread of her sex and age was constantly present to warn him that he was not tied to perfect sanity while the damsel Clara remained unmarried.'

OSWALD MILLBANK
Benjamin Disraeli, *Coningsby* (1844)

William Ewart Gladstone (1809–94)

Many of Disraeli's parliamentary contemporaries are portrayed in *Coningsby*, notably the young Gladstone, who appears as Oswald Millbank: 'the son of one of the wealthiest manufacturers of Lancashire. His father sent his son to Eton, though he disapproved of the system of education pursued there, to show that he had as much right to do so as any duke in the land. He had, however, brought up his only boy with a due prejudice against every sentiment or institution of an aristocratic character.... The character of the son ... tended to the fulfilment of these injunctions. Oswald Millbank was of a proud and independant nature; reserved, a little stern.... His talents were considerable, though invested with no dazzling quality.... But Millbank possessed one of those strong industrious volitions whose perseverence amounts almost to genius.... Millbank was not blessed with the charm of manner. He seemed close and cold; but he was courageous, just and flexible.' (*Coningsby*, Book I, ch. ix)

William Ewart Gladstone was born in 1809, the son of a successful Liverpool merchant, who traded successfully in the East and West Indies and defended the slave trade against the attacks of the reformers. An opponent of Corn Law Reform, he was Canningite MP for Lancaster. William was educated at Eton and Christ Church, Oxford. He took a double first in classics and mathematics and was president of the Union. He entered politics as Conservative MP for Newark in 1832, the seat he held between 1841–45. His first important speech, advocating a gradual winding down of the slave trade, was made in 1833. Peel made him Junior Lord of the Treasury in 1834, and he was later Under-Secretary for War and the Colonies in the same government. He opposed the Opium War with China in 1840 and was Vice-President of the Board of Trade and Privy Councillor in 1841. Peel made him President of the Board of Trade in 1843, and he introduced the first general railway bill in 1844. In 1845 he resigned over the Maynooth grant issue. He did not re-enter parliament until the struggle for the repeals of the Corn Laws was concluded. In 1847 he was elected MP for Oxford University, and was Chancellor of the Exchequer in Aberdeen's ministry. He became prime minister of the Liberal government in 1868–74, again in 1880 and again in 1886 and 1892–94. He died in May 1894 and was buried in Westminster Abbey.

MIRIAM LEIVERS
D. H. Lawrence, *Sons and Lovers* (1913)

Jessie Chambers (1887–1944)

D. H. Lawrence's *Sons and Lovers* shows the anguish the hero, Paul Morel, feels as he tries to reconcile his love for his mother with his passion for other women. At Willey Farm he meets Miriam Leivers and is enchanted by her: 'The girl was romantic in her soul.' For the remainder of the novel Paul and Miriam agonize over their relationship and end by agreeing to part.

Miriam is a recreation of Jessie Chambers, whose early influence on Lawrence was profound. He first met her in 1901, on her father's farm at Haggs, near Eastwood. Lawrence liked to visit the Haggites (as he called Jessie's family) and he shared with her a love of literature: as Jessie wrote in her *D. H. Lawrence: A Personal Record* (1935) 'It was entering into possession of a new world, a widening and enlargement of life.' Lawrence told Jessie of his ambitions and added 'Every great man . . . is founded in some woman. Why shouldn't *you* be the woman I am founded in.' When the two met at Lawrence's mother's funeral in 1911 Lawrence admitted to Jessie he had loved his mother 'like a lover. That's why I could never love you.' Jessie resented the rivalry of Lawrence's mother and noted that in *Sons and Lovers* he had 'handed his mother the laurels of victory'.

Jessie Chambers helped Lawrence by writing out passages which he adapted for use in *Sons and Lovers*; when he informed her of his 'new attachment' to Frieda Weekley in 1912 she was stunned but not surprised. She later said that on what turned out to be the day of Lawrence's death (2 March 1930) she heard him say 'Can you remember only the pain and none of the joy?' Before she died she burned many of the letters Lawrence had sent to her.

WALTER MITTY

James Thurber, *My World – and Welcome to It* (1942)

Charles Thurber (1867–1939)

'The original of Walter Mitty,' said James Thurber, is every other man I have ever known. When the story was printed . . . six men from around the country, including a Des Moines dentist, wrote and asked me how I had got to know them so well.' Thurber's classic account of the little man who escapes from everyday defeats by daydreaming himself into heroic situations was a sensation on its first appearance in the *New Yorker* on 18 March 1939. During the war, servicemen formed Mitty clubs and adopted catchphrases from the story.

Thurber's family realized that Mitty was based on the author's father. Charles Thurber had a difficult early life; his father was killed in a fall from a horse so Charles had to help support the family by selling newspapers. Anxious to make a name for himself as an actor, or a lawyer, his circumstances made him settle for the less glamorous job of clerk. Despite his dreams he never achieved fame though when he married Mary Agnes Fisher in 1892 he found himself connected to one of the most prominent families in Columbus, Ohio. His wealthy father-in-law offered him a job but Charles valued his independence and worked his own way up to become secretary to the Chairman of the Republican State Committee. However he lost that job (and several others) and was often dependent on the income his wife received from stock given to her by her father. Charles Thurber had a talent for defeatism: in 1912 he switched from the Republicans and became secretary of the Progressive Party's State Campaign thus ensuring he was unemployed come election day. On another occasion he inadvertently locked himself inside a rabbit pen for three hours. His fantasy life helped him win many newspaper competitions but he was unable to cope with the reality of his son's literary celebrity. Thurber used his father's idiosyncratic personality in several ways but never more memorably than as 'Walter Mitty, the undefeated, inscrutable to the last.'

MOBY DICK
Herman Melville, *Moby Dick* (1851)

Mocha Dick (circa 1820)

Moby Dick concerns the hunt for a fierce and dangerous white whale. He has caused many disasters to whalers and has become legendary, an object of fear and superstition. Captain Ahab of the *Pequod*, who lost a leg to Moby Dick in a previous encounter, has vowed to take him. After a hunt which takes him three quarters round the globe, Ahab finds the white whale and the contest for his life lasts three days. Moby Dick triumphs in the end, Ahab's neck is broken and the *Pequod* sinks. Ahab has come up against the ultimate force of the universe in his own refusal to accept any limits to his humanity in striving against the ultimate: 'I own thy speechless, placeless power,' he says, 'Thou canst blind. . . . Thou canst consume.' But even this acknowledgement does not compel him to limit his search for Moby Dick: 'There is some unsuffering thing beyond thee, thou clear spirit, to whom all thy eternity is but time, all thy creativeness mechanical.' Melville seems to be using the colour white in a startling reversal of traditional symbolism. Moby Dick is the consummate evil, but Moby Dick had a real source.

Mocha Dick was legendary among whalers before Melville's novel. Jeremiah N. Reynolds (1799–1858) published *Mocha Dick* in 1839. It is a narrative about a fierce and cunning white whale, based on his own personal experience of sea adventure and polar exploration. Reynolds wrote of: 'an old bull whale, of prodigious size and strength . . . known by awe-struck whale hunters as "Mocha Dick" and also, because of his colour, he was white as wool, as the "White Whale of the Pacific".' Early in his career, Edgar Allan Poe was a journalist and reviewer, and he reviewed essays, journals and accounts of sea adventures, including Reynolds's and he incorporated several of these ideas and incidents into his own fiction – *Unparalleled Adventures of One Hans Pfaal* (1835) and *The Narrative of Arthur Gordon Pym* (1835).

LORD MONMOUTH
Benjamin Disraeli, *Coningsby* (1844)

Francis Charles Seymour-Conway,
Third Marquis of Hertford (1771–1842)

Lord Monmouth is a wildly reactionary Tory parliamentarian, with ambitions for a dukedom and a lavish social life. Far
from seeing the 1832 Reform Act as an obstacle to his ambitions, it spurs him on: 'While all his companions in discomfor-
ture were bewailing their irretrievable overthrow, Lord
Monmouth became almost a convert to the measure, which
had furnished his devising and daring mind, pallid with prosperity, and satiated with a life of success, with an object, and
the stimulating enjoyment of a difficulty. . . . Lord Monmouth,
even to save his party and gain his Dukedom, must not be
bored. He therefore filled his castle with the most agreeable
people from London, and even secured for their diversion, a
little troop of French comedians. Thus supported he received
his neighbours with all the splendour befitting his immense
wealth and great position ... as he was extremely good-
natured, and for a selfish man even good-humoured, there was
rarely a cloud of caprice or ill-temper to prevent his fine
manners having their fair play. . . . Lord Monmouth, whose
contempt for mankind was absolute ... who never loved
anyone, and never hated anyone except his own children was
diverted by his popularity, but he was also gratified by it. . . .
Lord Monmouth worshipped gold, though, if necessary, he
could squander it like a caliph. He had even a respect for very
rich men; it was his only weakness, the only exception to his
general scorn for the species. Wit, power, particular friendships
. . . public opinion, beauty, genius, virtue, all these could be
purchased; but it does not follow that you can buy a rich man;
you may not be able or willing to spare enough. A person or a
thing that you could, perhaps, not buy, became invested, in the
eyes of Lord Monmouth, with a kind of halo amounting
almost to sanctity.'

This is a portrait of the third Marquis of Hertford, Francis
Charles Seymour-Conway, who was known as Lord Yar-
mouth before he took his title, was a friend of the Regent's,
moved in sporting circles, and entertained lavishly. (See LORD
STEYNE).

HUGH MORELAND

Anthony Powell, *Casanova's Chinese Restaurant* (1960), *The Kindly Ones* (1962), *The Valley of Bones* (1964), *The Soldier's Art* (1966), *The Military Philosophers* (1968), *Books Do Furnish a Room* (1971), *Temporary Kings* (1973), *Hearing Secret Harmonies* (1975).

Constant Lambert (1905–51)

The compositionally bright and conversationally brilliant Hugh Moreland, who appears in Anthony Powell's twelve-volume novel-sequence *A Dance to the Music of Time* (1951–75), is an affectionate portrait of the author's great friend Constant Lambert. Moreland first appears in *Casanova's Chinese Restaurant* as the embodiment of music: 'He was formed physically in a "musical" mould, classical in type, with a massive, Beethoven-shaped head, high forehead, temples swelling outwards, eyes and nose somehow bunched together in a way to make him glare at times like a High Court judge about to pass sentence.' In *The Kindly Ones* Moreland explains his intense approach to music: 'The arts derive entirely from taking decisions. . . . Having taken the decision music requires, I want to be free of all others.'

Powell met Lambert in 1927 and immediately formed a close friendship with him. At that time Lambert was already established as the outstanding young British composer; his ballet *Romeo and Juliet* had been commissioned for the Russian Ballet by Diaghilev and produced at Monte Carlo in 1926. Nevertheless Lambert was depressed at Diaghilev's authoritarian methods and there was always a melancholy side to his apparently outgoing nature. He scored a great success with his choral work *The Rio Grande* (1929) and was instrumental in encouraging the development of British ballet. His forthright opinions were entertainingly aired in his book *Music, Ho!* (1934) which discussed jazz and classical music with equal enthusiasm. Powell and Lambert liked to discuss literature and painting – as well as music – in pubs and at parties. In his autobiographical *Messengers of Day* (1978) Powell recalls 'Towards the end of his life especially, the laughter and talk of Lambert's light-hearted moods had an obverse side of periodical grumpiness and ill humour.'

DEAN MORIARTY
Jack Kerouac, *On the Road* (1957)

Neal Cassady (1926–68)

Jack Kerouac's *On the Road* is the restless story which narrator Sal Paradise tells as he takes off on a series of trips across America with his friend Dean Moriarty: 'With the coming of Dean Moriarty began the part of my life you could call my life on the road. . . . Dean is the perfect guy for the road because he actually was born on the road, when his parents were passing through Salt Lake City in 1926, in a jalopy, on their way to Los Angeles.' Dean Moriarty is a new kind of American hero: totally uninhibited and open to all sorts of outrageous experiences as he experiments with drink, drugs and sex. As Sal Paradise sees it, 'Dean just raced in society, eager for bread and love.' After the two men met, in New York in 1946, Kerouac became fascinated by Cassady as the embodiment of the beat generation.

Cassady, the 'Adonis of Denver', had the kind of experience Kerouac needed for his books: he had served reformatory terms, had a powerful physical presence, and was a great talker. He also wrote lively letters and Kerouac acknowledged 'The discovery of a style of my own based on spontaneous get-with-it came after reading the marvellous free-narrative letters of Neal Cassady, a great writer who happens also to be the Dean Moriarty of *On the Road*.' Living with the legend Kerouac had created for him, Cassady survived into the 1960s as a prophet of hippieness. In 1968 he was found unconscious near the railroad tracks outside San Miguel de Allende in Mexico and died in the local hospital from heart failure caused by exposure. Kerouac died one year later.

PETER MORRISON

Simon Raven, *Alms for Oblivion* (ten volumes, 1959–74)

James Prior (born 1927)

When he appears in *Sound the Retreat* (1971) – chronologically the second stage of Simon Raven's ten-volume *Alms for Oblivion* sequence – Peter Morrison is 'a large and slightly shambling Cadet with a huge round shining face . . . a young man of intelligence and iron will-power . . . a good-humoured boy who could take a joke at his own expense'. In *Friends in Low Places* (1965) he is 'Six foot two inches tall, broad both at chest and waist but giving no impression of overweight, carrying his huge round head thrown back like a guardsman's'. During the various stages of the story he rises step by step on the political ladder. By 1955 he is Conservative MP and leader of 'the Young England Group'; he returns to Parliament in a by-election of 1968 in a seat he retains at the general election two years later. On the death of his rival Somerset Lloyd-James he becomes, in 1972, Parliamentary Under-Secretary at the Ministry of Commerce. *The Survivors* (1976), the last novel of the series, has him as Minister of Commerce. Morrison is bright, if slightly devious, and tenacious.

Simon Raven has admitted that he based the character on James Prior, his contemporary at Charterhouse public school. Prior took a degree in Estate Management at Cambridge, was commissioned in the Royal Norfolk Regiment in 1946 and (like Morrison) looked after his East Anglian estate. He became an MP in 1959 and was closely associated with the rise to power of Edward Heath who (after winning the general election of 1970) made him Minister of Agriculture. Under Margaret Thatcher's premiership he served as Secretary of State for Employment and Secretary of State for Northern Ireland. His hobby is cricket and, in *Friends in Low Places,* he is seen – in a rare moment of relaxation – as he 'lumbered easily to the bowling crease and placed the ball just where he had told his son'.

SIR ROBERT MORTON

Terence Rattigan, *The Winslow Boy* (1946)

Sir Edward Carson (1854–1935)

Terence Rattigan's *The Winslow Boy* was, as the dramatist acknowledged, 'inspired by the facts of a well-known case'. George Archer-Shee (Ronnie Winslow in the play) was, in 1908, removed from the Royal Naval College at Osborne after being accused of stealing and cashing a five-shilling postal order belonging to Terence Back, a fellow cadet. The case against George rested on the memory of the local postmistress and the opinion of a handwriting expert, but George's elder brother, Major Martin Archer-Shee, was convinced of George's innocence. Accordingly he persuaded his father to consult Sir Edward Carson then widely regarded (as George's father puts it in the play) as 'the best advocate in the country [and] certainly the most expensive'. After interrogating George for three hours, Sir Edward decided to take the case and proceeded by Petition of Right and then, when this was initially dismissed, by going to the Court of Appeal. All his efforts, including his devastating cross-examination of the postmistress, resulted in the Crown accepting George's innocence and awarding his father £7,120 compensation. Four years after this legal victory of 1910 George died of wounds received in the first battle of Ypres.

Rattigan portrays Sir Edward as Sir Robert Morton who is 'a man in the early forties; tall, thin, cadaverous and immensely elegant. He wears a long overcoat and carries his hat. He looks rather a fop and his supercilious expression bears out this view.' Sir Edward Carson was a member of both the English and Irish Bars and his career as a lawyer was spectacularly successful. He played a major part in the downfall of Oscar Wilde and featured in many criminal and civil cases. He was also active politically and, as a leader of the Ulstermen, urged Ulster to support the British Government during the First World War. He was an MP from 1892 to 1921 and served as Attorney-General, First Lord of the Admiralty and member of the War Cabinet.

MOTH
William Shakespeare, *Love's Labours Lost* (1598)

Thomas Nashe (1567–1601)

Love's Labours Lost is, of all Shakespeare's comedies, probably the one most full of topical and contemporary references and allusions. Moth is the cheeky and delicately witty page to Don Armada – himself based on a celebrated contemporary (see DON ARMADO). His name amply suggests the felicitous and aerial nature of his ripostes. In the presentation of the Nine Worthies in Act V Moth plays the infant Hercules (see HOLOFERNES), but the general impression we carry away from the play is of his gossamer-like fanciful badinage: 'to jig off a tune at the tongue's end, canary to it with your feet, humour it with turning up your eye-lids, sigh a note and sing a note, sometimes through the throat, as if you swallowed love with singing love . . . with your hat penthouselike o'er the shop of your eyes. . . . These are complements, these are humours; these betray nice wenches.'

There are several references in the play to identify Moth with Thomas Nashe, who was a brilliant and witty controversialist and pamphleteer who associated with William Shakespeare. He was the son of a minister, educated at Cambridge and was publishing books and pamphlets by the 1580s in which he identified himself with the University Wits and made caustic and satiric attacks on actors and dramatists who were not university educated. Nashe collaborated with John Lyly to answer the attacks made by the anonymous puritan pamphleteer Martin Marprelate, and a paper war ensued which contained some of the best satiric writing of the period. Nashe's association with Greene and Lyly brought him up against Gabriel Harvey, the friend of Edmund Spenser, and a further flurry of savage pamphleteering followed which was finally ended as a public scandal in 1599 when Nashe's pamphlets were among those ordered to be burned. These controversies may well be the basis for the disputes between Moth and Don Armado. Moth is named 'juvenal' in *Love's Labours Lost*, and as a satirist Nashe was equated with Juvenal in his own day, notably in Robert Greene's *Groats-Worth of Wit* (1592), see *Love's Labours Lost* Act I, Scene 2, line 8 and Act III, Scene 1, line 67. Nashe's replies to Harvey were widely read and frequently reprinted in his day. He also wrote *The Unfortunate Traveller*, a picaresque novel (1594) and it has been suggested that he collaborated with Shakespeare on the Henry VI plays and *The Taming of the Shrew*. There are also echoes of Nashe in *Hamlet* and *Titus Andronicus*.

Oliver St John Gogarty (1878–1957)

In September 1904 James Joyce stayed with Oliver St John Gogarty in the Martello Tower at Sandycove, near Dublin. For a lease of eight pounds per year Gogarty had taken the tower in order to write and he put up with his difficult and demanding friend on condition that Joyce did the housework. Joyce and Gogarty soon found it impossible to live in the same place and Joyce left the Martello Tower. However, he returned to it imaginatively for the opening of *Ulysses*. In contrast to the sensitive, searching Stephen Dedalus (Joyce), 'Stately, plump Buck Mulligan' (Gogarty) is crude and complacent: 'Buck Mulligan at once put on a blithe broadly smiling face. He looked at them, his wellshaped mouth open happily, his eyes, from which he had suddenly withdrawn all shrewd sense, blinking with mad gaiety. He moved a doll's head to and fro, the brims of his Panama hat quivering, and began to chant in a quiet happy foolish voice'.

Like Joyce, Gogarty was born in Dublin but whereas Joyce chose 'Silence, cunning and exile' Gogarty acquired status, success and respectability. His wealthy parents sent him to Trinity College and, like Mulligan, he studied medicine. Because of his financial advantages he tended to patronize Joyce and encourage him to drink heavily; yet he sensed that Joyce's literary talent was greater than his own. After Joyce left Ireland, Gogarty pursued a distinguished career as a surgeon. In 1922 he was made a Senator of the Irish Free State but the same year *Ulysses* appeared and Gogarty was jealous of Joyce's international literary celebrity. When his country adopted the name Eire in 1936 Gogarty expressed his disapproval of new political developments and three years later he moved to the USA. His own works include the witty prose of *As I Was Going Down Sackville Street* (1937), *Tumbling in the Hay* (1939) and the verse of *Collected Poems* (1952).

MOLEY MYSTIC
Thomas Love Peacock, *Melincourt* (1817)

Samuel Taylor Coleridge (1772–1834)

Moley Mystic is the 'poeticopolitical, rhapsodicoprosaical, deisidaemoniaco-paradoxogeaphical, pseudolatreiological, transcendental-meteorosophist . . . of Cimmerian Lodge.' His Christian name, he believed, was improperly spelt with an 'e', and was in truth: 'nothing more nor less than/That Moly,/ Which Hermes erst to wise Ulysses gave', and which was, in the mind of Homer, *a pure anticipated cognition* of the system of Kantian metaphysics, or grand transcendental science of the *luminous obscure*; for it had a *dark root*, which was mystery; and a *white flower*, which was abstract truth; *it was called Moly by the gods*, who then kept it to themselves; and was *difficult to be dug up by mortal men*, having, in fact, lain *perdu* in subterranean darkness till the immortal Kant dug for it *under the stone of doubt*, and produced it to the astonished world as the *root of human science*. Other persons, however, derived his first name differently; and maintained that the 'e' in it showed it very clearly to be a corruption of *Mole-eye*, it being the opinion of some naturalists that the *mole* has *eyes*, which it can withdraw or project at pleasure, implying the faculty of wilful blindness, most happily characteristic of a transcendental metaphysician since, according to the old proverb, *None are so blind as those who won't see.*

This portrait of a pretentiously intellectual poet and philosopher whose discourse is almost totally incomprehensible, is Peacock's view of Coleridge. As Byron said in *Don Juan*, Coleridge explained Metaphysics to the nation, 'I wish he would explain his Explanation.' Hazlitt said he 'talked on for ever; and you wished him to talk on for ever'. Coleridge was a brilliant student but left Cambridge without graduating, introduced England to German metaphysics and the brilliant Shakespeare criticism of Schlegel, Lessing and Tieck, and became an influential lecturer and critic. A friend and collaborator of Wordsworth's, much of his own poetry was not completed, but is nevertheless powerful and moving. The *Ancient Mariner* is justifiably regarded as a classic, and *Biographia Literaria* a landmark in English romanticism. (See also FLOSKY.)

Ambrose Phillips (1675–1749)

Ambrose Phillips was a poet and fellow of St John's College, Cambridge, and a member of Joseph Addison's literary circle. His version of Racine's *Andromaque* (1712) entitled 'The Distressed Mother' was lauded in the *Spectator*. Pope and Addison were initially on good terms, but after their split, any friend of Addison's was a fair target for the satiric barbs of Alexander Pope (see ATTICUS) and so Phillips' *Pastorals*, in which he took Edmund Spenser as his model, were savagely received by Pope, who published his *Pastorals* a few years later. Pope took Virgil as his model and strove for elegance and harmony – he considered Ambrose Phillips' efforts were weak and simpering, especially as Phillips' verses were adulatory of public figures and politicians whom Pope despised. Phillips described Robert Walpole, manipulator of the system Pope decried, as 'steerer of the realm', for example. Henry Carey wrote: 'So the Nurses get by heart, Namby-Pamby's little rhymes.' But what put poor Phillips' cruel nickname into general circulation was a section in the 1733 version of Pope's *Dunciad*: 'Beneath is reign, shall Eusden wear the bays,/Cibber preside Lord Chancellor of Plays,/Benson sole judge of architecture sit,/And Namby Pamby be prefer'd for wit.'

By the middle of the 18th century, Ambrose Phillips' nickname had passed into the language as a term to describe anything weakly sentimental or affectedly childish. The quarrel between Phillips and Pope was a violent one, fanned by their deep political differences, and at one stage Phillips hung up a rod at Button's Coffee House, with which he threatened to chastise Pope. He tried, with success, to write dramas, and hoped for advancement when the Whigs came to power. He was in fact made a Justice of the Peace. Samuel Johnson's verdict: 'The pieces that please best are those which . . . procured him the name of Namby Pamby, the poems of short lines, by which he paid court to all ages and characters.'

Emile Zola, *Nana* (1880)

Cora Pearl (1835–86)

The heroine of Emile Zola's sensationally successful *Nana* is a harlot who wants to use her stunningly erotic beauty to take revenge on the sex that she feels has ruined her. At the Variety Theatre in Paris, where the book begins, Nana is due to appear in an operetta, 'The Blonde Venus'. Although she has no acting ability and no singing voice her presence electrifies the audience. When she flaunts her flesh a shiver goes round the house: 'She was wearing nothing but a veil of gauze; and her round shoulders, her Amazon breasts, the rosy points of which stood up as stiff and straight as spears, her broad hips, which swayed to and fro voluptuously, her thighs – the thighs of a buxom blonde – her whole body, in fact, could be divined, indeed clearly discerned, in all its foamlike whiteness, beneath the filmy fabric.' Nana is a woman with sexual power over men and attracts admirers like Count Muffat; yet she contrives to misuse her natural possessions and, after contracting smallpox, is ironically alone in her final disintegration.

Zola based Nana on the celebrated courtesan Cora Pearl, a woman whose erotic expertise earned her a fortune which she eventually squandered. Born Emma Elizabeth Crouch, the daughter of a popular composer, Cora became one of the most sought-after prostitutes in London. She transferred her business to Paris in 1858 and rapidly acquired what she referred to as her 'Golden Chain' of affluent and aristocratic clients. Her promotional activities were extraordinary: she once appeared naked on a silver platter as if being served to her dinner guests; she also bathed naked, before an invited audience, in champagne in her silver tub. Despite her many influential contacts Cora eventually lost her friends, and her fortune, when she lost her looks. She died of cancer in poverty and alone.

COLONEL THOMAS NEWCOME

William Makepeace Thackeray, *The Newcomes* (1853–55)

Henry Carmichael-Smyth (1778–1861)

The romantic aspects of Thackeray's novel *The Newcomes* literally begin and end with the character of Colonel Thomas Newcome who enters the book comically and leaves it tragically. Unable to marry the woman he loves, the Colonel settles for a life in India and marriage to a woman he wishes to help. As portrayed by Thackeray, Colonel Newcome is a paragon: 'Besides his own boy, whom he worshipped, this kind Colonel had a score, at least, of adopted children, to whom he chose to stand in the light of a father. . . . On board the ship in which he returned from Calcutta were a dozen of little children, of both sexes, some of whom he actually escorted to their friends before he visited his own.'

The Colonel is a tribute to the author's stepfather Henry Carmichael-Smyth. Thackeray's mother Anne Becher was sixteen when, in 1808, she fell in love with Lieutenant Henry Carmichael-Smyth who was staying in England after ten years' active service in India. As Grandmother Becher disapproved of his prospects she told Anne that the Lieutenant had died of a fever; Anne then went to Calcutta where she met and married Richmond Thackeray. A year after the birth of William Makepeace (on 18 July 1811) Anne discovered that her Lieutenant (now a Captain) was in fact alive and well and also living in India. The situation was only resolved when Richmond Thackeray died in 1815 and Anne married Henry Carmichael-Smyth. Three years after William Makepeace had been sent to England, his mother and stepfather came home. Major (as he now was) Carmichael-Smyth was a short man of military bearing and patriotic politics. Thackeray greatly admired his integrity and, when the Major was buried in his native Scotland, put on his gravestone the words with which the Colonel makes his exit in *The Newcomes*: '*Adsum* – And lo, he whose heart was as that of a little child, had answered to his name, and stood in the presence of The Master.'

ETHEL NEWCOME

William Makepeace Thackeray, *The Newcomes* (1853–55)

Sally Baxter (1833–62)

Ethel Newcome, the heroine of *The Newcomes*, is one of Thackeray's most attractive characters: 'Her eyes were grey; her mouth rather large; her teeth as regular and bright as Lady Kew's own; her voice low and sweet; and her smile, when it lighted up her face and eyes, as beautiful as spring sunshine; also they could lighten and flash often, and sometimes, though rarely, rain.'

Thackeray met Sally Baxter in New York, during his American tour of 1852, and knew immediately she would make a splendid heroine. All his romantic impulses soared at the sight of Sally and he wrote, in a letter, 'I have been actually in love for 3 days with a pretty wild girl of 19 (and was never more delighted in my life than by discovering that I could have this malady over again).' Sally teased Thackeray, whose work she admired enormously and told him how she expected to exploit her nubility. He was well aware of the dangers of his infatuation and did his best to control himself, writing to Sally 'My heart was longing and yearning after you full of love and gratitude for your welcome of me – but the words grew a little too warm. . . . When the destined man comes, with a good head and a good heart fit to win such a girl, and love and guide her; then old Mr Thackeray will make his bow and say God bless her.' When he returned to America, in 1855, he met Sally just after her marriage to Frank Hampton of South Carolina. He accepted the situation philosophically and was disturbed when the American Civil War meant that Sally's husband was actually fighting the part of the country that had produced Sally. While Frank Hampton was at war Sally, with fond memories of New York, was dying of tuberculosis on his plantation. Distraught by the news of Sally's death Thackeray wrote to her mother: 'What a bright creature! What a laugh, a life, a happiness! And it is all gone.'

Colonel Philip Toosey

In one of his greatest film roles, Alec Guinness played Colonel Nicholson, a British POW of the Japanese, who collaborates with the enemy and supervises the construction by allied prisoners of a railway bridge in Burma. He begins by defying the camp commandant, General Saito, but after being punished he returns triumphantly to build an even better bridge than the Japanese had originally designed, sited in a better place. The bridge becomes an obsession to him, and represents the full realization of the purpose of his life. Meanwhile British commando agents train to destroy the bridge. In the final moments of the film, the bridge is blown up and Nicholson dies of mortar fire, falling on one of the plungers which detonates his own bridge.

The film was written by Carl Foreman, based on Pierre Boulle's novel, *Le Pont de la Riviere Kwai*. Boulle placed the bridge near the Burmese border, though it was in fact constructed at Tha Makham, three miles west of Karnburi, Thailand, across the Khwae Yai. It was constructed to carry the railway from Bangkok to Rangoon. After the surrender of Singapore, the Dutch East Indies and the Philippines in 1942 the Japanese had over 200,000 POWs to look after. The inefficiencies and brutalities of POW camp life at Tha Makham were brought to an end by the extraordinary personality of Philip Toosey. He was not a professional soldier, but businessman and administrator with considerable industrial experience. Immediately before the war he had been a merchant banker and cotton merchant. He realized that escape was impossible and open defiance simply led to insufferable physical punishment. His negotiating skills enabled him to bargain with the Japanese and he effected an exchange of better living and working conditions, increased food and medical supplies, for the prisoners' organization of themselves to achieve work on the bridge. Toosey's aim was to work to guarantee the survival of as many POWs as possible. He was never accused by his fellow POWs of being 'Jap happy', but was considered, simply, as the one who could best handle the Japanese. Boulle never knew Toosey, was never a prisoner of the Japanese and had never been near the railway. His version of events is part based on the French stereotypical view of the British officer class and on the attitudes of French officers who collaborated with Vichy. The film version adds further distortions.

Mrs John (Elizabeth) Dickens (1789–1863)

Mrs Nickleby is the widow of Nicholas Nickleby, father of the hero of the novel, and of his sister Kate. She is a scatter-brained person, whose mind is a total jumble of inconsequential memories on which she has instant and copious recall. She is hopeless with money and when her irresponsible husband dies, she throws herself at the mercy of Ralph Nickleby, her husband's brother, a rich and miserly money-lender, whose machinations and their effect on Nicholas and Kate form the basis of the novel. Mrs Nickleby's character is bodied forth in a wild and brilliant profusion which, although to a large extent is meaningless to all but herself (and, occasionally, to members of her family), has a poetry all its own. She carries her gift for uncontrolled fancy into real life when she imagines she is wooed by the Gentleman in Small-clothes. 'I don't know how it is, but a fine warm summer day like this, with the birds singing in every direction, always puts me in mind of roast pig, with sage and onion sauce, and made gravy. . . . Roast pig; let me see. On the day five weeks after you were christened, we had a roast – no, that couldn't have been a pig, either, because I recollect there were a pair of them to carve, and your poor dear papa and I could never have thought of sitting down to two pigs – they must have been partridges. Roast pig! I hardly think we ever could have had one . . . for your papa could never bear the sight of them in the shops, and used to say that they always put him in mind of very little babies, only the pigs had much fairer complexions; and he had a horror of little babies, too, because he couldn't very well afford any increase to his family. . . . I recollect dining once at Mrs Bevan's, in that broad street round the corner by the coachmaker's where the tipsy man fell through the cellar flap of an empty house nearly a week before the quarter-day, and wasn't found till the new tenant went in – and we had roast pig there.'

She is based on Dickens's mother, who married John Dickens (see MICAWBER) in 1809 and became the mother of eight children, including the novelist. She seems to have been a loving mother who spent much time teaching Charles and encouraging his mental development and imagination, but she was rather shallow and vain. She read *Nickleby* and asked her brilliant son whether he thought anyone as silly as Mrs Nickleby could ever have existed.

NORA
Henrik Ibsen, *A Doll's House* (1879)

Laura Kieler

In 1870 Henrik Ibsen was sent a copy of Laura Petersen's *Brand's Daughters*, a feminist novel presented as a sequel to his play *Brand*. Ibsen replied on 11 June telling Laura 'The main thing is to be true and faithful to oneself. It is not a question of willing to go in this direction or that, but of willing what one absolutely must, because one is oneself and cannot do otherwise. The rest is only lies.'

Laura first visited Ibsen in Dresden in 1871 and he was attracted to her, calling her his 'skylark'. Again, after her marriage to Danish schoolteacher Victor Kieler, she called on Ibsen in 1876 and told him of her personal problem: since her tubercular husband needed an Italian holiday to improve his health Laura had secretly borrowed the money to pay for it. Two years later she was obliged to return the money and hoped that Ibsen would help her by recommending her new novel to a publisher. He declined, telling her 'In a family where the husband is alive it can never be necessary for the wife to sacrifice her heart's blood as you have done.' Distressed by Ibsen's attitude Laura burned her manuscript and forged a cheque to repay the debt; when she was found out her husband rejected her and, when she suffered a nervous breakdown as a result, had her placed in a public asylum while he sought a separation. Reluctantly he took her back when she implored him to do so.

Laura was appalled at *A Doll's House* because she realized how closely Ibsen had modelled his drama on her own trauma. Her connection with the play continued to disturb her and in 1891 a critical article suggested she was less idealistic than Ibsen's heroine Nora. Ibsen refused to issue a public denial that Nora was indeed Laura and told a friend: 'she herself or her husband, preferably both are the only people able to kill these rumours by an open and emphatic denial. I cannot understand why Herr Kieler has not long since taken this course, which would immediately put an end to the gossip.'

Dominic Cervoni (born 1834)

Nostromo is the captain of the dock workers at the port of
Sulaco in Costaguana. He is handsome, proud and a born leader
of men, but he has one fatal flaw – vanity. The dictator of
Costaguana dies and there is a power struggle which really
centres on the power represented by the Sant Tomé silver
mine. At one stage the struggle is won by the forces of Ribera,
backed by the mine owner, Gould. There is then a further
revolution, led by General Montero, which aims to drive
Europeans out of this South American nation. The Europeans
then support a counter revolution aimed at keeping Montero
from gaining control of the San Tomé mine. The silver has to
be hidden and contact has to be made with forces outside. The
venture is entrusted to Nostromo and a French boulevadier,
Decoud. Under strain of this mission, Decoud's nerve snaps
and he shoots himself. Nostromo is corrupted by the silver and
resolves to hide it and preserve it as a means to his own
advancement. Later to his horror he learns that a lighthouse is
to be built on the island where he has hidden the silver. To
gain access to his hoard he affects to be courting one of the two
daughters of old Viola, the lighthouse keeper. Nostromo
begins to realize that he is really in love with the younger
daughter and they agree to run away together. But on the
night when he goes to regain his hoard, Violo shoots him in
mistake for someone else – a former suitor of his younger
daughter. The gallant, flamboyant exterior personality of
Nostromo has always hidden his essential foolishness, which is
now tragically rewarded.

Nostromo was based on Dominic Cervoni, the Corsican first
mate of the *Saint Antoine*, a vain and colourful forty-two year
old, whom Conrad described in these words: 'His thick black
moustaches, curled every morning . . . seemed to hide a per-
petual smile. But nobody, I believe, had ever seen the true
shape of his lips. From the slow, imperturbable gravity of that
broad-chested man you would think that he had never
smiled. . . . In his eyes lurked a look of perfectly remorseless
irony . . . the slightest distension of his nostrils would give to
his bronzed face a look of extraordinary boldness.' Conrad
sailed with him to the West Indies in 1876.

EDIE OCHILTREE
Sir Walter Scott, *The Antiquary* (1816)

Andrew Gemmels (1687–1793)

Sir Walter Scott's third novel *The Antiquary* is one of his
warmest thanks to the presence of Edie Ochiltree who, as a
bedesman, receives the royal bounty to beggars. Scott describes
Edie's extraordinary appearance thus: 'A slouched hat of huge
dimensions; a long white beard, which mingled with his
grizzled hair; an aged, but strongly marked and expressive
countenance, hardened, by climate and exposure, to a right
brick-dust complexion; a long blue gown, with a pewter
badge on the right arm; two or three wallets, or bags, slung
across his shoulder, for holding the different kinds of meal,
when he received his charity in kind from those who were but
a degree richer than himself, – all these marked at once a beggar
by profession, and one of the privileged class which are called
in Scotland the King's Bedes-men, or, vulgarly, Blue-gowns.'

As a child Scott stayed with his aunt in Kelso and thus saw
some of the colourful characters who moved back and for-
wards over the Scottish Border. One of these was Edie's original
– Andrew Gemmels from Old Cumnock near Ochiltree in
Ayrshire. After serving in the army, and fighting at Fontenoy,
Andrew found himself penniless and so naturally took to
begging since there was no shame attached to the practice at
that time. As the most celebrated mendicant, or gaberlunzie,
of his day Andrew was a welcome figure in Border towns like
Galashiels where he was once observed playing cards with the
Laird of Gala. Through the power of his personality and his
entertaining ability to sing and spin stories he was well rewarded and became affluent enough, on his death at the age of
106, to leave a tidy sum of money to a nephew. As Edie says,
in Scott's novel, 'what wad a' the country about do for want o'
auld Edie Ochiltree, that . . . kens mair auld sangs and tales than
a' the barony besides, and gars ilka body laugh whereever he
comes?'

JONATHAN OLDBUCK

Sir Walter Scott, *The Antiquary* (1816)

George Constable (1719–1803)

Jonathan Oldbuck, Laird of Monkbarns, is *The Antiquary* in Sir Walter Scott's novel. He is a fussy old bachelor of radical views and a forceful turn of phrase ('his Scottish accent predominating when in anger'), a figure of some importance in Fairport (actually Arbroath). 'The country gentlemen,' writes Scott, 'were generally above him in fortune, and beneath him in intellect.' He had, however, the usual resources, the company of the clergyman, and of the doctor, when he chose to request it, and also his own pursuits and pleasures, being in correspondence with most of the virtuosi of his time, who, like himself, measured decayed entrenchments, made plans of ruined castles, read illegible inscriptions, and wrote essays on medals in the proportion of twelve pages to each letter of the legend.'

Scott acknowledged that Oldbuck was derived from George Constable, 'an old friend of my father's, educated to the law, but retired upon his independent property and generally residing near Dundee'. As a child Scott saw Constable as a man anxious to escape his bachelor status as he was in the habit of calling on Scott's Aunt Jenny when she was over fifty and he almost sixty, but the romance came to nothing. When Constable visited the Scotts he would expound his antiquarian interests, to the delight of young Walter, and also told the story that Scott later shaped into 'The Two Drovers'. Constable bought the estate of Wallace-Craigie near Dundee and held court there. Scott was fascinated by the man and once watched Constable dispute with the female proprietor of a stagecoach, a scene he subsequently fashioned into the opening of *The Antiquary* in which Oldbuck appears as 'a good-looking man of the age of sixty [whose] countenance was of the true Scottish cast, strongly marked, and rather harsh in features, with a shrewd and penetrating eye, and a countenance in which habitual gravity was enlivened by a cast of ironical humour'.

OPHELIA
William Shakespeare, *Hamlet* (1602)

Katharine Hamlet (died 1579)

Ophelia is the daughter of Polonius, and sister to Laertes. She is loved by Hamlet and in turn, loves him. Polonius and his son are suspicious of Hamlet's attentions to her, and Laertes attempts to warn Ophelia off him, and to suggest that the liaison is a dangerous one. On the other hand, Polonius is quite prepared to use Ophelia to find out things about Hamlet and to report back his findings to Claudius. Hamlet's behaviour towards Ophelia also confuses her, and this complex of stress and contradiction is too much for her and she loses her reason, goes mad, and drowns herself. This is reported by Queen Gertrude: 'There is a willow grows aslant the brook/That shows his hoar leaves in the glassy stream;/Therewith fantastic garlands did she make/Of crowflowers, nettles, daisies, and long purples. . . . There, on the pendent boughs her coronet weeds/Clamb'ring to hang, an envious sliver broke;/When down her weedy trophies and herself/Fell in the weeping brook.'

Katharine Hamlet was a resident of Tiddington, which lay some two miles from Stratford. She was drowned in the Avon on 17 December 1579. At the inquest held at the offices of the Stratford town clerk, it was declared that her death was accidental and not suicide. The gravediggers in Hamlet Act V, Scene 1 debate whether Ophelia's death was suicide or an accident, and the priest who conducts the burial service says that: 'Her obsequies have been as far enlarg'd/As we have warrantise. Her death was doubtful.' The coincidences between Katharine's death and the death of Ophelia, as well as the astonishing coincidence of the name Hamlet, are very striking.

SIR ORAN HAUT-TON
Thomas Love Peacock, *Melincourt* 1817

Orang-outang owned by James Burnett,
Lord Monboddo (1714–99)

Sir Oran-Haut-ton is an orang-outang owned by Mr Sylvan Forester, a wealthy young philosopher. He has educated it, taught it manners and how to move in high society and has bought him a baronetcy and a seat in parliament. Unfortunately, the orang-outang has not mastered human speech.

This is a satiric attack on the social standards of the day, the wildness of some theories then current in the sciences, and the political system of the time, with rotten boroughs, etc. Although he is an animal, he has all the surface qualities which would make him a gentleman, hence the essential punning nature of his name. As Forester says of him, when he is first seen sitting under a tree in a green coat and nankeens, looking 'very thoughtful', he is of a 'very contemplative disposition . . . you must not be surprised if he should not speak a word. . . . The politeness of his manner makes amends for his habitual taciturnity.' One of the visitors, though too polite to laugh, 'could not help thinking there was something very ludicrous in Sir Oan's physiognomy, notwithstanding the air of high fashion which characterized his whole deportment'. His manners at table are exemplary, though he shows a weakness for wine. He was liable, without warning, having taken too much, to rise from the table and take a flying leap through the window, and go 'dancing along the woods like a harlequin'. Forester asserts that he is a specimen of 'natural and original man'. He learns to play the flute and the French horn by ear 'with great exactness and brilliancy of execution'.

This extraordinary creature is a portrait of Lord Monboddo's orang-outang. Monboddo was a Scottish judge and scientist whose ideas to some extent predated Darwin's origin of species. His ape could play the flute, but never learned to speak. Human language, Monboddo believed, was the outcome of man's social needs. If he lived in a natural state, his language would disappear. Apes, he held, showed intelligence, affection, gentleness and 'a perception of numbers, measure and melody' (*Origin and Progress of Language*, 1773–92).

Vita Sackville-West (1892–1962)

Orlando's adventures through time in Virginia Woolf's prose
fantasy *Orlando* range from a sixteenth-century encounter with
'the great Queen herself' to a sudden realization that 'It was the
eleventh of October. It was 1928. It was the present moment.'
Initially, Orlando is a boy but after a seven-day trance in the
seventeenth-century he changes into a woman: 'Orlando stood
stark naked. No human being, since the world began, has ever
looked more ravishing. His form combined in one the strength
of a man and a woman's grace.' In her diary for 5 October 1927
Virginia Woolf recorded her plans for 'a biography beginning
in the year 1500 & continuing to the present day, called
Orlando: Vita.'

Vita Sackville-West, Lord Sackville's daughter, was born at
Knole, Sevenoaks, Kent; this ancestral home of the Sackvilles
is duly celebrated in *Orlando*. Although well aware of her
lesbian inclinations, Vita married Harold Nicolson in 1913;
their son Nigel Nicolson called *Orlando* 'the longest and most
charming love-letter in literature'. Virginia Woolf, who married Leonard Woolf in 1912, was undoubtedly in love with
Vita though Virginia's frigidity probably prevented the affair
from coming to a physical conclusion. Other literary women
came closer.

Vita's passionate involvement with novelist Violet Trefusis
features in the intimate diary kept by Vita and incorporated in
Portrait of a Marriage (1973) by Nigel Nicolson. Vita's lesbian
affair with Mary Campbell, wife of the poet Roy Campbell, is
the subject of her verse-collection *King's Daughter* (1929).
Campbell retaliated furiously in *The Georgiad* (1931) by setting the satire in the Nicolsons' half-timbered house Long Barn
(two miles from Knole) and describing Vita as 'Too gaunt and
bony to attract a man/But proud in love to scavenge what she
can.'

PETER PAN

J. M. Barrie, *Peter Pan* (1904), *Peter and Wendy* (1911)

Peter Llewelyn Davies (1897–1960)

At a New Year's Eve dinner party of 1897 J. M. Barrie met a lady he considered 'the most beautiful creature' he had ever seen. Sylvia's husband Arthur Llewelyn Davies was a barrister and her father was George du Maurier. Sylvia had named her youngest son Peter (born in 1897) after her father's novel *Peter Ibbetson* and Barrie, when walking through Kensington Gardens with his dog Porthos (named after the dog in *Peter Ibbetson*), had seen this baby boy with his brothers George and Jack and their nurse Mary. Barrie, though impotent, adored children; Sylvia produced two more boys, Michael and Nicholas, and Barrie attached himself to the family, lavishing his attention on the five boys.

Peter Pan portrays Arthur and Sylvia as Mr and Mrs Darling and, as he told the boys, 'I made Peter by rubbing the five of you violently together, as savages with two sticks produce a flame. That is all he is, the spark I got from you.' After the death of Arthur Llewelyn Davies (from sarcoma in 1907) and Sylvia (from cancer in 1910) Barrie adopted the five boys and was twice devastated by tragedy: in 1915 George was killed in action and in 1921 Michael was drowned at Oxford in what was possibly a suicide pact with a friend. Peter Llewelyn Davies, then a successful publisher, killed himself in 1960 by throwing himself under a train in the London underground. He suffered for his namesake for he was ragged at Eton as the real Peter Pan. 'What's in a name?' Peter asked in the family *Morgue* he kept from 1945 onwards, 'My God, what isn't? If that perennially juvenile lead, if that boy so fatally committed to an arrestation of his development, had only been dubbed George, or Jack, or Michael, or Nicholas, what miseries would have been spared me.' He thought the play he had helped to inspire was a 'terrible masterpiece'.

DR PANGLOSS

François-Marie Arouet Voltaire, *Candide* (1759)

Johann Christian von Wolff (1679–1754)

Candide, a philosophical tale by Voltaire, satirizes the optimism of Rousseau and Leibnitz. Candide is the illegitimate son of the sister of the Baron Thunder-ten-tronckh. He is brought up in the Baron's household with Dr Pangloss, an incurable optimist whose motto is 'All is for the best in this best of all possible worlds', as his tutor. Catastrophe after catastrophe happens to the pair on their journey through life. Candide experiences the brutality of war, the Lisbon earthquake, the drowning of dear friends and Pangloss contracts syphilis, which rots his nose, covers him in sores and blackens his teeth. Dr Pangloss is finally hanged for heresy.

Voltaire was not attacking the philosophy of Leibnitz, but the popular notion of it, a kind of senseless optimism which accepted the belief that a benevolent providence was in command of the world. Pangloss teaches Candide: 'Metaphysico-theologo-cosmolonigology. He proved admirably that there is no effect without a cause and that ... things cannot be otherwise; for, since everything is made for an end, everything is necessarily for the best end ... noses were made to wear spectacles and so we have spectacles. Legs were visibly instituted to be breeched, and we have breeches.'

Christian von Wolff was the influential popularizer of the philosophy of Leibnitz. He was born at Breslau and educated at Jena. He taught at the universities of Leipzig and Halle and his system of philosophy soon spread. He was attacked by pietistic colleagues and expelled from Prussia in 1723 but got a chair at Marburg. In 1740 Frederick the Great recalled him and he became Professor of the Law of Nations and Chancellor of the University of Berlin in 1743. His most influential publication was his *Theologica Naturalis* of 1737.

Pangloss survives hanging, finishes up serving in the galleys and experiences many hardships, but even then will not recant, for – as he tells Candide – 'after all I am a philosopher; and it would be unbecoming of me to recant, since Leibnitz could not be in the wrong.' *Candide* was made into a comic operetta with book by Lillian Hellman, lyrics by Richard Wilbur and music by Leonard Bernstein.

PAOLO AND FRANCESCA
Dante Alighieri, *Divina Commedia, Inferno* (1314)

Paolo Malatesta da Verrucchio (died 1285) and Francesca da Rimini (died 1285)

Francesca is the daughter of the Count of Ravenna, and she is given in marriage by her father to Giovanni Malatesta (who is known as Sciancato, the Lame) for political and military reasons. But she falls in love with her husband's handsome younger brother, Paolo. They were reading together the story of Launcelot and Guinevere. Dante, at the end of the fifth canto of the *Inferno*, tells of Paolo's meeting with Francesca, who rehearses to him her temptation and sin as a result of reading the illicit love story of Launcelot and Arthur's Queen: 'The bitterest woe of woes,' she says in her torment, 'is to remember in our wretchedness/Old happy times.' Her fall was such a casual thing: 'One day we read for pastime how in thrall/Lord Launcelot lay to love, who loved the Queen; We were alone – we thought no harm at all./As we read on, our eyes met now and then,/And to our cheeks the changing colour started,/But just one moment overcame us – when/We read of the smile, desired of lips long-thwarted,/Such smile, by such a lover kissed away,/He that may never more from me be parted/Trembling all over, kissed my mouth.' They are discovered by Francesca's husband, who kills them both, and now they suffer endless torment in the howling darkness of helpless discomfort.

Francesca was the daughter of Guido Vecchio di Polenta of Ravenna, and aunt to Guido Novella di Polenta, who was a friend of Dante, and his host at the end of his life. Francesca was married to Gianciotto, son of Malatesta da Verrucchio, Lord of Rimini. The marriage was an arranged one, in return for military services. She fell in love with his younger brother, Paolo. The lovers were discovered by Gianciotto, who stabbed them both to death. Dante had the story, therefore, at first hand.

MR PAPERSTAMP

Thomas Love Peacock, *Melincourt* (1817)

William Wordsworth (1770–1850)

Paperstamp is one of the Lake poets. He is 'chiefly remarkable for an affected infantine lisp in his speech, and for always wearing waistcoats of a duffel grey'. He hears Mr Feathernest give vent to self-praise at dinner at Melincourt Castle, and this is too good an example to be thrown away: 'and Mr Paperstamp followed it up with a very lofty encomium on his own virtues and talents, declaring he did not believe so great a genius, or so amiable a man as himself, Peter Paypaul Paperstamp, Esquire, of Mainchance Villa, had appeared in the world since the days of Jack the Giantkiller, whose *coat of darkness* he hoped would become the costume of the rising generation.' He strongly supports Mr Antijack's case that the wise man is he who appropriates as much of the public money as he can, 'saying to those from whose pockets it is taken: "I am perfectly satisfied with things as they are. Let *well* alone!".' To this he adds some useful political sophistry: 'you must not forget to call the present public distress an awful dispensation: a little pious cant goes a long way towards turning the thoughts of men from the dangerous and jacobinical propensity of looking into moral and political causes for moral and political effects.'

This is Wordsworth, who in earlier days had supported radical causes but grew reactionary in direct proportion to his public success, despite affecting to choose his poetical subject matter among the poor and the humble. He was made Distributor of Stamps for the County of Westmoreland in 1813 (a post he held until 1842) hence his name 'Paperstamp'. Browning immortalized the turncoat in Wordsworth: 'Just for a handful of silver he left us;/Just for a riband to stick in his coat.' Keats wrote (letter 3 February 1818): 'Every man has his speculations, but every man does not brood and peacock over them till he makes a false coinage and deceives himself.'

DON PARRITT

Eugene O'Neill, *The Iceman Cometh* (1946)

Louis Holliday

Eugene O'Neill's *The Iceman Cometh* deals with various personal, political and philosophical 'pipe dreams' as embodied in the assembled drinkers at Harry Hope's saloon-hotel. Whereas the regulars betray themselves, the newcomer Don Parritt has committed an archetypal act of treachery by going to the police and informing on his anarchist mother who is then imprisoned. Ironically, Parritt says to Larry Slade, his mother's old lover, that to her the anarchist movement is like a religion and 'Anyone who loses faith in it is more than dead to her; he's a Judas who ought to be boiled in oil.' Parritt, the Judas of the piece, is 'eighteen, tall and broad-shouldered but thin, gangling and awkward. . . . There is a shifting defiance and ingratiation in his light-blue eyes and an irritating aggressiveness in his manner.' At the end of the play Parritt kills himself by jumping off a fire escape.

O'Neill gradually evolved the character out of a traumatic memory of his drinking friend Louis Holliday, a young New York radical who was one of the first intellectuals to frequent Greenwich Village bars. After meeting a girl he wanted to marry Louis stopped drinking and began to make himself a career in the West as a fruit grower. In January 1918 he told his friends he was coming to New York to celebrate the fact that he had saved enough money to get married; so the evening started at the Hell Hole (the real Harry Hope's). After a while Holliday succumbed to despair and admitted that his girlfriend had left him for another man. Holliday asked his friend Terry Carlin (the prototype of Larry Slade) for enough heroin to kill himself and Terry obliged. Louis died in Romany Marie's cafe at six-thirty in the morning of 23 January. O'Neill's histrionic version of the tragic evening made Don Parritt a man determined to die and Larry Slade his judge and executioner who tells him to 'Get the hell out of life'.

Harold Johnsrud

One week after graduating from Vassar College in 1933 Mary
McCarthy married the actor Harold Johnsrud. As the first
sentence of McCarthy's *The Group* puts it: 'It was June, 1933,
one week after Commencement, when Kay Leiland Strong,
Vassar '33, the first of her class to run around the table at the
Class Day dinner, was married to Harald Petersen, Reed '27,
in the chapel of St George's Church, P. E., Karl F. Reiland,
Rector.' The novel spans seven years (from Kay's marriage to
her funeral, both services taking place in the same church) in
the lives of eight girls from Vassar and in this excessively
feminine world Harald stands as the representative of his sex.
As such he is a failure: unimaginative, unpleasant and unfaith-
ful to Kay (Mary McCarthy).

Like his fictional counterpart Harold Johnsrud was condi-
tioned to failure; his father, a school administrator, had been
involved in an academic scandal and Harold protected himself
through a cynically hard exterior. His ambitions as a dramatist
came to nothing but when Mary McCarthy first saw him, in
Seattle in 1929, he impressed her as an actor – a career she
herself considered. When she came to New York, Johnsrud
befriended her and kept in touch when he went, briefly, to
Hollywood in 1932 to work as a scriptwriter for MGM.
During her three years of marriage to Johnsrud, Mary Mc-
Carthy was influenced by his leftist political sympathies but
disturbed by his violent moods of depression. Perhaps partly
on account of his odd appearance – prematurely bald, with a
broken nose – he was unsuccessful as an actor. In the novel he
is fired from a musical show by a homosexual director, which
is probably a colourful version of the truth. In 1936 Mary
McCarthy decided to divorce Johnsrud. After leaving her,
Johnsrud's life continued towards catastrophe: he wrote plays
that were never produced and was burned to death in the
Hotel Breevort fire during the war. Apparently he had returned to the burning building to rescue some of his manuscripts.

JASPER PETULENGRO

George Borrow, *Lavengro: the Scholar, the Gipsy, the Priest*
(1851)

Ambrose Smith (1804–78)

Lavengro combines fiction with autobiography. The hero is
the son of an officer in the army, who spends much of his
military career guarding French prisoners, and moving from
one station to another. The son develops a wandering nature
and *Lavengro* is the story of his travels, adventures and the
characters he meets. Among the most memorable people he
gets to know is a family of gipsies, with a son, Jasper, slightly
younger than himself: 'A queer look had Jasper; he was a lad
of some twelve or thirteen years, with long arms, unlike the
singular being who called himself his father; his complexion
was ruddy, but his face was seamed.' His face was 'roguish
enough' without being evil, and he 'wore drab breeches, with
certain strings at the knee, a rather gay waistcoat, and tolerably
white shirt; under his arm he bore a mighty whip of whalebone
with a brass knob, and upon his head was a hat without either
top or brim'.

Borrow was almost an adopted member of the Romany race,
having learned the language and the way of life from personal
experience, and his works – *Lavengro* and *Romany Rye* in
particular – put into circulation a great deal of the initial
information on which British conception of the Romany life
was based.

Jasper is one of his finest portraits. He was based on Borrow's
friend Ambrose Smith, son of Faden and Mirella Smith, gipsies
of East Anglia. Ambrose's uncle, also called Ambrose, was
transported for stealing. This episode is also used in *Lavengro*,
though it is transferred to Jasper's father. After the publication
of *Lavengro* Ambrose Smith became something of a celebrity.
The *Athenaeum* reviewer had written that Borrow 'is never
thoroughly at his ease except when among Gipsies'. Ambrose
Smith was, in fact, presented to Queen Victoria at Knockenhair
Park in 1878, the year of his death.

SAMUEL PICKWICK

Charles Dickens, *The Posthumous Papers of the Pickwick Club*
(1836)

John Foster

Pickwick is one of the immortals of literature, a figure instantly and universally recognizable by his 'bald head and circular spectacles . . . gigantic brain beneath that forehead . . . beaming eyes . . . twinkling behind those glasses' and his inviable tights and gaiters. He is described, when we first see him in action standing on a Windsor chair to address the Club which he had founded, as presenting a subject suitable for the study of an artist 'with one hand gracefully concealed behind his coat tails, and the other waving in air, to assist his glowing declamation; his elevated position revealing those tights and gaiters, which, had they clothed an ordinary man, might have passed without observation, but which, when Pickwick clothed them – if we may use the expression – inspired voluntary awe and respect'.

The figure of Pickwick, now so familiar to us, was made from a description of one John Foster, who was a friend of the book's publisher, Edward Chapman. Robert Seymour, the original illustrator, first sketched a long thin man, but, as Chapman recorded: 'The present immortal one was made from my description of a friend of mine at Richmond, a fat old beau, who would wear, in spite of the ladies' protests, drab tights and black gaiters. His name was John Foster.' Thus was born the short and plump Pickwickian prototype. As Dickens says: 'I thought of Pickwick and wrote the first number, from the proof sheets of which Mr Seymour made his drawing of the Club, and that happy portrait of its founder by which he is always recognised.' Writer and illustrator seemed harmonious and in accord with their creation. Dickens took the name from Moses Pickwick, a coach proprietor at Bath. Sam Weller, in the book, is somewhat indignant to see the name on the outside of a coach at Bath, taking it to be a personal reflection upon his employer.

PIED PIPER OF HAMELIN
Robert Browning, *The Pied Piper of Hamelin* (1845)

Nicholas, leader of the Children's Crusade (1212)

The town of Hamelin is plagued by rats. The mayor and corporation strike a bargain with a mysterious piper who has promised to rid them of the rats by means of a mysterious charm. He takes out a pipe, which he plays, and all the rats follow him to the River Weser where they are all drowned. When the piper returns to claim his reward the mayor then argues with him and offers him considerably less than he'd been promised. At this, the piper plays again and all the children run out into the streets and follow him : 'All the little boys and girls,/With rosy cheeks and flaxen curls,/And sparkling eyes, and teeth like pearls,/Tripping and skipping, ran merrily after/ The wonderful music with shouting and laughter.' They follow him to the Koppenberg, here 'a wondrous portal opens wide' and the piper and the children go in, the door closes behind them, and they are never seen again. The poem ends by suggesting that the children come out in Transylvania, where their descendants still live.

There are several explanations for this story, variants of which are found in other parts of the world. One is that it is historically true and it happened in 1284; the man's name is given as 'Bunting' – on account of his parti-coloured costume (German, *bunte*, brightly coloured, cf bunting). Another explanation is that this is a mythological rendering of the German colonial settlement of Sudetenland in Bohemia during the Premyslid dynasty in the middle ages, when Germans settled in colonies near the German frontier formed by the Sudetic Mountains. Before the Second World War, Sudetan Germans numbered some four millions. Another explanation is that it is an account of the Children's Crusade of 1212 when a child called Nicholas, of Cologne, assembled 20,000 children as young crusaders. Many died on the way to the Italian coast, the rest boarded ship, but when they got to Alexandria they were sold into slavery.

John Forster (1812–76)

John Podsnap is a complacent businessman, firm-handed and very self-opinionated: 'Mr. Podsnap was well-to-do, and stood very high in Mr. Podsnap's opinion. Beginning with a good inheritance, he had married a good inheritance, and had thriven exceedingly in the Marine Insurance way, and was quite satisfied. He never could make out why everybody was not quite satisfied, and he felt conscious that he set a brilliant social example in being particularly well satisfied with most things, and, above all other things, with himself.' He was intolerant of the opinions of others about anything, and developed mannerisms and gestures for sweeping others' opinions aside, in which he 'settled that whatever he put behind him he put out of existence: "I don't want to know about it; I don't choose to discuss it; I don't admit it!" Mr. Podsnap had even acquired a peculiar flourish of his right arm in often clearing the world of its most difficult problems by sweeping them behind him (and consequently sheer away) with those words and a flushed face.'

He is modelled on Dickens's close friend and biographer, John Forster. A barrister at the Inner Temple by 1843, he developed a distinguished literary career, as drama critic for the *Examiner*, editor of several journals and contributor to learned publications. He was a friend of Lamb, Bulwer Lytton, Landor, Tennyson, Carlyle, Leigh Hunt and others of the Dickens circle. He wrote *The Life of Charles Dickens*, a valuable, detailed and influential biography of the novelist, which excludes any breath of scandal or blemishes on Dickens's life or character. He was a bossily loquacious man, who would not brook interruption or contradiction, and would literally shout down all opposition with loud explosions of 'Don't tell me!' – 'Incredible!' – 'Monstrous!'. Having beaten opponents into the ground, he would then simply reiterate his own assertions and opinions in his loud sarcastic tones, seasoned with mocking laughter and dismissive snorts. Robert Browning commented on his 'rhinoceros-laugh', and William Macready termed it a 'horse-laugh'. All the same, this pompous and dominating character aroused deep and lasting affection amongst a wide group of sensitive and intelligent people. At table on one occasion he demanded carrots, only to be told by the maid that there were none. With a wave of his hand he exclaimed: 'Mary! Let there be carrots!'.

William Cecil, Lord Burghley (1520–98)

Polonius is the Lord Chamberlain of Denmark, and father to Laertes and Ophelia. He is a complex character, a wily and mature politician who has grown old and whose acumen is affected by senility. At the same time he is a man of considerable – if rather worldly – experience and insight. His long-windedness and pomposity make him an easy butt of the comedy of others, of Prince Hamlet in particular. His most famous speech is the advice he gives his son as he leaves to return to France: 'Neither a borrower nor a lender be;/For loan oft loses both itself and friend,/And borrowing dulls the edge of husbandry,/ This above all – to thine own self be true,/And it must follow, as the night the day,/Thou canst not then be false to any man.' He diagnoses the cause of Hamlet's supposed madness – his unrequited love for Ophelia. He and Claudius attempt to overhear Hamlet and Ophelia conversing. He is slain by Hamlet, in mistake for the King, while hiding behind the curtains in the Queen's room. Here he had hoped to spy on Hamlet as he spoke with his mother. Hamlet sums him up, as a 'rash, intruding fool'.

Burghley had a reputation for investigating the conspiracies of others, and organized what was in effect a secret police to detect plots against Queen Elizabeth, tracking down all the clues and threads in the labyrinthine entanglement of intrigues surrounding Mary Queen of Scots. His main opponent at Elizabeth's court was the Earl of Essex, whom Shakespeare supported. The evidence for the dramatist's satirizing Burghley in the character of Polonius is considerable. Burghley was the author of *Certaine Preceptes, or Directions*, which he wrote for his son and which Shakespeare may have had privy sight of in manuscript. Polonius begins his advice to Laertes by saying: 'these few precepts in thy memory/Look thou character'. And the nature of Burghley's precepts is close to those trotted out by Polonius. Hamlet is deliberately rude to Polonius and mistakes him for 'a fishmonger' – an obvious reference to Lord Burghley's celebrated attempts while treasurer to foster and stimulate the fish trade. He was a renowned busybody. One of his household described him as 'never less idle than when he had most leisure to be idle' and Robert Naunton (1563–1635) commented on his ability to 'unlock the counsels of the Queen's enemies'.

ALETHA PONTIFEX
Samuel Butler, *The Way of All Flesh* (1903)

Mary Ann Savage (1836–85)

The only human warmth which Ernest Pontifex experiences in his schooldays is that lavished on him by his good aunt, Aletha. His father has attempted to beat scholarship, obedience and the Christian religion into him, ably assisted by his hypocritical wife, Christina, and at boarding school he experiences the commendable harshness of school discipline. Aunt Aletha moves from London to be near her favourite nephew, as she recognizes Ernest's qualities and encourages his love of music. With her active support he constructs an organ, which shows his skill in carpentry as well as music. His father holds music to be sinful and degenerate. On her death she leaves him £15,000 which he is to inherit when he is twenty-eight. Aletha represents the qualities of good sense and good nature in a world frequently dominated by the hard and the unyielding.

This is an affectionate portrait of Butler's life-long friend Mary Ann Savage, whom he met at Heatherley's Art School in 1870. She had been a governess and was professionally associated with several clubs for young ladies. She was an intelligent and witty person and a brilliant letter-writer. They corresponded until her death and he consulted her about all his writings. He wrote of her after her death: 'I never knew any woman to approach her at once for brilliancy and goodness.' After her funeral he said: 'I felt that I was attending the funeral of incomparably the best and most remarkable woman I have ever known.' He was asked if he had been in love with her, and he replied: 'I never was and never pretended to be. I valued her, and she perfectly understood that I could do no more. I can never think of her without pain.' He wrote several extraordinary sonnets inspired by their relationship, one of which contains the honest lines: 'I liked, but like and love are far removed;/Hard though I tried to love I tried in vain./For she was plain and lame and fat and short,/Forty and over-kind. Hence it befell/That though I loved her in a certain sort,/Yet did I love too wisely but not well.'

THEOBALD PONTIFEX
Samuel Butler, *The Way of All Flesh* (1903)

Thomas Butler (1806–86)

Samuel Butler's novel was written between 1873 and 1885 and not published until 1903, a year after the author's death. The novel deals with the life and career of Ernest Pontifex, the son of the Revd Theobald Pontifex and his wife Christina. Ernest's father is the rector of Battersby on the Hill and is brought up on strict Victorian middle-class and religious principles. The constant and harsh discipline inflicted on the boy by his father successfully crushes any affection he might have for his father, who crams him with Greek and Latin and the scriptures, driven home by frequent thrashings. On one occasion he is beaten within an inch of his life for mispronouncing a word. He is sent away to a boarding school which is almost as harsh as his home and his love of music is his sole consolation apart from the warmth and affection he has from his aunt, who encourages him in his music and his ambitions to build an organ (see ALETHA PONTIFEX). The nadir of the father/son relationship is reachèd when Ernest witnesses his father's dismissing a pregnant servant girl. Overcome with compassion for her, Ernest gives her his watch and his pocket-money, and his father immediately suspects Ernest to be responsible for Ellen's condition.

This dreadful picture of a Victorian pater familias is based on Butler's own father, Thomas Butler, who was educated at Shrewsbury, under his father, Dr Samuel Butler, and at St John's College, Cambridge. Thomas Butler taught at Shrewsbury and was later rector at Langar-with-Bramston and eventually made Canon of Lincoln. The novelist wrote of him in his notebooks: 'He never liked me, nor I him; from my earliest recollections I can call to mind no time when I did not fear and dislike him . . . no matter whose [fault] it is, the fact remains that for years and years I have never passed a day without thinking of him . . . as the man who was sure to be against me, and who would see the bad side rather than the good of everything I said and did.'

ALISON PORTER
John Osborne, *Look Back in Anger* (1956)

Pamela Lane (born 1930)

John Osborne's *Look Back in Anger* brought a sense of excitement to the complacent English theatre. In the play Jimmy
Porter often imposes his opinions on a captive audience of two
comprising his submissive wife Alison and his friend Cliff
Lewis. Jimmy resents the fact that Alison's background is more
privileged than his: whereas his upbringing has been drab and
his education undistinguished ('not even red brick, but white
tile') she has been raised by affluent upper-class Colonel and
Mrs Redfern. In a typical outburst against Alison's mother
Jimmy explains that he has long hair because he likes it: 'But
that obvious, innocent explanation didn't appeal to Mummy
at all. So she hires detectives to watch me, to see if she can't
somehow get me into the *News of the World*. All so that I shan't
carry off her daughter on that poor old charger of mine.'

Before his dramatic success with the play, John Osborne was
an obscure actor who, in 1951, found himself playing in
Bridgwater in a family comedy opposite Pamela Lane. She
was a Bridgwater girl who had made good at the Royal
Academy of Dramatic Art and had returned to perform before
the suspicious locals. Pamela's parents, who ran a draper's
business, disapproved of Osborne and hired a private detective
to probe into his supposedly disreputable life. In his autobiography *A Better Class of Person* (1981) Osborne says 'Mr and
Mrs Lane were much coarser characters than Alison's mother
and father, but their tactics were similar. They were certainly
farther down in the class scale, firmly entrenched in trade for
generations.' Still, Osborne married Pamela and took her to
live with him in London; she brought 'her twenty-first birthday present from her parents, a portable typewriter on which
I was to type *Look Back in Anger*'. The couple separated in
1954.

SIR JOSEPH PORTER, KCB, FIRST LORD OF THE ADMIRALTY

Opera, *HMS Pinafore* (1878, music by A. S. Sullivan, libretto by W. S. Gilbert)

William Henry Smith (1825–91)

The portrait of the First Lord of the Admiralty is a satiric attack on the political system which allowed those to be in charge of departments of government who had little or no professional experience of their affairs. Sir Joseph sings a celebrated patter song which describes his brilliant career from office boy in a lawyer's firm, through junior clerk, articled clerk, legal partnership, on to a seat in the Commons by means of a pocket borough, party stalwart and finally to the position of First Lord: 'I grew so rich that I was sent/By a pocket borough into Parliament./I always voted at my party's call,/ And never thought of thinking for myself at all./I thought so little, they rewarded me/By making me the Ruler of the Queen's Navee!'

Although Gilbert made some efforts to deny it, this was clearly a portrait of W. H. Smith. Gilbert wrote to Sullivan in 1877: 'Among other things there is a song for the First Lord – tracing his career as office boy in a cotton broker's office, clerk, traveller, junior partner, and First Lord of Britain's Navy. I think a splendid song can be made of this. Of course there will be no personality in this – the fact that the First Lord in the opera is a Radical of the most pronounced type will do away with any suspicion that W. H. Smith is intended.' But the character who sang urging those who wished to follow his success should stick close to their desks 'and never go to sea' was all too obviously based on W. H. Smith. He entered his father's news agency business in the Strand in 1841 and was a junior partner by 1846. By securing the railway bookstall monopoly he developed the profits of the firm enormously and later developed a circulating library. In 1868 he was elected MP for Westminster and was a member of the first London School Board in 1871. In 1877, only a year before the premier of *HMS Pinafore*, he entered Disraeli's Cabinet as First Lord of the Admiralty. Gilbert commented: 'You would naturally think that a person who commanded the entire British Navy would be the most accomplished sailor who could be found, but that is not the way in which such things are managed in England.'

Oliver Goldsmith (1728–74)

George Primrose is the eldest son of the Vicar of Wakefield, who lives a vagabond life in search of a living, and finally joins the army after trying his hand at all manner of careers. As he says: 'travelling after fortune, is not the way to secure her; and, indeed . . . I have desisted from the pursuit'. But throughout it all he is buoyantly optimistic: 'No person ever had a better knack at hoping than I. The less kind I found fortune at one time, the more I expected from her another.' His early attempts take him to London, where he hopes to prosper as an usher in a school. He then tries authorship. He fails to earn recognition, lacking influential friends. He tries hack writing. He becomes a family servant. He attempts to move into a grand household, but fails to gain entrance and nears despair. Then he hears of opportunities for British citizens to be transported as slaves to America, but he is saved from this fate and given the chance to sail for Amsterdam, where he is assured of a living teaching English. He then finds that he needs to learn Dutch first: 'How I came to overlook so obvious an objection, is to me amazing.' A fellow Irishman tells him there is a need for professors of Greek, and being a scholar, he tries this. To no avail. He manages to earn his bed and food by singing, and makes his way to France. In Paris he is involved in buying and selling paintings. For a time he is a travelling tutor, but is abandoned by his charge at Leghorn. He gets back to England and joins a troop of players.

This is a comic version of Goldsmith's own life. His father was a curate of Kilkenny West, and he ran away from college, returned and graduated, was rejected for holy orders, resolved to go to America but got no further than Cork. He was given £50 to study in London, but gambled this away in Dublin. He went to Edinburgh to study medicine, but excelled socially rather than academically. He drifted to Leyden and again gambled his funds. He attempted the Grand Tour on foot but returned penniless in 1756. He was then successively poor doctor, proofreader, teacher, hack-writer and failed to leave the country. After pawning his clothes he was nearly imprisoned for debt until finally he succeeded as a writer, after Dr Johnson got a publisher to accept *The Vicar of Wakefield*.

221

D. H. Lawrence (1885–1930)

Although it has a plot involving political assassination the point of Aldous Huxley's *Point Counter Point* is the satirical treatment of various aspects of life in the 1920s when intellectual ideals were treated as playthings by the privileged. Huxley constructed the story round a series of portraits of recognizable characters: John Bidlake, for example, is the painter Augustus John: 'handsome, huge, exuberant, careless; a great laugher, a greater worker, a great eater, drinker, and taker of virginities'. Everard Webley, the Fascist leader who is murdered in the book, is based on Sir Oswald Mosley.

The most incisive portrait, however, shows D. H. Lawrence as the writer Mark Rampion: 'His profile was steep, with a hooked fierce nose like a cutting instrument and a pointed chin. The eyes were blue and piercing, and the very fine hair, a little on the reddish side of golden, fluttered up at every moment, every breath of wind, like wisps of blown flame.' Rampion's affirmative utterances provide the novel with a visionary alternative to the mental confusion of the other characters. As Rampion tells the evil Spandrell: 'You hate the very source of your life, its ultimate basis – for there's no denying it, sex *is* fundamental. And you hate it, *hate* it.' At the end of the book, when Spandrell is about to be shot by members of Webley's Brotherhood of British Freemen, Rampion is still hammering home his opinions on life and art. Lawrence was aware of Huxley's use of his opinions as an important part of *Point Counter Point* but wrote to the writer William Gerhardi on 14 November 1928: 'I refuse to be Rampioned. Aldous' admiration for me is only skin-deep, and out of a Mary Mary quite contrary impulse.' Mary was Maria Huxley who was devoted to Lawrence and typed parts of his novels.

Julia Stephen (1846–95)

The central figure and source of the emotional light in Virginia Woolf's *To the Lighthouse* is Mrs Ramsay who copes with her idiosyncratic husband and with eight children. On the Isle of Skye, Mrs Ramsay holds out hopes that a trip to the lighthouse might be possible whereas Mr Ramsay, who 'never altered a disagreeable word to suit the pleasure or convenience of any mortal being', insists that the weather will make a journey impossible. Mr Ramsay, the prominent writer, is correct but it is Mrs Ramsay who provides human warmth and comfort: 'Flashing her needles, confident, upright, she created drawing-room and kitchen, set them all aglow ... there was scarcely a shell of herself left for her to know herself by; all was so lavished and spent'.

In her novel Virginia Woolf drew Mr and Mrs Ramsay as portraits of her father Leslie (who was also the model for Vernon Whitford in Meredith's *The Egoist*) and her mother Julia. When her first husband, Herbert Duckworth, died in 1870 Julia (née Jackson) was a young woman of twenty-four with three children to care for. In 1875 she met Leslie Stephen, a literary journalist whose wife died that year. Widow and widower found they first had sorrow, and then love, in common and were married on 26 March 1878. Between them, like Mr and Mrs Ramsay, they were responsible for eight children though Julia always felt her greatest duty was to protect her sensitive husband from his worries. While he exhausted himself in his work on the *Dictionary of National Biography* (which he began in 1882, the year of Virginia's birth) she bore the family's emotional burdens. On 5 May 1895 she died, after an attack of rheumatic fever, and for Virginia this was 'the greatest disaster that could happen'. As well as sustaining a personal shock she had to endure the sight of her father suffering as he succumbed to the grief that overwhelmed him.

REBECCA

Sir Walter Scott, *Ivanhoe* (1819)

Rebecca Gratz (1781–1869)

Rebecca, the daughter of Isaac of York in *Ivanhoe*, is one of Sir Walter Scott's most compelling female characters as she displays both physical and moral beauty: 'Her form was exquisitely symmetrical, and was shown to advantage by a sort of Eastern dress, which she wore according to the fashion of the females of her nation. . . . The brilliancy of her eyes, the superb arch of her eyebrows, her well-formed aquiline nose, her teeth as white as pearl, and the profusion of her sable tresses which, each arranged in its own little spiral of twisted curls, fell down upon as much of a lovely neck and bosom as a simarre of the richest Persian silk, exhibiting flowers in their natural colours embossed upon a purple ground, permitted to be visible – all these constituted a combination of loveliness, which yielded not to the most beautiful of the maidens who surrounded her.'

Scott conceived the character after a meeting, at Abbotsford in 1817, with Washington Irving. In one of their many conversations the American author told Scott about a tragedy that dominated his life: in 1809 his fiancée, Mathilda Hoffman, had died of consumption at the age of eighteen. On her deathbed Mathilda had been looked after by her close friend Rebecca Gratz and the devotion of this lady – known as 'the good Jewess' and 'the beautiful Jewess' in Philadelphia – deeply impressed Scott. Irving further revealed that Rebecca Gratz had renounced a financially and emotionally tempting offer of marriage rather than compromise her religion. Instead she dedicated herself to philanthropic pursuits and died (as she said) 'believing with firm faith in the religion of my fathers'. When Scott's medieval romance was published he sent a copy to Irving with the question 'How do you like your Rebecca? Does the Rebecca I have pictured, compare well with the pattern given?'

ARCHIE RICE
John Osborne, *The Entertainer* (1957)

Max Miller (1894–1963)

John Osborne's second play, *The Entertainer*, takes place in an English coastal resort. As young Mick Rice is fighting in Suez the political crisis impinges on the whole Rice family and Osborne arranges his play as a domestic drama interrupted by Archie Rice's stage-act. At home Archie is an obvious failure but when he performs he comes alive with his music-hall patter: 'I bet you think I have a marvellous time up here with all these posing girls, don't you? . . . You're dead right! You wouldn't think I was sexy to look at me, would you! No, lady.'

Archie's act, consisting of sexual innuendo aimed at the audience, is a deliberate parody of the outrageous approach of the Cheeky Chappie, Max Miller. Archie is, however, third-rate; a pathetic version of Miller who was, in John Osborne's opinion, a genius – 'flashiness perfected'. In *A Better Class of Person* (1981) Osborne compares his fictional failure with the real thing: 'Archie was a man. Max was a god, a saloon-bar Priapus. Archie never got away with anything properly. Life cost him dearly always. When he came on, the audience was immediately suspicious or indifferent. Archie's cheek was less than ordinary. Max didn't have to be lovable. . . . His humanity was in his cheek.'

Archie's father, Billy Rice, is an old performer of some style; he is a 'part-portrait' of William Crawford Grove, Osborne's maternal grandfather. Grandpa Grove managed a pub in London 'but unlike Billy Rice he could not be regarded as having been a star, except in a very small way at the height of his career as a publican, when there were hansom cabs, cigars and his famous breakfast'. The sheer vulgar energy of working-class entertainment delighted Osborne and of Max Miller he says 'hardly a week passes when I don't miss his pointing star among us.'

ROBIN HOOD

Sir Walter Scott, *Ivanhoe* (1819), Francis James Child, *The English and Scottish Popular Ballads* (1882–98)

Robin Hood

'Call me no longer Locksley, my Liege,' says the Outlaw in Scott's *Ivanhoe* when the Black Knight reveals that he is Richard Coeur de Lion: 'I am Robin Hood of Sherwood Forest.' Scott adds that a full pardon was granted to Robin but that 'Richard's good intentions towards the bold Outlaw were frustrated by the King's untimely death. . . . As for the rest of Robin Hood's career, as well as the tale of his treacherous death, they are to be found in those black-letter garlands, once sold at the low and easy rate of one halfpenny.'

There are several Robin Hoods in the manorial rolls and court records of medieval England and any one of them might have been the original outlaw. However, as the great scholar Francis James Child points out in *The English and Scottish Popular Ballads* 'Robin Hood is absolutely a creation of the ballad-muse'. Robin Hood is the only character who appears in a large number of ballads (Child Nos 117–54); he was the darling of the minstrels since his name was enough to sell a song. Robin is a simple soul piously devoted to Our Lady. He loves individual combat, is more than a match for his adversary the Sheriff of Nottingham, and is 'a gode yeoman' as the minstrels affirm. In the thirty-eight ballads that comprise the Robin Hood sequence the good yeoman assumes disguises, steals the king's deer but honours the king himself, abuses the clergy but respects the poor. He is an outlaw with a heart of gold: 'Cryst have mercy on his soule,/That dyed on the rode!/For he was a good outlawe,/And dyde pore men moch god.' So says 'A Gest of Robyn Hode'. The Robin Hood legend has circulated at least since the fourteenth century for Sloth, in the poem *Piers Plowman* (1362), mentions 'rymes of Robyn Hood'.

ROCKY

Sylvester Stallone, *Rocky* (1976), *Rocky II* (1979),
Rocky III (1982)

Rocky Marciano (1923–69)

In *Rocky* an unknown Philadelphia club fighter, Rocky Balboa, gets the chance of a lifetime and decides to 'go for it' (the motto of the three *Rocky* films): through sheer determination and courage he becomes the first man to go the distance with fast-talking world champion Apollo Creed (modelled on the flamboyant Muhammad Ali). In *Rocky II* the 'Italian stallion' wins the title, in *Rocky III* he loses and regains it.

Although Sylvester Stallone (creator and star of the films) drew the loser-as-winner theme from his own life as a poor Italian attempting to break through to stardom in America – and partly from watching club fighter Chuck Wepner go fifteen rounds with Ali in March 1975 – the fighting character was suggested by the apparently indestructible Italian-American heavyweight champion Rocky Marciano. In the first *Rocky* film the hero is visited by Mickey, an old trainer, who wants to manage Rocky for the big fight. Pointing to a photograph of Marciano on the wall, Mickey says 'Ah, Rocky Marciano. You know, you kinda remind me of the Rock, you know that. You move like him, you got heart like he did.' Like Rocky Balboa, Marciano lacked technical skill but more than made up for this by his ability to take (as *Rocky II* has it) a 'terrific beating' before winning by the relentless power of his punching.

Marciano became heavyweight champion of the world on 23 September 1952 by defeating Jersey Joe Walcott. For twelve rounds Walcott completely outclassed Marciano. Then, in the thirteenth round, Marciano threw a short right-hand punch that caught Walcott coming off the ropes and floored him. Marciano defended his title six times and retired undefeated in 1956. He was killed in an aeroplane accident the day before his forty-sixth birthday.

Lady Ottoline Morrell (1873–1938)

Women in Love brings D. H. Lawrence's heroines, the sisters Gudrun and Ursula Brangwen, to Willey Green. Here, Ursula is fascinated by Hermione Roddice: 'She was rich. . . . She was impressive, in her lovely pale-yellow and brownish-rose, yet macabre, something repulsive. . . . She was a *Kulturtrager*, a medium for the culture of ideas.' Later in the novel Gudrun and Ursula visit Breadalby where Hermione wilts before the presence of Rupert Birkin (a self-portrait of Lawrence): 'he caught her, as it were, beneath all her defences, and destroyed her with some insidious occult potency'.

Lady Ottoline Morrell recognized herself as the ridiculous Hermione; felt Lawrence's wife Frieda was responsible for the malice of the portrayal; and called *Women in Love* 'horrible . . . a wicked chaotic spiteful book'. Lawrence had written to Lady Ottoline on 1 February 1915, urging her 'to form the nucleus of a new community which shall start a new life amongst us – a life in which the only riches is integrity of character'. Coincidentally her husband Philip Morrell, a Liberal member of parliament, had a 500-acre estate – Garsington Manor near Oxford – suitable for the cultural community Lawrence envisaged. Lady Ottoline brought to Garsington such celebrities as Bertrand Russell (Sir Joshua Mattheson in *Women in Love*) and Lawrence himself. At first grateful for Lady Ottoline's generosity, Lawrence turned on her in a letter of 23 April 1915: 'Why must you always use your *will* so much, why can't you let things be, without always grasping and trying to know and to dominate'. By 1929 Lawrence had re-established relations with Lady Ottoline who was (so he wrote to a friend) 'a queen, among the mass of women'.

RODOLPHE

Henry Murger, *La Vie de Bohème* (1849 play) and opera, *La Bohème* (1896, music by *Puccini*, libretto by Giacosa and Illica)

Henry Murger (1822–61)

Scènes de la Vie Bohème was a series of sketches of Bohemian life in Paris serialized in the journal *Corsaire* 1847–49. They catalogue the fortunes and misfortunes of a group of poverty stricken students and artists – would-be poets, painters, philosophers, writers – their loves, hopes, amusements and catastrophes. It was adapted for the stage by Murger with the assistance of Théodore Barrière and was a resounding success from its premier at the Variétiés on 22 November 1849. The operatic version, with libretto based on the stage version by Giacosa and Illica and music by Puccini, was premiered at Turin under Toscanini on 1 February 1896. The main thrust of the narrative is the tragic love affair between Rodolphe, the young poet, and Mimi. The relationship is always a difficult one and the quarrels are frequent, aggravated by the poverty in which they and their companions – Marcel, the painter, and his old flame Musette, Colline, the philosopher and Schaunard, the musician, live. Mimi is taken seriously ill with consumption, and Colline sells a precious overcoat to buy her medicine, but it is too late. Rodolphe realizes what the others have already seen – that Mimi is dead.

Murger based the character of Rodolphe on himself. He was born in Paris of German descent, and at one time was secretary to Count Alexei Tolstoy. He always lived in grinding poverty. Mimi was based on Lucile Louvet and Musette on Marie Christine Roux, famous for her wit and charming voice. Colline was based on Jean Wallon, who eventually became Directeur de l'Imprimerie Impériale. When his work had made him wealthy and secure Murger wrote of the Bohemians: 'The great family of poor artists, whose destiny is to be unknown, because they do not know . . . the means to attest their existence in art. . . . They are the race of stubborn dreamers, for whom art remains a faith and not a trade.'

Henry John Temple, Third Viscount Palmerston (1784–1865)

Endymion and Myra are two children of William Pitt Ferrars, an ambitious and rising politician, who dies in poverty after just failing to enter the Cabinet. Endymion plods away at a clerkship in Somerset House; his sister enters social eminence by marrying Lord Roehampton, then Foreign Secretary. She later marries a second time, Florestan, a parvenu king. The period Disraeli portrays in *Endymion* is the late 1830s and early 1840s, when he himself had failed to gain preferment under Robert Peel. Endymion rises as a result of his own efforts and the influence of his wife, rather than because of his powerful brother-in-law, Lord Roehampton, 'the strongest member of the government, except, of course, the premier himself. He was the man from whose combined force and flexibility of character the country had confidence that in all their councils there would be no lack of courage yet tempered with adroit discretion. Lord Roehampton, though an Englishman, was an Irish peer, and was resolved to remain so, for he fully appreciated the position, which united social distinction, with the power of a seat in the Commons. He was a very ambitious and ... worldly man, deemed even by many to be unscrupulous, and yet he was romantic. A great favourite in society, and especially with the softer sex, somewhat late in life, he had married suddenly a beautiful woman, who was without fortune, and not a member of the enchanted circle in which he flourished ... [he] was gifted with a sweet temper, and, though people said he had no heart, with a winning tenderness of disposition.'

This is Lord Palmerston, who was of the Irish branch of an ancient English family, educated at Edinburgh and Cambridge, a life-long parliamentarian, Foreign Secretary and a master of foreign affairs in several governments, and Prime Minister when he died in 1865. This kindly portrait is of the young Palmerston; later in life Disraeli said he was 'at best only ginger beer and not champaign, and now an old painted Pantaloon.'

MARIE ROGET
Edgar Allan Poe, *The Mystery of Marie Roget* (1843)

Mary Cecilia Rogers (1820–41)

Marie Roget is a pretty young *grisette* who works in a Parisian perfumery. She is popular with the customers, and good for trade. She disappears for a few days but when she returns she tells her widowed mother that she had been to stay with friends: 'It was about five months after this return home, that her friends were alarmed by her sudden disappearance for the second time. Three days elapsed. . . . On the fourth day her corpse was found floating in the Seine.' Poe's celebrated detective, Dupin, unravels the mystery, concluding that Marie had been killed by someone who knew her, and not a stranger; that he was probably a former lover; that the murder was committed to conceal a pregnancy. The murderer had a swarthy complexion and the knot tied in the bandage found with the body suggested a serving member of the navy. He was probably an officer and his position prevented his coming forward and identifying himself.

Poe based the story on that of the murder of the New York tobacconist's salesgirl Mary Cecilia Rogers, who worked at the counter in Anderson's shop on Broadway, where Poe was a customer. He read in the newspapers that her body had been found in the Hudson. She had apparently left home with a young man on the Sunday before the Thursday when her body was found. Like Marie, she had previously disappeared for a week, claiming that she had stayed with friends in Brooklyn. Poe transfers the story to Paris. John H. Ingram, whose biography of Poe was published in 1880, claimed that the naval officer responsible for Mary's death was named Spencer. William Kurtz Wimsatt Jr of Yale has examined the naval records of the time and has concluded that the suspect was one Philip Spencer, son of the Secretary of State for the US Navy, John Canfield Spencer. Philip Spencer had an unfortunate record of drunkenness and disorderly conduct and was expelled from several colleges. He was hanged for his part in a mutiny.

FAIR ROSAMOND

Samuel Daniel, *The Complaint of Rosamond* (1592); Thomas
Deloney, *Fair Rosamond* (1612); opera, *Rosamond* (libretto by
Joseph Addison, music by Thomas Arne, 1733)

Rosamond de Clifford (died 1176)

Rosamond was the subject of several traditional and well-loved
ballads, all of which told a fairly consistent story. She was the
beloved mistress of King Henry II who was so desperate as to
her safety that he had constructed a house which was impossible
to get into unless one had the key to the labyrinth. Queen
Eleanore gained access through the maze by means of a thread
or a silk and was able to poison the beautiful damsel: 'But when
the queene with stedfast eye/Beheld her beauteous face,/She
was amazed in her minde/At her exceeding grace. Cast off
from thee these robes, she said,/That riche and costlye bee;/
And drink thou up this deadly draughte,/Which I have
brought to thee. Then presently upon her knees/Sweet Rosa-
monde did falle;/And pardon of the queen she crav'd/For her
offences all.' This is how Deloney gives us the climax of the
story. There is strong historical evidence for the authenticity
of this story.

Rosamond was the daughter of Walter de Clifford (died 1190)
who inherited estates in Herefordshire and other counties and
was Baron de Clifford by 1138. He owned estates in Shropshire
and fought against the Welsh. His daughter was acknowledged
as mistress of Henry II by 1174. Ranulf Higden, the chronicler,
has an account of the story in his *Polychronicon*, which would
date the story certainly before 1364. This was translated by
John Trevisa in 1387, and this was used as the basis of the
version found in John Stow's *Chronicles of England*: 'Rosamond
the fayre daughter of Walter Lord Clifford, concubine to
Henry II (poisoned by Queen Elianor as some thought) dyed
at Woodstocke where King Henry had made for her a house
of wonderful working, so that no man or woman might come
to her but he that was instructed by the King. This house was
named by some Labyrinthus . . . wrought like unto a knot in a
garden, called a maze, but it was commonly said that lastly the
Queen came to her by a clue of thredde or silke.' Rosamond's
body was buried in the choir of Godstow Abbey and her
remains later removed to the chapter house in 1191.

Nikolai Ivanovich Bukharin (1888–1939)

Arthur Koestler, once a prominent Marxist intellectual who put his faith to the test in Germany and Spain (where the fascists kept him in a death cell for three months before releasing him), renounced communism in 1938 after recoiling from the spectacle of the Moscow show trials. Koestler believed that Marxist theory had been distorted in practice, and that in Stalin's Soviet Union communism had been reduced to a brutal creed willing to use the most appalling means in pursuit of some impossible end. *Darkness at Noon*, the author's most devastating critique of communism, portrays Rubashov, an old Bolshevik, as he undergoes arrest, imprisonment, interrogation and trial for treason. Rubashov realizes that the revolutionary means determine the political ends and that a revolution in the name of humanity has perpetrated the most atrocious offences against the individual who is seen as a unit – a millionth part of a million. Before he is shot in the back of the head Rubashov understands that the unprincipled use of expedients during the revolution has created the perfect conditions for Stalinism.

When Koestler started work on the novel he conceived Rubashov as 'a member of the Old Bolshevik guard, his manner of thinking modelled on Nikolai Bukharin's'. Nikolai Ivanovich Bukharin was a prominent Party member: theorist, author of the Soviet constitution, member of the Politburo, general secretary of Comintern, editor-in-chief of *Izvestia*. Despite his record of loyalty and his personal friendship with Stalin he was expelled from the Party, accused of treason at a show trial in 1938 and executed. In *The Gulag Archipelago,* Alexander Solzhenitsyn praises Koestler's 'talented inquiry' and points out that Bukharin constantly 'renounced his views in order to remain in the Party'.

Mikhail Bakunin (1814–76)

The tragi-comic hero of Ivan Turgenev's *Rudin* has been taken as a representative of the 'superfluous man' whose Hamlet-like indecision was a feature of the intellectual life of pre-revolutionary Russia. Rudin's arrival at a prominent Russian household is both fortuitous and forceful for he enters as 'a man of about thirty-five, tall, slightly round-shouldered, curly-haired, swarthy, with irregular, but expressive and intelligent features and a liquid brilliance in his lively dark-blue eyes, with a straight broad nose and finely chiselled lips'. Rudin impresses all by his faith in the future and his astonishing eloquence: 'Image after image poured out; analogies, now unexpectedly bold, now devastatingly apt, rose one after another. . . . He did not seek after words: they came obediently and freely to his lips and each word, it seemed, literally flowed straight from his soul and burned with all the heat of conviction.' Eventually Rudin is shot on the barricades during the 1848 Revolution in Paris.

As Turgenev acknowledged, Rudin is a portrait of Mikhail Bakunin, the celebrated Russian anarchist and once Turgenev's best friend. After meeting in Berlin in 1840 the two men shared a flat, read Hegel together and regularly went to listen to the music of Beethoven. In 1848 Bakunin was expelled from France; in 1849 he was sentenced to death for participating in a Dresden revolt and, when this sentence was commuted to imprisonment, was sent to Siberia in 1855. After escaping to Switzerland in 1861 Bakunin was recognized as the leader of the anarchist movement but Turgenev said, in a letter of 1862, that his old friend was simply a 'Rudin who was not killed on the barricades . . . a spent agitator'. Bakunin joined the First International in 1869 but was expelled in 1872 after ideological confrontations with Marx.

SAMSON

John Milton, *Samson Agonistes* (1671)

John Milton (1608–74)

Samson, the great hero and wrestler, is a prisoner of the Philistines. He was betrayed to his enemies by the woman who loved him. He has been blinded: 'O dark, dark, dark, amid the blaze of noon,/Irrecoverably dark, total Eclipse/Without all hope of day!/O first created Beam, and thou great Word,/Let there be light, and light was over all;/Why am I thus bereav'd thy prime decree? The Sun to me is dark/And silent as the Moon.' He is visited by his friends and father who seek to comfort him and finally by Dalila, who hopes for his forgiveness. She finally taunts him. The tragedy ends when he is brought forth to entertain his captors at a feast to their god and realizing the purpose he has to fulfil Samson pulls down the pillars holding the roof and totally destroys his enemies.

Milton himself was blind by 1652. In writing *Samson* he is writing from personal experience of his affliction. Also strongly present in *Samson Agonistes* is Milton's awareness of the irresistible attraction of women, and the sense that the attraction was dangerous to full realization of a man's destiny. He had early resolved to remain celibate to devote himself to study, teaching and writing, but in 1642 he married Mary Powell, then less than seventeen. Milton was a passionate man. He wrote of feminine charm as a young man: 'I do not let spring time pass by me in vain' and he describes watching 'groups of girls stroll by, stars that breathe out tempting flames'. This marriage failed and Mary left him as they had deep political differences (her family were Royalist). He married Catherine Woodcock, who died in 1658, and in 1662 he married Elizabeth Minshull, who outlived him. He published pamphlets on divorce which were very advanced for their day. Also present in *Samson* is Milton's almost Calvinistic belief that whatever we are, however weak, or strong, we are all part of God's purpose, and that we should wait, and endure until that purpose be revealed. This is the same theme found in the sonnet on his blindness, which ends: 'they also serve who only stand and wait'. Samson waits. And he serves his moment.

Lady Mary Wortley Montagu (1689–1762)

Pope portrays Sappho as one who had been beautiful in her day but is now certainly past it. A former poetess, she is described as being none too careful about her appearance. Pope refers to her habit of wearing: 'diamonds with her dirty smock' and pictures her at her 'toilet's greasy task' in preparation for a day's socializing which will conclude with her 'Fragrant at an evening masque;/So morning insects that in muck begun,/ Shine, buzz and flyblow in the setting sun.'

This is a malicious portrait of Lady Mary Wortley Montagu, who – like Sappho – was a famous beauty and poetess, who grew somewhat slatternly of her appearance in later life. She was born in 1689, the daughter of Evelyn Pierreoint (later Duke of Kingston) and married Edward Wortley Montagu, MP for Huntingdon, in 1712. She travelled with him to Constantinople when he was in the diplomatic service, and on her return to England she introduced inoculation for smallpox, which she had observed being used abroad. She was a celebrated figure in the social life of the day, and was courted by Edward Young, the poet, and on good terms with Sarah, Duchess of Marlborough (see ATOSSA). It was said that she rebuffed Pope's amorous advances by laughing in his face. She lived in Brecia, Venice and Avignon, and published *Court Poems* and *Letters From the East*. Her beauty, when she was a young woman, was said by all to have been quite striking, and the carelessness of her appearance in later life equally famous. Horace Walpole said of her: 'She was always a dirty little thing. This habit has continued with her.' He met her during her exile in Rome and left this account of her: 'Her dress, her avarace and her impudence must amaze anyone that never heard her name. She wears a foul mob that does not cover her greasy black locks, that hang loose, never combed or curled, an old mazarine blue wrapper, that gapes open and discovers a canvas petticoat. Her face swelled violently on one side, partly covered with a plaster, and partly with white paint, which for cheapness she has bought coarse.' Pope alludes to her unfavourably also in *The Dunciad* and in his *Imitation of the First Satire of the Second Book of Horace*. Her verse was invariably accomplished and frequently witty and is often deservedly anthologized.

CAPTAIN SAVAGE
Frederick Marryat, *Peter Simple* (1834)

Thomas Cochrane, Tenth Earl of Dundonald (1775–1860)

Peter Simple is usually regarded as Marryat's masterpiece. It tells the story of a young man – the fool of his family – and his gradual maturity into becoming a first-class naval officer. The book is packed with notable characters, Chucks the boatswain, Swinburne, the quartermaster, O'Brien, the plucky Irishman, Captain Kearney, the habitual liar, and the incomparable Captain Savage: 'A sailor every inch of him. He knew a ship from stem to stern, understood the character of seamen and gained their confidence. He was besides a good mechanic, a carpenter, a rope-maker, sail-maker, and cooper. He could hand-reef and steer, knot and splice: but he was no orator. He was good-tempered, honest and unsophisticated, with a large proportion of common sense and free with his officers.'

Thomas Cochrane was the son of Archibald Cochrane, Ninth Earl of Dundonald, and originally held a commission in the army. He joined his first ship, the *Hind*, in 1793. He served in North America and on the French and Spanish coasts 1796–1800. As commander of the *Speedy* he captured several enemy vessels, and was captain by 1801. He was captured by the French but exchanged in 1801. He cruised in the Azores, Bay of Biscay and the Mediterranean. He put forward plans to destroy the French fleet in Aix in 1809, but this was ruined by petty jealousies among senior officers. His criticisms for a time got him placed on half-pay and after service with his uncle, Sir Alexander Forrester Inglis Cochrane, he was expelled from the navy, from his seat in parliament and other honours for his alleged part in a stock exchange fraud in 1814. He served with the Chilean navy, and became admiral in the Brazilian and Greek navies. He was a pioneer supporter of steam-power and an original naval strategist. By 1832 he was a rear-admiral in the British Navy, and admiral by 1851. Marryat had served with Cochrane from 1806 on the *Impérieuse*.

May Dickinson

On hearing that her sister Helen has impetuously fallen in love with young Paul Wilcox of Howards End, Hertfordshire, Margaret Schlegel feels drawn to her 'at this crisis of her life'. Introducing Margaret in *Howards End* E. M. Forster describes her as 'not beautiful, not supremely brilliant, but filled with something that took the place of both qualities – something best described as a profound vivacity, a continual and sincere response to all that she encountered in her path through life'. Margaret is also impulsive – 'She did swing rapidly from one decision to another' – and lets her aunt go in her place and so the events of the novel are set in motion. Destined to inherit Howards End, Margaret is convinced she can improve the lot of those she encounters: 'Only connect! That was the whole of her sermon. Only connect the prose and the passion, and both will be exalted, and human love will be seen at its highest.'

Forster modelled Margaret on one of the three sisters of his great friend G. L. Dickinson. At the Dickinson family home near Langham Place in London, Forster observed May, Janet and Hester and noted their habit of slumming in order to uplift the so-called lower orders. May – as P. N. Furbank observes in *E. M. Forster: A Life* (1977–78) – was 'ugly, intelligent and something of an intellectual manqué'. Apparently she was in the habit of marking, in the margins of books she could not understand, the comment 'Some confusion of thought here.' Assured and eccentric, and yet alert enough to study Greek at the age of eighty, she was known as an accomplished hostess with an interest in cultural self-improvement. On 17 March 1931 Forster wrote to Dickinson about the genesis of his novel and acknowledged that 'May was, perhaps, more definitely Margaret than anyone else was anything else in those two worlds'.

Sir Joseph Paxton (1801–65)

Roger Scratcherd, a stonemason, takes to drink but nevertheless becomes a 'great man in the world' by dint of his own
efforts. His sister, Mary, is seduced by Thorne's brother, and
Dr Thorne brings up the child which results from this union.
No one in the community is aware of her origins. Meanwhile
Roger Scratcherd becomes a contractor, 'first for little things,
such as half a mile or so of a railway embankment, or three or
four canal bridges, and then a contractor for great things, such
as Government hospitals, locks, docks, and quays, and had
latterly had in his hands the making of whole lines of railway'.
He becomes a very rich man. But he gains more than wealth:
'There had been a time when the Government wanted the
immediate performance of some extraordinary piece of work,
and Roger Scratcherd had been the man to do it. . . . He went
up one day to Court to kiss Her Majesty's hand, and came
down to his new grand house . . . Sir Roger Scratcherd, Bart.'
But he does not change in essentials: 'he was the same man at
all points that he had been when formerly seen about the streets
of Barchester with his stone-mason's apron tucked up round
his waist'.

The character of Scratcherd was based on Joseph Paxton, who
was a gardener and architect, and an example of a man who
rose from humble origins and manual work to a position of
wealth and public acclaim. He was born at Milton Bryant,
near Woburn. He worked in the arboretum at Chiswick and
became intimate with the Duke of Devonshire, who made him
superintendent of his gardens and grounds at Chatsworth. He
became manager of his estates at Derbyshire. In 1836 he began
work on the three-hundred-foot conservatory which became
the prototype of the design of the Great Exhibition building
in 1851, for which he was knighted. He also designed the
mansion at Ferrières for Baron James de Rothschild. He was
MP for Coventry from 1854 until his death. Ruskin considered
the Crystal Palace simply a large greenhouse.

Arthur Koestler (1905–83)

At the beginning of Simone de Beauvoir's *The Mandarins* the heroine, Anne, is aware of the excitement associated with the liberation of France. Married to Robert Dubreuilh, a prominent intellectual interested in a united front with the communists, she functions as an observer of ideological ferment. She is flattered when approached by Victor Scriassine, a writer fiercely critical of communism: 'I liked his brusque manner. Like everyone else, I had read his famous book, *The Red Paradise*. But I had been especially moved by his book on Austria under the Nazis. . . . I studied his triangular face with its prominent cheekbones, its hard, fiery eyes, its thin, almost feminine mouth. It wasn't at all the face of a Frenchman. To him Russia was an enemy nation, and he did not have any great love for the United States. There wasn't a place on earth where he really felt at home.'

Scriassine is a political portrait of Arthur Koestler and his hostility to Dubreuilh's plans conveys Koestler's dislike of Sartre's political tolerance of communism. In the novel Scriassine's dogmatic anti-communism is reinforced by his clinically cold approach to human relationships and Anne finds his attempt at seduction distasteful. Everything Scriassine does is conceived in terms of confrontation as he is unable to compromise. As Simone de Beauvoir says: 'He always created the impression that everything happening where he chanced to be and even where he chanced not to be – was his personal concern.' Koestler got to know the French intellectuals – Sartre, Camus, de Beauvoir – after the liberation of France and alienated them by his assertive manner and vanity. In her autobiography Simone de Beauvoir writes of Koestler: 'we were a bit embarrassed by his self-taught pedantry, by the doctrinaire self-assurance and the scientism he had retained from his rather mediocre Marxist training'.

Charles Dickens (1812–70)

The basis of the plot in *The Warden* is the controversy over Hiram's Hospital, a charitable foundation. The property of the charity has increased in value and now yields an income of £800 a year to the warden, the Revd Septimus Harding. This sinecure is attacked by a journalist, John Bold, who writes for the *Jupiter* (*The Times*, which was nicknamed the 'Thunderer'). The theme of the almshouse controversy is taken up and used as the basis of a sensational 'reforming' novel, published in monthly instalments, by Popular Sentiment.

This was a satiric attack by Trollope on his contemporary radical, reforming and humanitarian novelist, Charles Dickens, who attacked one social abuse after another. Trollope writes of Popular Sentiment: 'In former times great objects were attained by great work. When evils were to be reformed, reformers set about their heavy task with grave decorum and laborious argument. . . . We get on now with a lighter step, and quicker: ridicule is found to be more convincing than argument, imaginary agonies touch more than true sorrows, and monthly novels convince, when learned quartos fail to do so. If the world is to be set right, the work will be done by shilling numbers. Of all such reformers Mr. Sentiment is the most powerful. It is incredible the number of evil practices he has put down: it is to be feared he will soon lack subjects, and that when he has made the working classes comfortable, and got bitter beer put into proper sized pint bottles, there will be nothing further for him left to do. Mr. Sentiment is certainly a very powerful man, and perhaps not the less so that his good poor people are so very good; his hard rich people so very hard; and the genuinely honest so very honest. . . . If his heroes and heroines walk upon stilts, as heroes and heroines, I fear, ever must, their attendant satellites are as natural as though one met them in the street.' (See DR PESSIMIST ANTICANT.)

JUSTICE SHALLOW

William Shakespeare, *Henry IV*, Part II, *The Merry Wives of Windsor* (1597–1600)

Sir Thomas Lucy (1532–1600) **or perhaps William Gardner** (1531–97)

Robert Shallow is a country justice. In *Henry IV* he recruits a group of bumpkins for service of the King under Sir John Falstaff. Falstaff lodges with him and borrows £1,000 from him. He is a foolish old fellow who constantly harps on the exploits and daring of his youthful days: 'Jesu, Jesu, the mad days that I have spent! And to see how many of my old acquaintance are dead!' In *The Merry Wives of Windsor* he is even more grotesquely senile, but brags of the days when he could make 'fellows skip like rats' and claims that his fingers itch whenever he sees a sword drawn. Falstaff has fallen into his bad books for killing his deer, breaking open his lodge and assaulting his servants. He is also engaged in some complex love intrigue with Anne and his cousin, Slender.

It was traditionally assumed that Robert Shallow was based on Sir Thomas Lucy, who owned the great estate of Charlcote, near Stratford, where the young Shakespeare – legend has it – was caught poaching deer. Lucy was educated by John Foxe, the martyrologist and became a puritan. He rebuilt the great manor house at Charlcote 1558–59. He was knighted in 1565 and was MP for Warwick in 1571 and 1584. He is reputed to have prosecuted Shakespeare in 1585. Shallow threatens to make Falstaff's deer-poaching episode a matter for the Star Chamber, and following his outburst in *Merry Wives* there is a reference to the 'dozen white luces' in the coat-of-arms of Shallow's family. The Lucy coat-of-arms shows three luces (pike fish) in each quarter, that is to say, a dozen luces. Shallow is also fond of archery, as was Sir Thomas Lucy himself.

Leslie Hotson argues, however, that Shallow is really a satiric attack on another justice, William Gardner (Hotson, *Shakespeare versus Shallow*, 1931). Gardner's coat-of-arms had three luces, as he had married into the family of Sir Robert Luce. Gardner became justice of the peace for Brixton Hundred (which included Southwark) and high sheriff of Sussex and Surrey. Shakespeare lived at Southwark and was an associate of one Langley, owner of the Swan theatre. Langley and Gardner were engaged in acrimonious litigation and the portrait of Shallow may be interpreted as a satiric squib as Shakespeare's part in their quarrel.

MRS ELIZABETH SHANDY
Laurence Sterne, *Tristram Shandy* (1760–67)

Mrs Elizabeth Sterne (1714–73)

In Sterne's *Tristram Shandy* Walter Shandy habitually amuses himself at the expense of his wife who 'knew no more than her backside what my father meant' (as the narrator puts it). Mrs Elizabeth Shandy is portrayed as a wearisome wife: 'A temperate current of blood ran orderly through her veins in all months of the year, and in all critical moments both of the day and night alike; nor did she superinduce the least heat into her humours from the manual effervescencies of devotional tracts'.

The only wife in Sterne's fiction is based on his own wife. Sterne was a clergyman when he met Elizabeth Lumley, a vicar's daughter, in York; when the couple married on 30 March 1741 she was already aware of his amorous reputation. When word of the match reached her relatives they had reservations and Mathew Robinson wrote to his sister that 'our cousin Betty Lumley is married to a Parson who once delighted in debauchery, who is possessed of about £100 a year in preferment, and has a good prospect of more. What hopes our relation may have of settling the affections of a light and fickle man, I know not, but I imagine she will set about it not by means of the beauty but of the arm of flesh.' Sterne's delight in debauchery survived the marriage and Elizabeth's increasing irritability may well have been provoked by the frequency of her husband's extramarital affairs. She was known for being easily offended and for her quarrelsome nature; and she was generally considered to be dull, which she doubtless was in comparison to her brilliant and accomplished husband. Like many of the women of her time Elizabeth had problems with childbirth; one daughter, Lydia, survived but there were two miscarriages, the one of 1751 probably ending her sexual relationship with Sterne. Sterne left his widow in poverty and she and Lydia had to make the most of the famous author's literary remains.

TAM O' SHANTER

Robert Burns, *Poetical Works* (1904)

Douglas Graham (1738–1811)

In the summer of 1775 Robert Burns left the drudgery of Mount Oliphant farm in Ayrshire to go to school on the 'smuggling coast' of Kirkoswald; he later recalled that he did well at his studies and made even more progress in 'the knowledge of mankind'. Among scenes of 'swaggering riot and roaring dissipation', the sixteen-year-old found out how to 'mix without fear in a drunken squabble'.

One local who participated enthusiastically in the 'roaring dissipation' of Kirkoswald was Douglas Graham who rented the farm of Shanter (*seann tor* means 'old mound') and had a boat called the *Tam O' Shanter* for the purposes of smuggling. The village inn, adjacent to the church, was called the Kirkton; as the landlady Jean Kennedy affected airs her hostelry was known as 'The Leddies' House'. In Burns's poem about 'Tam O' Shanter' the hero 'at the Lord's house, even on Sunday . . . drank wi' Kirkton Jean till Monday'. As well as farming (and smuggling) Graham was a dealer in malt so every market day he would go to Ayr accompanied by his 'ancient, trusty drouthy crony', the shoemaker John Davidson (1728–1806) – Souter Johnny. These excursions were anathema to Graham's wife Helen (*née* M'Taggart) who thus became a 'sulky sullen dame' in his absence. Years after his visit to Kirkoswald, Burns leased Ellisland Farm in Dumfriesshire where he became friendly with the antiquarian Captain Francis Grose who was working on his *Antiquities of Scotland*. Burns asked Grose to include an illustration of Kirk Alloway (where his father was buried); Grose agreed on condition that Burns would provide a witch story to go with the picture. A letter to Grose beginning 'On a market day, in the town of Ayr, a farmer from Carrick . . .' contains the narrative germ of 'Tam O' Shanter', in which Douglas Graham's homeward ride from Ayr to Shanter Farm becomes a drink-induced nightmare vision.

Roger Sterne (1692–1731)

'My uncle TOBY SHANDY,' declares the narrator of Laurence Sterne's *Tristram Shandy*, 'was a gentleman, who, with the virtues which usually constitute the character of a man of honour and rectitude, – possessed one in a very eminent degree, which is seldom or never put into the catalogue; and that was a most extreme and unparallel'd modesty of nature ... which happening to be somewhat subtilized and rarified by the constant heat of a little family pride'. After being wounded in the groin at the siege of Namur, Toby begins to ride a hobby-horse by studying the science of attacking fortified towns.

With his military obsession and curious character, Toby is a caricature of Laurence Sterne's own father. Roger Sterne broke with family tradition by enlisting in Marlborough's army and serving as an ensign in the 34th Regiment of Foot. By the time he was ready for action the great battles (Blenheim, Ramillies) had been fought and the English army had settled down to a series of sieges. Roger Sterne was at the siege of Douay in 1710 and then at the sieges of Bethune, Aire, St Venant and Bouchaine – where he married Agnes Hebert, Laurence Sterne's mother. In 1727 Roger Sterne was with the 34th at Gibraltar and there he was (as his son recorded in a letter) 'run through the body by Captain Phillips, in a duel (the quarrel begun about a goose), with much difficulty he survived – tho' with an impaired constitution'. Weakened by the wound ensign Sterne nevertheless resumed active service and was posted, in 1731, to Jamaica where he died 'by the country fever, which took away his senses first, and made a child of him, and then, in a month or two, walking about continually without complaining, till the moment he sat down in an arm chair, and breathed his last.' Sterne remembered him as 'a little smart man – active to the last degree, in all exercises ... he was in his temper somewhat rapid, and hasty – but of a kindly, sweet disposition.'

John Bright (1811–89)

Jawster Sharp is a 'radical shopkeeper . . . who had taken what is called "a leading part" in the town on every "crisis" that had occurred since 1830; one of those zealous patriots who had got up penny subscriptions for gold cups to Lord Grey; cries for the Bill, the whole Bill, and nothing but the Bill . . . a worthy who makes speeches, passes resolutions, votes addresses, goes up with deputations, has at all times the necessary quantity of confidence in the necessary individual; confidence in Lord Grey; confidence in Lord Durham; confidence in Lord Melbourne; and can also, if necessary, give three cheers for the King or three groans for the Queen.'

This is an unflattering portrait of John Bright, who was no hero of Disraeli's. He was the son of a Rochdale miller and worked at his father's mill for a time. He gained a reputation as an orator in the temperance cause and in opposition to the principle of church rates in 1834. He supported the Reform Bill and abolition of capital punishment. He was friend and supporter of Richard Cobden in the Anti Corn Law struggle and by 1843 was MP for Durham. He opposed the Maynooth Grant and the Ten Hour Bill, the former as a non-conformist with no time for Catholicism, and the latter as a believer in leaving the management of industry to industrialists. As a Liberal-Whig Bright was inevitably bound not to appeal to Disraeli and their mutual opposition was to show itself during the Turkish crisis of 1876 and the Transvaal issue in 1881. He was a sincere anti-imperialist and resigned over British policy in Egypt in 1882. With Cobden he seemed to embody the ideology of the new manufacturing classes. His opinion of himself was rather more flattering than Disraeli's: 'I have seen so much intrigue and ambition, so much selfishness and inconsistency in the character of so-called statesmen, that I have always been anxious to disclaim the title. I have been content to describe myself as a simple citizen, who honestly examines such questions as affect the public weal and honestly offers his counsels to his countrymen.'

Sir Osbert Sitwell (1892–1969)

Wyndham Lewis's novel *The Apes of God* satirizes the artistic affectations of the English aristocracy who are condemned as Apes of God – 'those prosperous mountebanks who alternately imitate and mock at and traduce those figures they at once admire and hate'. As the novel moves towards its mock-heroic catastrophe the innocent Dan Boleyn is inexorably drawn towards the Lenten Party held by the supreme ape, 'the figurehead, the host, the famous Chelsea Star of "Gossip", Lord Osmund Finnian Shaw'. Lewis draws attention to Lord Osmund's 'carefully-contained obesity' and then describes him in some detail: 'In colour Lord Osmund was a pale coral, with flaxen hair brushed tightly back, his blond pencilled pap rising straight from his sloping forehead: galb-like wings to his nostrils – the goat-like profile of Edward the Peacemaker. . . . Eyes, nose, and lips contributed to one effect, so that they seemed one feature. It was the effect of the joissant animal – the licking, eating, sniffing, fat-muzzled machine – dedicated to Wine, Womanry, and Free Verse-cum-soda-water.'

When the novel was first published this was instantly recognized as a malicious portrayal of Sir Osbert Sitwell who – with his sister Edith and brother Sacheveral – escaped from the claustrophobic atmosphere of the family home at Renishaw Hall and created the rarefied English cultural climate of the 1920s which was anathema to a modernist such as Lewis. By way of revenge Sir Osbert printed copies of a picture postcard, showing two actors dressed in the sinister hat-and-cloak outfit favoured by Lewis, then had these mysteriously mailed to Lewis from various parts of Europe.

HAMER SHAWCROSS
Howard Spring, *Fame is the Spur* (1940)

James Ramsay MacDonald (1866–1937)

Howard Spring's novel, *Fame is the Spur*, charts the career of a young man, born in humble life in Manchester, who gradually rises to political eminence. Initially he is spurred on by apparently sincere feelings motivated by his compassion for the poor and a burning sense of social injustice. He inherits a sword from a relative which was used at the Peterloo massacre, and this sword symbolizes for him the struggle against oppression which must never be abandoned until social equality and the dignity of life have been guaranteed to all. He is a brilliant and moving orator. Early in his career to public office he witnesses the tyranny of management and owners during the mining strike and he vows not to rest until his aims have been realized. However, as he becomes a successful politician and a writer, he gradually sheds his zeal, becomes cautious and compromising in his political stance, and betrays his original principles. He has forgotten his origins.

Hamer Shawcross was based on Ramsay MacDonald, who was born illegitimately in Morayshire of farming stock, experienced great poverty and hardship in his early days and became politically active in the Labour movement. He married Margaret Ethel Gladstone, daughter of a scientist and became gradually more middle-class and respectable himself. He was a natural parliamentarian, with greatly attractive eloquence. He was MP for Leicester 1906–18 and wrote several books of political theory. He gradually developed a sure instinct for moderation, and was actively anti-communist in the 1920s and by 1922 was leader of the opposition in the Commons as MP for Aberavon. He formed an all-party government with the Conservatives and Liberals in 1931 and a permanent breach with his own party was the cost. He was described by Winston Churchill as a 'boneless wonder' who had the gift of 'compressing the largest amount of words into the smallest amount of thought'.

Emily Brontë (1818–48)

Shirley takes place in Yorkshire during the Napoleonic wars. The wool industry is suffering severely from lack of exports. Robert Gérard attempts to modernize his production by means of machinery and is threatened by Luddites. He needs capital and therefore proposes marriage to Shirley Keeldar, who has wealth. He is really loved by Caroline Helstone. Shirley rejects him, and he marries Caroline, after the end of the war terminates his business difficulties. Shirley marries Louis, Robert's brother, who – like her – is a proud and headstrong person with judgement of his own. Shirley is described as a handsome young woman, 'agreeable to the eye. Her height and shape were not unlike Miss Helstone's; perhaps in stature she might have the advantage by an inch or two. She was gracefully made, and her face, too, possessed a charm as well described by the word grace as any other. It was pale naturally, but intelligent, and of varied expression. . . . Clear and dark were the characteristics of her aspect as to colour. Her face and brow were clear, her eyes of the darkest gray . . . and her hair of the darkest brown. Her features were distinguished . . . mobile they were, and speaking; but their changes were not to be understood nor their language interpreted all at once.'

Charlotte is describing her sister Emily, who together with Anne, made up that trio of extraordinary genius. Emily was a strong-willed young woman of tremendous and original imagination. Emily survived the rigours of Cowan Bridge school (see BROCKLEHURST) and became a governess in Halifax, went to the Heger Pensionat in Brussels and after 1845 devoted herself to writing. *Wuthering Heights* (1847) was her masterpiece and she wrote several outstanding poems. Her last poem opens: 'No coward soul is mine/No trembler in the world's storm-troubled sphere/I see heaven's glories shine,/And faith shines equal, arming me from fear.' She died of consumption, worsened by a cold caught at her brother Branwell's funeral in September 1848.

SHYLOCK
William Shakespeare, *The Merchant of Venice* (1597)

Roderigo Lopez (died 1594)

Shylock, although he is one of Shakespeare's most impressive creations, appears in only five scenes of *The Merchant of Venice*. His character remains a puzzle. On one level he seems to be a characteristic Elizabethan stage-villain who out-Herods Herod and would have been hissed and hooted off the stage, but on another level the irony of his presentation and the pathos of his persecution at the hands of the Christians, make him seem almost more sinned-against than sinning. Our reaction to his treatment by the court is bound to be tinged with post-Nazi guilt and unease.

Shylock is abused by the businessmen and merchants of Venice, and long endures their taunts. Bassanio wants to borrow from Antonio in order to court Portia. To support his friend, Antonio, who hopes his trading enterprises are about to pay off, borrows 3,000 ducats from Shylock, the Jewish money-lender. If the debt is not repaid, then Antonio will have to repay the bond with a pound of flesh. Antonio's ships are lost and Shylock demands his pound of flesh. Portia, in disguise as a lawyer, appears in the court, begs for mercy for Antonio, and, when this fails, asserts that in payment of the bond Shylock must not spill one drop of blood. Shylock is defeated and loses his wealth – half to Antonio and half to the state. Antonio graciously declines the fortune provided that Shylock turns Christian and gives his property to his daughter Jessica, whom he had disinherited for eloping with a gentile. Anti-semitic feeling was strong in England at this time.

Roderigo Lopez was a Jewish doctor who settled in England and was house physician at St Bartholomew's Hospital and a member of the Royal College of Physicians before 1569. He became Elizabeth I's chief physician in 1586, but was implicated in a plot to murder the Queen and executed at Tyburn in 1594.

Benjamin Disraeli (1804–81)

Sidonia is a central character in *Coningsby*, used by the author to put forward – often in dialogue form – the leading ideas of the Young England movement, a revival of the aristocracy and of the chivalrous ideas they represent, the support of the old social order which preceded the factory system and the Manchester school, a revitalizing of the Church and the consequent rebirth of the true and innate greatness of Britain. 'He was above middle height, and of a distinguished air and figure; pale, with an impressive brow, and dark eyes of great intelligence.' Harry Coningsby asks him whether he believes in the influence of the individual character, even though it may not be the Spirit of the Age. Sidonia answers: 'The Age does not believe in great men, because it does not possess any. . . . The Spirit of the Age is the very thing that a great man changes. . . . From the throne to the hovel all call for a guide.' Coningsby then asks him: 'What is an individual, against a vast public opinion?' and receives Sidonia's reply: 'Divine . . . God made Man in his own image; but the Public is made by Newspapers, Members of Parliament, Excise Officers, Poor Law Guardians. Would Philip have succeeded, if Epamanondas had not been slain? . . . Would Prussia have existed had Frederick not been born?'

Sidonia is Disraeli's portrait of himself. The name 'Sidonia' suggests Sidney, and Sir Philip Sidney (1554–86) evoked the chivalrous and aristocratic qualities which motivated the Young England movement. He was particularly bitter at not being given Cabinet office by Robert Peel and by 1842 he was leader of a new force in British conservatism, and he used the novels *Coningsby* and *Sybil*, which appeared in the mid-1840s, to put his faith in Tory radicalism before the public. He attacked Peel's policy of Corn Law repeal and led the Protectionist faction in the Commons. He was Chancellor under Derby in 1852 and again in the Cabinet in 1858 and 1866. Briefly Prime Minister in 1868 his great administration was from 1874–80, and among the measures associated with him are reform at home, expansion abroad, the purchase of the Suez Canal shares and his handling of the Balkan crisis.

LONG JOHN SILVER
Robert Louis Stevenson, *Treasure Island* (1883)

W. E. Henley (1849–1903)

When Jim Hawkins, in *Treasure Island*, approaches the Spy-glass tavern he sees Long John Silver: 'His left leg was cut off close by the hip, and under the left shoulder he carried a crutch, which he managed with wonderful dexterity, hopping about upon it like a bird. He was very tall and strong, with a face as big as a ham – plain and pale, but intelligent and smiling.'

The description fits W. E. Henley who, at the age of sixteen, had his left leg amputated beneath the knee and thereafter walked with a crutch or a stick (and sometimes both). Stevenson admitted that Henley's 'maimed masterfulness gave me the germ from which John Silver grew'. Henley was born in Gloucester and, after English doctors recommended the amputation of his right leg when the tubercular infection became active, he moved to Edinburgh to be treated by Joseph Lister at the Royal Infirmary. Lister saved Henley's leg, and probably his sanity, by his expertise and his example. Henley idolized Lister and evolved, as a result of his triumph over mental anguish and physical agony, a heartily heroic attitude to life best summed up in the closing lines of his poem 'Invictus': 'I am the master of my fate:/I am the captain of my soul.'

He acted as Stevenson's agent, collaborated with him on the play *Deacon Brodie* and in 1889 became editor of the *Scots Observer*. His positive attitude to life enabled him to surmount adversity and he can be well-imagined, like Long John Silver in *Treasure Island*, dreaming his dreams: 'Why, it makes me young again. I was going to forget my timber leg, I was. It's a pleasant thing to be young, and have ten toes, and you may lay to that. When you want to go a bit of exploring, you just ask old John, and he'll put up a snack for you to take along.'

JOCK SINCLAIR
James Kennaway, *Tunes of Glory* (1956)

Captain Jock Laurie

James Kennaway's first novel *Tunes of Glory* opens atmospherically in Campbell Barracks (actually Queen's Barracks, Perth) with the snow sealing the soldiers in their own small world. In command of the battalion is acting-colonel Jock Sinclair, a war hero who intimidates friend and foe alike with his aggressive behaviour. In peacetime Jock is an anachronism with more muscles than manners and no sense of decorum : all the graces he lacks are supplied by the new colonel – Basil Barrow of Eton, Oxford and Sandhurst. Jock, by contrast, rose to command 'by way of Sauchiehall Street, Barlinnie gaol, and the band. I was a boy piper.' Campbell Barracks is not big enough for both men and Jock drives Colonel Barrow to suicide and himself to distraction.

James Kennaway did his national service with the Queen's Own Cameron Highlanders. In 1948 he was attached to the 1st Battalion, Gordon Highlanders, with the British Army on the Rhine at Essen. Since drink was cheap and the men were not allowed to fraternize with the Germans the evenings were spent in the barracks in alcoholic self-indulgence ; occasionally the men ventured out to pick a fight with Germans just for the fun of it. One of the men Kennaway observed was Captain Jock Laurie, a tough character who had been a sergeant in the 8th Argylls. During the war his heroism earned him promotion and he was greatly admired for his courage. In peacetime, however, he undermined the authority of the senior officers with his belligerent behaviour and his insistence on hard competitive drinking. Laurie's activities caught up with him and he was eventually cashiered and ended his days in Barlinnie gaol. Kennaway found the whole atmosphere alarming and told his mother he would 'rather serve in the Argentine police than in this regiment'.

Hugh MacDiarmid (1892–1978)

Eric Linklater's comic novel *Magnus Merriman* describes the hero's experiences as a successful Orkney novelist at large in Scotland as he fights for national autonomy and loses his own independence to a farmer's daughter. In Edinburgh, where he mingles with the literati, he meets the poet Hugh Skene: 'In Scotland the chief exponent of literal revolution was Hugh Skene, and he ... attempted to revive the ancient Scottish forms of speech. They had this advantage, at least, that they were fully as obscure as Joyce's neologisms or the asyntactical compressions of the young English poets. But as Skene's genius matured he discovered that the Scots of Dunbar and Henryson was insufficient to contain both his emotion and his meaning, and he began to draw occasional buckets from the fountains of other tongues. At this time it was not uncommon to find in his verse, besides ancient Scots, an occasional Gaelic, German, or Russian phrase. The title-poem of his new volume, *The Flauchter-spaad*, was strikingly polyglot, and after three hours' study Magnus was unable to decide whether it was a plea for Communism, a tribute to William Wallace, or a poetical rendering of certain prehistoric fertility rites.'

Skene is Hugh MacDiarmid whose Synthetic Scots poems of the 1920s, particularly *A Drunk Man Looks at the Thistle* (1926), created a new style of Scottish poetry, international in range and modernistic in approach. MacDiarmid's volume *Scots Unbound and Other Poems* (1932) used what the poet called Aggrandized Scots to extend the idiom and this is the experiment Linklater satirizes – his description of Skene's title-poem refers to a MacDiarmid poem 'Tarras' with its line 'Nor wi' their flauchter-spades ettle to play'. MacDiarmid (who was born Christopher Murray Grieve and adopted the pseudonym in 1922) thoroughly approved of the fictional portrayal: 'That's me to a T' he said in his autobiography *Lucky Poet* (1943).

HAROLD SKIMPOLE
Charles Dickens, *Bleak House* (1852)

James Henry Leigh Hunt (1784–1859)

Harold Skimpole is a protégé of John Jarndyce, who hides his utter irresponsibility, especially of money matters, under the guise of an assumed childish innocence. He attacks Jarndyce, accusing him of selfishness: 'He was a bright little creature, with a rather large head; but a delicate face, and a sweet voice, and there was a perfect charm in him. All he said was so free from effort and spontaneous, and was said with such a captivating gaiety, that it was fascinating to hear him talk. . . . He had more the appearance, in all respects, of a damaged young man, than a well preserved elderly one. There was an easy negligence in his manner, and even in his dress (his hair carelessly disposed, and his neck-kerchief loose and flowing, as I have seen artists paint their own portraits), which I could not separate from the idea of a romantic youth who had undergone some unique process of depreciation.'

This is a rather unflattering portrait of Henry Leigh Hunt, brilliant essayist and friend of several distinguished men of letters, including Keats, Byron, Shelley and Lamb, as well as Dickens. He was a distinguished journalist and editor, who ran the *Examiner* and the *Reflector* at various times in his career. A man of great personal charm, he had been imprisoned in 1813 for making derogatory remarks about the Regent. He was distressed to realize Dickens had caricatured him as Skimpole, though Dickens's biographer, John Forster, claims that the novelist: 'erred from thoughtlessness only'. Dickens, Forster said: 'yielded to the temptation of too often making the character speak like his old friend'. Dickens tried to mollify Hunt and to justify the portrait, but the damage was done. At first the original had not recognized himself: 'but good natured friends in time told Hunt everything'.

LARRY SLADE
Eugene O'Neill, *The Iceman Cometh* (1946)

Terry Carlin

In 1915 Eugene O'Neill, finding himself down and almost out in New York, began to drink heavily at the Hell Hole, as the regulars called the Golden Swan saloon-hotel in Greenwich Village. This alcoholically extreme period is recreated in *The Iceman Cometh* in which O'Neill appears as Willie Oban, one of the roomers at Harry Hope's saloon-hotel. Another is the 'grandstand philosopher' Larry Slade whose drunkenness is an attempt to escape from his Syndicalist-Anarchist past. 'He stares in front of him,' reads O'Neill's stage-direction on Larry, 'an expression of tired tolerance giving his face the quality of a pitying but weary old priest's.'

O'Neill met Terry Carlin, Larry's original, in the Hell Hole and instantly adopted him as friend, philosopher and surrogate father. Terry, who was born Terence O'Carolan, had an Irish peasant background (as had O'Neill's father) and had come to America as a child in the 1860s. He worked for ten years, as a tanner, then opted out of what he regarded as a rat race. He was brought back into the commercial world when his brother Jim, a stockholder in a tannery, persuaded him to advise the firm. Although Terry's suggestions were profitable the owner of the firm refused to reward him and this caused Jim to resign and thus bring financial ruin on himself and his family. Terry returned to his former poverty and dreamed of an art that would encompass his experience: 'Oh,' Terry wrote, 'that I might expand my written words into an Epic of the Slums, into an Iliad of the Proletaire!' O'Neill articulated this ambition for him and later went with Terry to Provincetown in search of theatrical fame and fortune. Terry had a powerful influence on O'Neill who felt responsible for him; when O'Neill left Provincetown he maintained an account for Terry at a general store. 'I am free and always drunk,' maintained Terry.

JULIUS SLINKTON
Charles Dickens, *Hunted Down* (1859)

Thomas Griffiths Wainewright (1794–1847)

Julius Slinkton is a murderer. He murders one of his nieces, and has designs on the other, Margaret. He stands to gain from their insurance money. His crimes are detected by Meltham, who is the actuary of the insurance company Slinkton had hoped to defraud. Meltham was in love with Slinkton's first victim, and uses various disguises in the pursuit of the criminal, including that of Major Banks and Alfred Beckwith. Slinkton assumes that Beckwith is what he pretends to be – a drunkard near to death – and insures him preparatory to his attempt to poison him. Slinkton's villainy is revealed, and he takes his own life. Dickens describes him as: 'About forty or so, dark, exceedingly well dressed in black, – being in mourning, – and the hand he extended with a polite air, had a particularly well fitting black-kid glove upon it. His hair, which was elaborately brushed and oiled, was parted straight up the middle; and he presented this parting to the clerk, exactly . . . as if he had said, in so many words: "You must take me, if you please, my friend, just as I show myself. Come straight up here, follow the gravel path, keep off the grass, I allow no trespassing".'

Dickens based Slinkton on the painter, art critic and forger Wainewright, who was also alleged to have murdered his uncle, mother-in-law, sister-in-law as well as other victims. His sister-in-law, Helen, he had insured for £16,000. The company refused to pay, and Wainewright took them to court and nearly won his case. He was sentenced to transportation in 1837 and continued to paint. Dickens may also have had the notorious William Palmer of Rugely in mind (1825–56) who was hanged for the murder of John Parsons Cook but probably poisoned his brother and his wife in order to collect insurance to finance horse-racing and gambling. Dickens followed these cases and wrote about Palmer in *Demeanour of Murderers* (*Miscellaneous Papers*).

DR SLOPER
Henry James, *Washington Square* (1881)

William James (1842–1910)

Henry James discovered the plot of *Washington Square* in a conversation with the actress Fanny Kemble who told an anecdote about her brother jilting an Oxford heiress on hearing that her father would disinherit her rather than sanction the marriage. In the novel, Catherine Sloper's romance with Morris Townsend is destroyed by the arrogant actions of her distinguished father. Dr Austin Sloper is a famous New York physician who is faithful to the memory of his wife, a rich woman who died a week after giving birth to Catherine. He cannot accept that Catherine is attractive in herself and generally ridicules her efforts to be individual. Commenting on his daughter's prospects Dr Sloper says 'You must remember that she has the prospect of thirty thousand a year. . . . I don't mean that is her only merit; I simply mean that it is a great one. . . . Catherine is not unmarriageable, but she is absolutely unattractive.'

The relationship between the diffident Catherine and her father recalls the tension between Henry James and his brother William, sixteen months his senior. William James was, as psychologist and pragmatic philosopher, one of the most accomplished intellectuals of his time and, like Dr Sloper, 'a thoroughly honest man'. He was, however, easily irritated and given to pouring scorn on what he thought of as brother Henry's literary pretensions. He was astonished at Henry's stunning success as a novelist and eventually found himself in the disagreeable position of being eclipsed by his younger brother. In 1905 William was elected to the American Academy of Arts and Letters but the honour came two months after it had been conferred on Henry. Accordingly William refused the election – ostensibly because he felt the James' family influence would be excessive. He added, with typical sarcasm, 'I am the more encouraged in this course by the fact that my younger and shallower and vainer brother is already in the Academy.'

MR SLUDGE

Robert Browning, *Mr Sludge 'The Medium'* (1864)

Daniel Dunglas Home (1833–86)

In this dramatic monologue the fraudulent medium, Sludge, defends the course of his career. He urges that we cannot blame him too fiercely, as a large part of the responsibility for what seems to be his guilt, is the fact that the public are so anxious to be deceived. They desperately want to believe what he attempts to fool them with: 'It's fancying, fable-making, nonsense work – /What never meant to be so very bad – /The knack of story-telling, brightening up/Each dull old bit of fact that drops its shine./One does see somewhat when one shuts one's eyes,/If only spots and streaks; tables do tip/In the oddest way of themselves: and pens, good Lord,/Who knows if you drive them or they drive you?'

This is a portrait of Daniel Dunglas Home, the doyen of Victorian spiritualism. He was at the height of his fame in the decade 1860–70. Browning was particularly distrustful of those who claimed to be able to contact the 'other world' – and regarded them as little better than magicians. Home was born near Edinburgh, and claimed to be related to the Earls of Home. His mother took him to the USA when he was quite young, and it was in America that he made his initial reputation. He came to Britain in 1855 and held numerous seances, which attracted large audiences and many of the famous, including the historian H. T. Buckle, who was present when Home caused a dining table to leave the floor and float in mid-air. In Florence he demonstrated his powers to English expatriots and the American sculptor, Hiram Powers, was present when he produced spirit hands. Lord Lyndhurst, Lord Dufferin, Landseer, Henry Grattan, the Duchess of Somerset, Lady Salisbury, Lady Londonderry and Lady Mitford were among other celebrities who saw Home in action. In 1867 he was taken to court by a wealthy widow, after claiming he had messages from her husband involving her handing over to him cash and property of considerable value. The case ruined his reputation, he had already been expelled from the Catholic church as a sorcerer. He died in France.

Laurence Sterne, *A Sentimental Journey through France and Italy*
(1768)

Tobias Smollett (1721–71)

A Sentimental Journal was to have consisted of four volumes, but Sterne lived to complete only two. They recount travels through Calais, Amiens and to Paris, through the Bourbonnais and on to Lyons, en route to Italy. The narrative is packed with sentimental adventures, and the narrator, presumed to be Mr Yorick, finds everything to his taste, unlike Smelfungus, whom he meets. Smelfungus travels from Boulogne to Paris, and from Paris to Rome, but sees everything through the distortions of his own irascibility and spleen: 'I pity the man who can travel from Dan to Beersheba, and cry: "Tis all barren" – and so it is; and so is all the world to him who will not cultivate the fruit it offers . . . was I in a desert, I would out wherewith in it to call forth my affection.' By contrast, Smelfungus writes an account of his travels which is 'nothing but the account of his miserable feelings'. Of the Pantheon he said: ' 'Tis nothing but a huge cockpit.'

This is a malicious portrait of Tobias Smollett, the Scottish novelist, journalist and historian, who had a rather jaundiced view and an acid wit. Sterne met Smollett at Montpellier in 1763. Smollett published his *Travels in France and Italy* in 1766, to which Sterne directly replies in *A Sentimental Journey*, at times echoing Smollett's own words, as he had written: 'I was most disappointed at sight of the Pantheon, which, after all that has been said of it, looks like a huge cockpit, open at top. . . . I cannot help thinking that there is no beauty in the features of Venus, and that the attitude is awkward and out of character.' It is true to say, however, that Smollett was in very poor health at this time, and no doubt this considerably coloured his view. The character Mundungus in *A Sentimental Journey*, is a characterization of Dr Samuel Sharp, who went across Europe 'without one generous connection or pleasurable anecdote to tell of'. He published *Letters From Italy* in 1766, and died in 1778. Smollett wrote on returning: 'You cannot imagine what pleasure I feel while surveying the White cliffs of Dover.'

GEORGE SMILEY

John Le Carré, *Tinker Tailor Soldier Spy* (1974), *The Honourable Schoolboy* (1977), *Smiley's People* (1980)

Revd Dr V. H. H. Green (born 1915)

John Le Carré's subtle spymaster George Smiley has the appearance of an academic and the cunning of a vastly experienced operator. In *Tinker Tailor Soldier Spy* Le Carré mentions his 'Buddha-like inscrutability' and in *The Honourable Schoolboy* he is described with 'a sheet of notes before him. . . . As he spoke, he was actually marking something with his pencil.'

Interviewed on the subject of Smiley, Le Carré mentioned 'my mentor at Oxford' and in a letter of 24 January 1983 named the original as Vivian Green: 'it was Green's quiet, and shrewdness, which I liked'. When David Cornwell (John le Carré) went to read Modern Languages at Oxford in 1952 he was admitted to Lincoln College by Green, then Senior Tutor. The Revd Dr Vivian Hubert Howard Green is a historian who became Sub-Rector of Lincoln in 1970, and Rector in 1983. He has published books on *The Young Mr Wesley* (1961), *Martin Luther and the German Reformation* (1964) and *Religion at Oxford and Cambridge, c. 1160–1960* (1964). He names his recreation as 'mountain walking in Switzerland'. Smiley himself is an Oxford man though his interest is in philosophy rather than ecclesiastical history. In a letter of 30 January 1983 Dr Green commented on his connection with Smiley: 'I understand that such likeness as there is is in some facets of character, more especially, I am told, in being a good listener! Obviously Smiley is a compound of many ingredients, the author's among them, but it seems that somewhere there is at least a minimal something of myself. . . . I have known David Cornwell for a very long time, and been a close friend. . . . I remember reading the first Smiley MS as I came back from visiting him in London in the train from Paddington. . . . When David and his wife stayed with me last October, they brought a present of caviare and vodka with a card reading "With love from Karla".'

JULIEN SOREL
Stendhal, *Scarlet and Black* (1830)

Antoine Berthet (executed 1827)

Julien Sorel is an ambitious young Bonapartist, humbly born, but hoping to rise in society by adopting the priesthood. As a tutor to the Renal family, he seduces Madame de Renal. After returning to the seminary, he leaves to take up a post at the family of the de la Moles, where he has a love affair with their young daughter. He loses his post, believing that he has been betrayed by Madame de Renal. He attempts to shoot her out of vengeance, while she is attending church. He is condemned to death. While awaiting execution he is visited by the confessor who says to him: 'Your youth . . . the attractive face with which Providence has endowed you, the motive itself of your crime, which remains a mystery, the heroic efforts which Mademoiselle de la Mole has not spared on your behalf . . . have all combined to make you the hero of the young women of Besancon. . . . Your conversion would find an echo in their hearts and would leave a deep impression. . . . You can be of the greatest service, to religion.' Julien answers: 'And what shall I have left, if I despise myself? I have been ambitious, I am not going to blame myself for that; I acted then in accordance with the demands of the time. Now I live for the day, without thought of the morrow. . . . I should be making myself extremely unhappy if I allowed myself to slide into any act of cowardice.' He is beheaded.

Stendhal found the story in several issues of a newspaper, the *Gazette de Tribuneaux*, during December 1827. Antoine Berthet was the good-looking, ambitious son of a blacksmith at Grenoble. With the help of a priest he obtained the post of tutor in the family of a well-to-do lawyer, Michaud. Berthet seduced Madame Michaud. He got bored with her and left to enter the local seminary. He later took another post as tutor in the aristocratic family of de Cordet. Here he had an affair with their young daughter. He was dismissed from his post and was no longer able to continue in the priesthood. He was convinced that it was his former mistress, Madame Michaud, who had betrayed him. In revenge he shot her in church and later attempted suicide. At his trial he argued that his mistress, more worldly than he was, had corrupted him. All attempts to gain a reprieve failed, and he was executed.

SIR PATRICK SPENCE

Francis James Child, *The English and Scottish Popular Ballads*
(1882–98)

Sir Patrick Spence

Traditional ballads that tell the story of the drowning of Sir Patrick Spence agree that Sir Patrick was reluctant to accept the King's commission for a sea voyage and that his fears were shared by his men, one of whom says prophetically: 'I saw the new moon late yestreen,/Wi' the auld moon in her arms;/And if we gang to sea, master,/I fear we'll suffer harm.'

The King who sat in Dunfermline town drinking the blood-red wine was Alexander III (1241–86) during whose reign Scotland enjoyed a golden age of prosperity. As his daughter Margaret (1261–83) was to marry King Erik of Norway in 1281 the King sent courtiers to attend the ceremony scheduled for August. The variant of 'Sir Patrick Spence' collected in Robert Jamieson's *Popular Ballads and Songs* (1806) duly sends Sir Patrick Spence on the voyage north: 'They mounted sail on Munenday morn,/Wi' a' the haste they may,/And they hae landed in Norraway,/Upon the Wednesday.' According to this version the Scots encountered hostility in Norway: 'They hadna been a month, a month/In Norraway but three,/Till lads of Norraway began to say,/"Ye spend a' our white monie".' Indignant at this insult Sir Patrick and his men make haste to return to Scotland; and it is an historical fact that courtiers who went with Margaret to Norway were drowned on the return voyage. Sir Patrick Spence's name does not appear in the chronicles but survives in the oral tradition, which underlines the contrast that distinguishes the ballad: the King drinks wine, Sir Patrick swallows salt water. Margaret died giving birth to the Maid of Norway who herself died of seasickness on a voyage from Norway to Scotland in 1290.

RODERICK SPODE
P. G. Wodehouse, *The Code of the Woosters* (1938)

Sir Oswald Mosley (1896–1980)

In P. G. Wodehouse's novel *The Code of the Woosters* there appears the fascist leader, Roderick Spode. In Bertie Wooster's words, Spode has 'succeeded in inducing a handful of half-wits to disfigure the London scene by going about in black shorts. . . . You hear them shouting "Heil Spode!" and you imagine it is the voice of the people. This is where you make your bloomer. What the Voice of the People is saying is: "Look at that frightful ass Spode swanking about in footer bags. Did you ever in your puff see such a perfect perisher?"' Jeeves later discovers that Spode is secretly a dealer in lingerie.

Roderick Spode is a satiric portrait of the British politician, Sir Oswald Mosley. He was educated at Winchester and the Royal Military College at Sandhurst. He was Conservative MP for Harrow between 1918 and 1922 and then sat as an Independent. Between 1924 and 1930 he sat as a Labour MP. In December 1930 he issued a manifesto which put forward his own plans for dealing with the economic crisis. His advice was not heeded and he and a few supporters left the Labour party to form a group of their own, as Ramsay MacDonald resigned and later became Prime Minister of a National government. In the election of 1931 Mosley's new party failed to win a single seat at the election. The British Union of Fascists, as it was called, held some of the biggest public political meetings in history, and occasioned mob riots and public disturbances in the run up to the Second World War. Under the Defence Regulations Mosley was arrested in May 1940 and he and a number of his fellow party members were interned during the war. He subsequently lived in exile in France. In 1968 he declared: 'I am not, and never have been, a man of the right. My position was on the left and is now in the centre of politics.' He published his political ideas in *My Answer* (1946) and *Mosley-Right or Wrong?* (1961).

SPORUS
Alexander Pope, *Epistle to Dr. Arbuthnot* (1735)

John Hervey, Baron Hervey of Ickworth (1696–1743)

The *Epistle to Dr. Arbuthnot* was written by Pope as an answer
to his critics and a defence of his literary career. In addressing
it to Dr Arbuthnot (1667–1735) the poet was able to establish
some virtue by association, as Arbuthnot was a man of great
respect and probity. Among the persons attacked in the *Epistle*
is Sporus, whom the poet particularly chides for weakness and
cowardice, and one who incites others to attack him. In the
dialogue, Dr Arbuthnot asks why Sporus should be attacked,
when he was a 'thing of silk' and a 'mere white curd of ass's
milk'. What point is there in breaking 'a butterfly upon a
wheel?' he asks. Pope answers: 'Yet let me flap this bug with
gilded wings,/This painted child of dirt, that stinks and stings;/
Whose buzz the witty and the fair annoys,/Yet wit ne'er tastes,
and beauty ne'er enjoys.' He hints strongly at Sporus's sexual
ambiguity, and likens him to Milton's Satan, tempting Eve,
beautiful to look upon yet vile in spirit: 'A cherub's face, a
reptile all the rest./Beauty that shocks you, parts that none will
trust,/Wit that can creep, and pride that licks the dust.' He is
seen as the tempter of Queen Caroline, wife of George II.

This is a portrait of Lord Hervey, who acted in consort with
Lady Mary Montagu (see SAPPHO) to attack Pope. The attacks
on Pope had been no less personal and abusive: 'as thou hat'st,
be hated by all mankind,/Marked on thy back, like Cain, by
God's own hand,/Wander like him accursed through the land.'
The allusion to Pope's deformity is particularly distasteful. As
Pope wrote in a letter: 'There is a woman's war declared against
me by a certain Lord. His weapons are the same which women
and children use: a pin to scratch, and a squirt to bespatter.'
The result of this quarrel has been Hervey's assured immortality in Pope's poetry. As Vice Chamberlain Hervey had particular influence over Queen Caroline. He was a close friend
of Lady Mary Montagu. He had been granted a pension by
George II when he deserted Frederick, Prince of Wales, and as
a supporter of Robert Walpole and friend of Lady Mary soon
fell foul of Pope, who attacked him as Lord Fanny in *Bathos,
the Art of Sinking in Poetry* and in *The Dunciad*. Hervey's
Memoirs of the Reign of George II remain a vivid portrait of the
times.

EVERARD SPRUCE
Evelyn Waugh, *Sword of Honour* (1965)

Cyril Connolly (1903–74)

Everard Spruce is the founder and editor of *Survival*: 'A man who cherished no ambitions for the future, believing, despite the title of his monthly review, that the human race was destined to dissolve in chaos.' He is one of those intellectuals whom war brought to an eminence they might not otherwise have enjoyed: 'Those of his friends who had not fled to Ireland or America had joined the Fire Brigade.' In the years preceding the war Spruce had emphatically not been the most esteemed of his coterie of 'youngish, socialist writers'. His journal had announced itself devoted to 'the Survival of Values' and had been protected by the Ministry of Information, exempted its staff from other duties and granted it a generous allowance of paper. It had also been privileged by being exported in bulk to countries still open to British shipping. A chapter of accidents, then, created the literary persona of Everard Spruce, who: 'was in his middle thirties. Time was, he cultivated a proletarian, youthful, aspect; not successfully; now, perhaps without design, he looked older than his years and presented the negligent elegance of a fashionable don . . . he wore a heavy silk, heavily striped shirt and a bow tie above noncommittal trousers.'

This is a portrait of Cyril Connolly, seen by Waugh as one who created a legend of his own brilliance and then failed to live up to it. Waugh's friend Hubert Duggan described Connolly as one who looked as if he'd 'been kicked in the face by a mule'. He did have a snub nose and shaggy eyebrows, and his eyes were set rather far apart. Connolly and Waugh met at Oxford and remained friends, though Waugh constantly provoked and needled him. Connolly was one of the founders and editor of *Horizon*, a journal which was intended to 'give to writers a place to express themselves, and to readers the best writing we can obtain'. It lasted from 1940 until 1950. He was literary editor of *The Observer*, and author of several novels and a fascinating autobiography, *Enemies of Promise*. Waugh's *Black Mischief* has a character called General Connolly, and Apthorpe in *Sword of Honour* has a luxury portable lavatory, *Connolly's Chemical Closet*.

SS *CABINET MINISTER*

Compton Mackenzie, *Whisky Galore* (1947)

SS *Politician*

Compton Mackenzie's farce *Whisky Galore* opens in 1943 with the people of the Hebridean island of Little Todday lamenting the lack of whisky owing to wartime restrictions: there has not been a drop of whisky on the island for twelve days. Suddenly, like manna from heaven, whisky is delivered on (as it were) the islanders' doorstep when the SS *Cabinet Minister*, carrying a cargo of 50,000 cases of whisky, strikes a reef in the Minch. The islanders are quick to use all their native ingenuity to dispose of the hard stuff in the most suitable way. Mackenzie presents the treasure thus: 'Many romantic pages have been written about the sunken Spanish galleon in the bay of Tobermory. That 4000-ton steamship on the rocks of Little Todday provided more practical romance in three and a half hours than the Tobermory galleon has provided in three and a half centuries. Doubloons, ducats, and ducatoons, moidores, pieces of eight, sequins, guineas, rose and angel nobles, what are these to vaunt above the liquid gold carried by the *Cabinet Minister*?' Put in that golden light the SS *Cabinet Minister* emerges as the heroine of Mackenzie's novel and she had an historical counterpart.

In February 1941 the SS *Politician*, a ship considered fast enough to outrun the U-boats in the Atlantic, foundered on a reef in the Sound of Eriskay with her cargo of 264,750 bottles of whisky. Inevitably, the men of Eriskay illegally salvaged the 'liquid gold'. Mackenzie, who settled in the Hebridean island of Barra in 1928, changed one local detail for comic effect: Eriskay is a Roman Catholic island whereas Little Todday is depicted as a Presbyterian stronghold. This causes some problems since the islanders are obliged to observe the Sabbath – the day on which the SS *Cabinet Minister* is wrecked.

ELENA STAHOV
Ivan Turgenev, *On the Eve* (1860)

Anita Garibaldi (1821–49)

Elena Stahov, heroine of Ivan Turgenev's *On the Eve*, is an earnest woman in search of an heroic ideal: 'Weakness of character made her indignant, stupidity angered her, a lie she would not forgive "as long as she lived". . . . A person had but to lose her respect – and she passed judgement quickly, often too quickly – and at once he ceased to exist for her. Every impression was imprinted sharply on her soul; life, for her, was no light matter.' Elena finds the cause she is looking for when she falls in love with Insarov, a Bulgarian patriot exiled in Russia. Henceforth she devotes her life to him and, when he dies, takes his body to Bulgaria and prepares to participate in the war of liberation.

In creating Elena, Turgenev drew on the inspirational figure of Anita Garibaldi, wife of the great Italian patriot. Born in a Brazilian village (now named after her) Anita had been married for four years when Garibaldi noticed her in Laguna in 1839. In his memoirs he described the meeting: 'We both remained enraptured and silent, gazing on each other like two people who had met before, and seeking in each other's faces something which makes it easier to recall the forgotten past. . . . I had formed a tie, pronounced a decree, which only death could annul. I had come upon a forbidden treasure, but yet a treasure of great price!!!' Anita eloped with Garibaldi and married him, in Montevideo, in 1842. She was subsequently his most passionate supporter, insisting on being present in the most demanding and dangerous actions such as the defence of Rome, and the march to San Marino although at the time she was pregnant and suffering from fever. After her death she was celebrated as a great woman of the people. Turgenev's hero, Insarov, had nothing to do with Garibaldi: the prototype was Katranov, a Bulgarian poet, whose love story Turgenev learned about in a notebook given to him by Vassili Karatyeev, a landowner he knew at Spasskoye.

Irving Thalberg (1899–1936)

Despite (or, as he thought, *because*) of his great literary style, F. Scott Fitzgerald was a failure in Hollywood terms; though he worked as a writer in Hollywood in 1927, 1931 and 1937 his only screen credit was for his work on the MGM movie *Three Comrades* (1938). Moreover, Fitzgerald's alcoholic excesses made him an embarrassing figure at Hollywood parties where one could be flamboyant but not frankly vulgar. At one party (described in his story 'Crazy Sunday') Fitzgerald offended the guests of producer Irving Thalberg and was dismissed by MGM a week later.

When Fitzgerald conceived what was to be his final novel, *The Last Tycoon*, he portrayed Thalberg as an artist carefully controlling his sensitivity in order to survive in a viciously competitive business. Monroe Stahr, the hero of the novel, is described in terms exactly applicable to Thalberg: 'He was a marker in industry like Edison and Lumière and Griffith and Chaplin. He led pictures way up past the range and power of the theatre, reaching a sort of golden age, before the censorship.' In fact Thalberg was the brains behind the MGM successes of the 1930s, bringing artistic quality to such films as *The Barretts of Wimpole Street* (1934) and *Romeo and Juliet* (1936).

In Fitzgerald's fiction the Thalberg–Stahr figure assumes certain of the author's own characteristics for he falls in love with a young English girl, Kathleen Moore, who is clearly an affectionate portrait of Sheila Graham, the woman Fitzgerald lived with at the end of his life. In a synopsis of his novel Fitzgerald said 'Thalberg has always fascinated me. His peculiar charm, his extraordinary good looks, his bountiful success, the tragic end of his great adventure. The events I have built around him are fiction, but all of them are things which might very well have happened.'

MAJOR GENERAL STANLEY

Opera, *The Pirates of Penzance* (1879, music by A. S. Sullivan, libretto by W. S. Gilbert)

Sir Garnet Wolseley (1833–1913)

Major General Stanley introduces himself with one of the most famous patter songs in the Savoy operas: 'I am the very model of a modern Major-General,/I've information vegetable, animal, and mineral,/I know the kings of England, and I quote the fights historical,/From Marathon to Waterloo, in order categorical;/I'm very well acquainted too with matters mathematical,/I understand equations, both the simple and quadratical,/About binomial theorem I'm teeming with a lot o' news –/With many cheerful facts about the square of the hypoteneuse.'

Stanley is based on Garnet Wolseley, the most renowned Victorian major-general and trouble-shooter of imperialism. When George Goldsmith appeared in the premier of *The Pirates* in this role he was made up to look like Wolseley, who was a household name after exploits in India, Burma, China, the Ashanti wars, Natal, the Transvaal and Cyprus. The general delighted in singing this song to entertain family and friends at his home, happy to declare himself 'the very model of a modern Major-General'. Indeed there was something of the braggart in Wolseley's character which Gilbert wholly captured. Disraeli wrote of him in a letter to Queen Victoria: 'It is quite true that Wolseley is an egotist and a braggart . . . men of action when eminently successful in early life are generally boastful and full of themselves.'

Wolseley was born in County Dublin, of a long line of military men. His early career was one long series of brilliant exploits, he was dangerously wounded during the Crimean war, and his promotion was rapid – Assistant Quarter Marshall General in Canada 1861, Colonel 1865, Deputy Quarter Master General 1867, Commander of the Red River expedition 1870, KCMG and CB 1870, Assistant Adjutant General at the War Office 1871, Commander of the Ashanti expedition 1873, Major-General GCMG and KCB 1874, General Commanding in Natal 1875, First Administrator in Cyprus 1878, sent to retrieve the situation in the Zulu wars in 1879 and Adjutant General by 1882, victor at Tel-el-Kebir 1882 and the leader of the expedition finally sent to relieve Gordon at Khartoum. A Viscount by 1885, he was Commander-in-Chief in Ireland 1890–95 and finally Commander-in-Chief of the British Army.

WILLIE STARK
Robert Penn Warren, *All the King's Men* (1946)

Huey Long (1893–1935)

All the King's Men is the life story of an honest man from a small town background who gets involved in politics. He gets elected mayor and gradually develops ambition, which fuels his career. He is eventually elected governor of the state and gradually power begins to corrupt him, and he destroys his own personality and ruins the lives of friends and family who have supported him. He is eventually assassinated. It is a classic study of the 'gothic' politics of the Southern United States.

The leading character, Willie Stark, is based on the Louisiana politician, Huey Long, known as the 'Kingfish'. He combined an apparently genuine concern for the ordinary citizen, with demagogic political ruthlessness. He was born in Wingfield, Louisiana. He left high school before graduating, was a salesman, and then went to law school. He was called to the Louisiana bar in 1915. He was soon fascinated by politics. Elected as state railroad commissioner in 1918 he soon showed what he could do; he transformed it into a properly energetic public agency, the Public Service Commission. His attacks on big business and the monopoly tactics of the large corporations earned him considerable public support. He was seen as the champion of the Little Man against the likes of Standard Oil. He was elected governor in 1928 and pushed through an extensive series of legislative measures affecting education and public health, in the face of considerable conservative opposition, maintaining his political influence with a machine which he created. Initially he supported Roosevelt, but presidential ambitions of his own as well as feelings that Roosevelt was insufficiently radical caused Long to break with him. In 1934 he declared his 'Share Our Wealth' campaign. His spectacular career was brought to an end by his assassination on 8 September 1935, when he was shot by Dr Carl A. Weiss. Weiss was killed by Long's bodyguard and the assassination has never really been explained. It might have been personal revenge (Weiss believed Long had insulted him) or it might have been a conspiracy to end Long's power. The novel was filmed in 1949 with Broderick Crawford as Willie Stark. Long is also the basis of Hamilton Basso's *Sun in Capricorn* (1942) and John Doss Passo's *Number One* (1943).

Penelope Rich (1562–1617)

Astrophel and Stella is a sequence of 108 sonnets and eleven songs which Philip Sidney wrote between 1581 and 1583 to celebrate his love for Penelope Devereux, the 'Stella' of the sequence. The story which holds the work together is a simple and moving one. Astrophel loves Stella. But Stella marries another, who is despised by Astrophel, who is tortured by the struggle which takes place in his bosom between passion and reason: 'When I say "Stella", I do mean the same/Princess of beauty for whose only sake/The reins of love I love, though never slake,/And joy therein, though nations count it shame./I beg no subject to use eloquence,/Nor in hid ways to guide philosophy;/Look at my hands for no such quintessence;/But know that I in pure simplicity/Breathe out the flames which burn within my heart,/Love only reading unto me this art.' Sidney's beloved 'Stella' was to marry Sir Robert Rich, who became Second Earl of Warwick. Sidney constantly puns on his name: 'Towards Aurora's court a nymph doth dwell,/Rich in all beauties which man's eyes can see;/Beauties so far from reach of words, that we/Abase her praise saying she doth excell;/Rich in the treasure of deserved renown,/Rich in the riches of a royal heart,/Rich in those gifts which give the eternal crown;/Who, though most rich in these and every part/Which makes the patents of true worldly bliss,/Hath no misfortune but that Rich she is.'

Penelope was the daughter of Walter Devereux, First Earl of Essex. When she was fourteen years old Philip Sidney fell in love with her, and her father was anxious that they should marry. But in 1581, she married Robert Rich. The marriage was an unfortunate one and she encouraged the attentions of Philip Sidney. After Sir Philip Sidney died of wounds received at Zutphen, she became the mistress of Lord Mountjoy. The couple lived together in open adultery. Her husband finally abandoned her after her brother, the celebrated Second Earl of Essex, was executed for treason in 1601, and in 1605 she married Mountjoy, who had now become Earl of Devonshire.

Francis Charles Seymour–Conway, Third Marquis of Hertford (1771–1842)

Vanity Fair details the various adventures of two young girls of very different character. The virtuous Amelia, daughter of a wealthy businessman, and the crafty Becky, daughter of an artist and an opera dancer. Becky attempts to entrap Amelia's brother, is then employed as a governess at the household of Sir Putt Crawley and secretly marries his second son and is then proposed to by Sir Pitt, whose wife dies suddenly. She seduces Amelia's husband, George, and gradually makes her way up in society, by manipulation and intrigue. Among her associates is Lord Steyne, with whom she enjoys a liaison which compromises her virtue. Steyne is one of the finest portraits of a society roué in Victorian fiction. He has a 'shining bald head, which was fringed with red hair. He had thick bushy eyebrows, with little twinkling bloodshot eyes, surrounded by a thousand wrinkles. His jaw was underhung, and when he laughed, two white buck-teeth protruded themselves and glistened savagely in the midst of the grin . . . he wore his garter and ribbon. A short man was his Lordship, broad-chested and bow-legged, but proud of the fineness of his foot and ankle, and always caressing his garter-knee. . . . Lord Steyne in early life had been notorious for his daring and his success at play. He had sat up two days and two nights with Mr. Fox at Hazard. He had won money of the most august personages of the realm; he had won his marquisate, it was said, at the gaming-table.'

This is a picture of the Third Marquis of Hertford, son of the Second Marquis. He was a BA of St Mary Hall, Oxford in 1796 and MP for Oxford, Lisburne and Camelford 1819–22. He was made a Knight of the Order of the Garter in 1822 and was an intimate friend of the Prince Regent and of the Duke of Wellington (see LORD MONMOUTH). Henry William Greville recorded of him: 'He was a *bon vivant*, and when young and gay his parties were agreeable . . . but he became puffed up with pride. . . . There has been . . . no such example of undisguised debauchery exhibited to the world.'

MRS ALGERNON STITCH

Evelyn Waugh, *Scoop* (1938), and *Sword of Honour* (1965)

Lady Diana Cooper (born 1892)

Mrs Stitch is the wife of the Cabinet minister, Algernon Stitch.
The hero of *Scoop*, the writer and journalist John Boot, is proud
of the fact that his novels sold 15,000 copies in their first year
and were read by people whose opinions John Boot respected.
Among them is 'the lovely Mrs. Algernon Stitch'. She is a
source of great comfort and support to him: 'Like all in her
circle John Boot habitually brought his difficulties to her for
solution.' She is a busy, involved and rather arty member of
the upper-class so well portrayed by Waugh: 'she was still in
bed although it was past eleven o'clock. Her normally mobile
face encased in clay was rigid and menacing as an Aztec mask.
But she was not resting. Her secretary . . . sat at her side with
account books, bills, and correspondence. With one hand Mrs.
Stitch was signing cheques; with the other she held the telephone to which, at the moment, she was dictating details of
the costumes for a charity ball. An elegant young man at the
top of a step ladder was painting ruined castles on the ceiling.'

Evelyn Waugh met Diana Cooper at Lady Cunard's and they
became life-long friends. She was the third daughter of the
Eighth Duke of Rutland and married Alfred Duff Cooper
(later Viscount Norwich) in 1919. She worked as a nurse at
Guy's Hospital in the First World War and went on the stage
after the war, mainly to finance her husband's political career.
She scored a noted success in Max Reinhardt's production of
The Miracle. She greatly amused Waugh by her imitations of
Edward and Mrs Simpson, with whom she had enjoyed a sea
voyage while her husband was in the government (Duff
Cooper resigned as First Lord of the Admiralty during the
Munich crisis, was Minister of Information and later British
Minister in Algiers during the Second World War). When
Waugh told her she was the original of Mrs Stitch she did not
mind at all. When she apologized for having made her behave
badly as Mrs Stitch in *Sword of Honour* in tearing up an official
letter of Guy Crouchback's she told the novelist she did not
mind at all, as she would have done the same. In old age she
became absent-minded and vague and often acted true to her
Mrs Stitch role. At the party to celebrate Sir Robert Mayer's
100th birthday she failed to recognize a lady who apparently
knew her well. It was only when she recognized the diamonds
she realized it was the Queen. She apologized, saying she did
not recognize her without her crown.

CHARLES STRICKLAND

W. Somerset Maugham, *The Moon and Sixpence* (1919)

Paul Gauguin (1848–1903)

Fascinated by the notion of artistic excess, W. Somerset Maugham decided in 1916 to write a novel based on the life of the painter Paul Gauguin who had (in 1881) given up a career in banking to dedicate himself to art. He worked in Brittany and with Van Gogh in Arles; then, in 1890, he left Paris for Tahiti where he executed a series of symbolically-charged compositions using scenes and figures from Tahitian life. As Maugham discovered, when he arrived in Tahiti in 1917 to research his novel, Gauguin's stay in Tahiti had been far from romantic. He was forty-two when he came to the island in bad health and without money; as usual he was obstreperous and had clashes with the local police and clergy. There was a suicide attempt in 1898 and he left Tahiti in 1901; he died of syphilis two years later in the Marquesas Islands. While on Tahiti, Maugham sent his friend Gerald Haxton round the bars picking up stories from people who had known Gauguin. He also discovered a house in which there was a door decorated by Gauguin, bought the door for two hundred francs, and sold it for $37,400 in 1962.

In Maugham's novel Charles Strickland, a London stock-broker, leaves his wife and goes to Paris to practise the art he knows is inside him. Despising domesticity he drives a woman, Blanche, to suicide and then heads for Tahiti where he marries a native girl. Now Strickland realizes pictorially his vision of the Garden of Eden: 'those nude men and women. They were of the earth, the clay of which they were created, and at the same time something divine'. Maugham commented on the title of his novel in 1923: 'It means reaching for the moon and missing the sixpence at one's feet.'

SUBTLE, THE ALCHEMIST
Ben Jonson, *The Alchemist* (1610)

Dr John Dee (1527–1608)

Jonson's comedy concerns the attempts made by Subtle, an alchemist, and his assistant, Face, to dupe gullible people by promising to transform base metals into gold.

According to John Aubrey, a nigh-on-infallible literary gossip, Jonson based Subtle on the Elizabethan mathematician, geographer, astronomer and astrologer, Dr John Dee. He was educated at St John's College, Cambridge 1542–45, and was one of the original fellows of Trinity in 1546. During a production of a comedy by Aristophanes, Dee earned a reputation for wizardry, by his demonstration of a mechanical beetle which flew as if by magic. He earned a European reputation as a scholar and scientist – travelling and lecturing in centres of learning as distant as Poland and Bohemia, as well as neighbouring European academies. Edward VI gave him a pension, but he was imprisoned by Mary I on suspicion of attempting to murder her husband. He was released after examination by the Star Chamber. Elizabeth I showed him favour and frequently consulted him. He was involved in the search for the Northwest passage. In 1578 he was consulted during the Queen's illness. In the 1580s he began to work with Edward Kelley, a mountebank who claimed to consult the angels. They were partners on a Subtle and Face basis for some twenty years. Prince Albert Laski, a bankrupt ruler of Siradz (Bohemia) was duped by the two who claimed to be able to restore him to fortune. Laski passed them on to the emperor Rudolph at Prague and they later attempted to impress King Stephen Bathory of Poland. The partnership broke up when Kelley claimed divine instructions for the sharing of their wives.

Although Dee asserted he had found quantities of the elixir at the ruins of Glastonbury, he died in poverty in 1608. His library numbered 4,000 volumes, and he left a collection of charts, astronomical and scientific paraphernalia. His 'speculum', a mirror – a solid piece of pinkish glass the size of an orange – is held by the British Museum.

ŠVEJK

Jaroslav Hašek, *The Good Soldier Švejk* (1930)

Private Strašlipka

Although he seems to be an unusually vulnerable individual in a cruel bureaucratic world, the hero of Jaroslav Hašek's *The Good Soldier Švejk* exists by imaginatively establishing his human rights in the most unlikely circumstances. For example when Švejk becomes batman to Lieutenant Lukáš, after being gambled away in a game of cards, he is told to look after a lady who comes to stay in his superior's apartment. When she sees Švejk she is described (in Cecil Parrott's translation) as wearing 'a transparent gown, which made her exceptionally alluring and attractive'; she orders him to do his duty 'And so it happened that the good soldier Švejk could report to the lieutenant when he returned from the barracks: "Humbly report, sir, I've fulfilled all the lady's wishes and served her decently according to your orders".' Švejk, in other words, is not as stupid as he looks so he survives war and what passes for peace in Czechoslovakia.

Jaroslav Hašek was known in Czechoslovakia as an anarchist and an eccentric who loved to play elaborate practical jokes on the authorities. He was called up in 1915 and drafted to Švejk's regiment – the 91st Infantry – but soon dropped when the army recalled his dangerous political opinions. While he was with the 91st Infantry, Hašek became friendly with his company commander, Lieutenant Lukáš, who appears in the novel under his own name: 'Lieutenant Lukáš was a typical regular officer of the ramshackle Austrian monarchy.' Lukáš's batman was a private named Strašlipka who displayed an endearing ingenuity. Thus this humble character was endowed, by Hašek, with the heroic qualities of the good soldier: 'His simple face, smiling like a full moon, beamed with enthusiasm. Everything was so clear to him.' In a surviving regimental photograph the face of Strašlipka conforms to the description of Švejk in the novel; when Hašek died, however, his friend Josef Lada chose to caricature Švejk rather than base his illustrations on Strašlipka.

SVENGALI
George du Maurier, *Trilby* (1894)

Felix Moscheles

George du Maurier's artistic career was threatened, in 1857, by the loss of sight in his left eye and for the next two years he consulted experts in Holland and Belgium before accepting that a detached retina would forever deprive him of the use of the eye. During this difficult period du Maurier stayed in Malines, Belgium, and formed a close friendship with Felix Moscheles who dabbled in art and the occult with equal enthusiasm: in a drawing he did of Moscheles, du Maurier added the caption 'Moscheles, or Mephistopheles?' Moscheles was an accomplished mesmerist who used his skill to entertain and astonish du Maurier. In his book *In Bohemia With Du Maurier* (1897) Moscheles describes one of the experiments he conducted in the back parlour of a tobacconist's store: 'There I am operating on [this] stupid little Flemish boy.... All I recollect is that I gave him a key to hold, and made him believe that it was red-hot and burnt his fingers, or that it was a piece of pudding to be eaten presently, thereby making him howl and grin alternately.' Du Maurier, who sketched this incident, was greatly impressed by the power of hypnotism and later wrote to Moscheles: 'You'll see that I've used up all your Mesmerism and a trifle more in my new book.'

The new book was *Trilby* in which the attractive heroine is transformed into a great singer by the mesmeric presence of Svengali who appears as a caricature of Moscheles: 'a tall bony individual of any age between thirty and forty-five, of Jewish aspect, well featured but sinister.... He went by the name of Svengali, and spoke fluent French with a German accent, and humorous German twists and idioms, and his voice was very thin and mean and harsh, and often broke into a disagreeable falsetto.' Moscheles was delighted with the novel and proud that his hypnotic demonstrations provided du Maurier with 'the germs that were eventually to develop into Trilbyism and Svengalism.'

ELLIOT TEMPLETON
W. Somerset Maugham, *The Razor's Edge* (1944)

Sir Henry Channon (1897–1958)

Elliot Templeton, the heroine's elegant uncle in Somerset Maugham's *The Razor's Edge*, is an American who does his best to live down what he regards as the vulgar connotations of his own country. Thanks to his expert knowledge of the art market and his love of social climbing he has established for himself, in Paris, impeccable social credentials. 'He was a colossal snob,' writes Maugham. 'He was a snob without shame. He would put up with any affront, he would ignore any rebuff, he would swallow any rudeness to get asked to a party he wanted to go to or make a connexion with some crusty old dowager of great name. . . . His French was fluent and correct and his accent perfect. He had taken great pains to adopt the manner of speech as it is spoken in England and you had to have a very sensitive ear to catch now and then an American intonation.'

Maugham modelled the character on Henry 'Chips' Channon as he once admitted over dinner to the original. Chips, a rich homosexual from Chicago, was always determined to identify himself with the English establishment. When prime minister Baldwin called for strike-breaking, special constables in 1926 both Maugham and Channon volunteered. In 1935 Maugham met Chips at a London lunch and was fascinated by the American's progress in English society. To add influence to his affluence Chips married into the aristocracy in 1933 and he and his wife, Lady Honour Guinness, made their home in Belgrave Square in a mansion next door to the Duke of Kent. 'I have put my whole life's work into my anglicization,' wrote Chips in his posthumously-published diary. His ambitions were gradually realized for he became a Conservative MP in 1936, served as private secretary to R. A. B. Butler, Under-Secretary of State for Foreign Affairs from 1938 to 1941, and was eventually knighted in 1957.

Mary Head Hardy (1772–1857)

Thomas Hardy's subtitle for *Tess of the d'Urbervilles* was 'A Pure Woman Faithfully Presented', a concept that caused some hostility when the book first appeared. Tragically, the tale catalogues Tess's tribulations: after being seduced by Alec d'Urberville she loses her child; after being married to Angel Clare he abruptly deserts her on hearing her confession. Eventually, in despair, Tess is driven to stab d'Urberville. There is an elemental quality to Tess as Hardy describes her: 'On these lonely hills and dales her quiescent glide was of a piece with the element she moved in. Her flexuous and stealthy figure became an integral part of the scene.'

Although Hardy's powerful conclusion to his novel is artistic invention, the basic pattern of a poor woman's suffering is taken from the life of his grandmother Mary Head Hardy. She was born in Fawley, Berkshire, and by the time she was twenty-four had moved to Reading where she gave birth to an illegitimate child in 1796. The following year she was charged with stealing a copper tea-kettle and sent to the House of Correction in Reading. At that time the penalty for larceny was hanging and Mary Head lived with this threat for three months until she was released after her accusers failed to bring evidence against her in the Quarter Sessions of 25 April. In 1799 Mary Head met Hardy's grandfather Thomas in Puddle-town, Dorset, and married him when she was already three months pregnant. Hardy was devoted to his grandmother who provided him with much material that he used in his poetry and fiction. In his poem 'One We Knew' he describes her: 'With cap-framed face and long gaze into the embers – /We seated around her knees – /She would dwell on such dead themes, not as one who remembers/But rather as one who sees.'

MILLY THEALE
Henry James, *The Wings of the Dove* (1902)

Minny Temple (1846–70)

Although the innocent American victim of an English plot in Henry James's *The Wings of the Dove*, millionairess Milly Theale achieves a posthumous victory of the spirit. On learning that Milly is dying of an incurable illness Kate Croy persuades the impecunious Merton Densher to feign undying affection for the American so that he will inherit her fortune and use it as the basis of a prosperous marriage to Kate. Milly is described as a young woman whose face 'was expressive, irregular, exquisite, both for speech and for silence. When Milly smiled it was a public event.' Although she discovers Kate's deception, Milly leaves her money to Merton and so her presence dwells with the other characters. Kate observes that, like a dove, Milly 'stretched out her wings, and. . . . They cover us' and tells Merton 'Her memory's your love.'

James based the character on his cousin Minny Temple who died of tuberculosis in 1870. In a letter to his mother James writes: 'As much as a human creature may, I fancy, she will survive in the unspeakably tender memory of her friends. No attitude of the heart seems tender and generous enough not to do her some unwilling hurt – now that she has melted away into such a dimmer image of sweetness and weakness! . . . She certainly never seemed to have come into this world for her own happiness – as that of others – or as anything but as a sort of divine reminder and quickness – a transcendent protest against our acquiescence in its grossness. To have known her is certainly an immense gain. . . . There is absolute balm in the thought of poor Minny and *rest* – rest and immortal absence.' James had been delighted when he met Minny in 1860 in Newport, Rhode Island, as she had both mental agility and social grace. It is possible that he never recovered from the shock of losing her and his most beautiful heroines – including Milly and the exuberantly open Isabel Archer in *The Portrait of a Lady* (1881) – are recreations of Minny.

THERESE
George Sand, *Elle et Lui* (1859)

Armandine Aurore Lucie Dupin, 'George Sand' (1804–76)

In her novel *Elle et Lui*, George Sand recounted her love affair with the poet and dramatist Alfred de Musset (see LAURENT) from her point of view. Thérèse is a young painter with a highly developed sense of duty to her art and a loving and forgiving heart. Laurent is a handsome but irresponsible young gigolo, who takes to drink and spends all the money Thérèse manages to earn selling her canvasses.

George Sand was brought up by her grandmother at Nohant. At one time intending to be a nun, she inherited her grandmother's property, married, had two children, and then left for Paris where her first novel, *Indiana*, made her famous in 1832. She had a riotous love-life. She was seduced at the age of sixteen, and never looked back. Among her lovers were Frederic Chopin, Prosper Mérimèe and Gustave Planche. She also enjoyed liaisons with lovers of her own sex, including the actress Marie Dorval.

Her relationship with Alfred de Musset was passionate and tempestuous. After one of their more serious breaks, she was in such despair that she cut off all her hair, stuffed it into a skull and had it sent to him. This was a direct imitation of an incident in her novel *Indiana*. In the version of the story written by Alfred's brother Paul, *Lui et Elle,* the hair is delivered in a parcel to Alfred, who is in company in his rooms. He begins to open the package, sees what it contains, and shoves it in a drawer. He later laments over the shorn locks. In the story as told by Alfred's later mistress, Louise Colet (see EMMA BOVARY) George Sand delivers the hair in person, sinking to the floor at the hero's feet: 'her eyes seemed dark and hollow. . . . She did not utter a word . . . but . . . touched me with her sinister offering. I brushed it aside and it rolled onto the floor at my feet. Out of it flowed a long black tress of hair.'

Aurore took her name Sand from the novelist Jules Sandeau, with whom she had developed an intimacy between 1831 and 1833. She wrote a string of novels, dealing with forbidden love and social revolt. She was an ardent feminist and enemy of bourgeois conventions. In old age she was transformed into a kind old lady.

SADIE THOMPSON

W. Somerset Maugham, *The Trembling of a Leaf* (1921)

Miss Thompson

In 1916, on his way to Tahiti for material for *The Moon and Sixpence*, Somerset Maugham took the steamer *Sonoma* to Pago Pago, capital of Eastern Samoa. Among his fellow passengers was a Miss Thompson, a prostitute who had lost her livelihood when the police had closed down Honolulu's red-light district. She was on her way to Western Samoa to work as a barmaid in Apia and quickly became conspicuous on board since she flaunted herself sexually and played her gramophone incessantly, to the novelist's great annoyance. Also on board were a medical missionary and his wife and they, like Maugham, found Miss Thompson's loud and flirtatious behaviour unacceptable. Because of a quarantine inspection all the passengers were delayed in Pago Pago and Maugham, again enduring the unavoidable presence of Miss Thompson, speculated on what might happen if the missionary and Miss Thompson competed in a contest for moral supremacy.

The result was 'Rain', included in the collection *The Trembling of a Leaf*, in which the missionary becomes Mr Davidson whose 'sincerity was obvious in the fire of his gestures and in his deep, ringing voice'. Miss Thompson was made unforgettably fictional by the addition of the first name Sadie: 'She was twenty-seven perhaps, plump, and in a coarse fashion pretty. She wore a white dress and a large white hat. Her fat calves in white cotton stockings bulged over the tops of long white boots in glacé kid.' In the story the Revd Davidson's obsessive attempts to impose his rigid notions of joykilling morality on Sadie Thompson bring him into intimate contact with her. Unable to practise what he preaches, he succumbs to Sadie's obvious charms and afterwards cuts his throat. As the story ends Sadie is once more 'dressed in all her finery, in her white dress' and aggressive in her attitudes: 'You men! You filthy, dirty pigs! You're all the same, all of you. Pigs! Pigs!'

Harriet Beecher Stowe, *Uncle Tom's Cabin* (1852)

Josiah Henson, a Maryland slave

Uncle Tom's Cabin or *Life Among the Lowly*, was first serialized in the *National Era* from June 1851, and in book form became an international bestseller, translated into twenty-three languages and praised by George Sand, Turgenev, Heine and Dickens.

The political impact of this anti-slavery novel was tremendous. It pictured in colour and vividness scenes which fuelled anti-slavery sentiments. Lincoln is reputed to have said on meeting Mrs Stowe: 'So this is the little lady who made this big war!' The theme of the book is the buying and selling of slaves as if they were so much cattle, the heartless dividing of their families and the brutal treatment of the slaves by their owners. The one scene remembered by all who read the book is Uncle Tom's being beaten to death by Simon Legree, deliberately portrayed as a Yankee come South to make his fortune. Mrs Stowe wrote later: 'Human nature is no worse at the South than at the North; but the law at the South distinctly provides for and protects the worst abuses to which that nature is liable.' (*Key to Uncle Tom's Cabin*, 1853.) Tom is portrayed as a true Christian martyr. He is converted at a revival meeting and subsequently acts in the manner of the primitive martyrs of the Christian church. In her view the churches of the North should defy the Fugitive Slave Law of 1850, educate escaped slaves, and help them get to Liberia and set up a true Christian republic there.The black man's ideal state was to be realized not in the USA but in Africa.

An apparently deeply religious woman, Mrs Stowe claimed that Uncle Tom was given to her in a vision during a communion service in Brunswick, Maine. Here she suddenly saw an old and ragged slave being cruelly beaten. The claim she was to make as being merely God's amanuensis must be seriously qualified by the fact that she met Josiah Henson earlier in her life. He had been abused while a slave in the South and had made his escape by the underground railway, up North to Canada, where he was instrumental in establishing an all-black Utopia in Ontario. He was something of a celebrity and was introduced to Queen Victoria in London. Mrs Stowe commented that she met him in Boston in 1850 at her brother's house and read his account of his life (seventy-six pages long) which: 'furnished me many of the finest conceptions and incidents of Uncle Tom's character.'

Carry of Malines

Trilby O'Ferrall, the heroine of George du Maurier's *Trilby*, enchanted America when the novel first appeared in the pages of *Harper's Magazine* and subsequently caused a sensation in England where the book came out in three volumes. The story of the poor, tone-deaf artist's model, transformed into a celebrated singer by Svengali, produced a Trilby craze. There were Trilby hats and Trilby songs, Trilby soaps and Trilby toothpastes; and a town in Florida, USA, was named Trilby.

Du Maurier conceived the character as a result of his stay in Malines, Belgium, in the late 1850s. With his great friend Felix Moscheles, du Maurier frequented the back parlour of a local tobacco store. Octavie, the daughter of the proprietress, was nicknamed Carry (a corruption of Cigar) by Moscheles and du Maurier who both adored her. Carry's tobacco store background is alluded to in the novel when Trilby 'sat herself down cross-legged on the model throne and made herself a cigarette'. As Moscheles wrote in *In Bohemia with Du Maurier* (1897) Carry 'looked upon us as superior beings, and, granting her points of comparison, not without cause; du Maurier could draw and I could paint; he could sing and I could mesmerize, and couldn't we just both talk beautifully!' Although Moscheles was unable to mesmerize Carry, du Maurier had the creative time of his life imagining what might happen to such a girl who succumbed to the hypnotic power of one she regarded as a 'superior being'. Daphne du Maurier, in *The Du Mauriers* (1937), supposes that when her grandfather came to write Trilby 'he brought [Carry of Malines] out and polished her and beautified her, and breathed a little of his own charm upon her, and Trilby, the freckled Irish giantess, was born, with her clubbed hair and fringe, her military coat, her exquisite feet thrust into a pair of men's slippers'.

TOM TULLIVER
George Eliot, *The Mill on the Floss* (1860)

Isaac Pearson Evans (1816–90)

Central to George Eliot's novel *The Mill on the Floss* is the relationship between Maggie Tulliver and her brother Tom. Maggie is, especially in the early stages of the book, a self-portrait of Mary Ann Evans (as the author was called before adopting the pseudonym George Eliot in 1857); Tom, the obstinate brother, is Isaac Pearson Evans.

As Mary Ann's senior by three years Isaac was the object of her adoration as *The Mill on the Floss* and the sonnet-sequence 'Brother and Sister' (1874) show. When Isaac turned against her, Mary Ann must have reacted like Maggie Tulliver who 'felt the hatred in his face, felt it rushing through her fibres'. In June 1840 Isaac married Sarah Rawlins and, when Mary Ann offended her father in 1842 by her refusal to go to church, he invited his sister to Griff House (her childhood home) and persuaded her to make the gesture of accompanying her father to church – which she did until his death in 1849.

A more serious crisis arose in 1854 when Mary Ann decided to live with Henry George Lewes; three years later she wrote to Isaac explaining the situation and he broke off all relations with her. A Tractarian, he did not relent and only resumed contact with her on 17 May 1880 when Lewes was dead and Mary Ann married her admirer J. W. Cross. On 29 December, that same year, Mary Ann was buried in Highgate Cemetery; among the mourners there was, said George Eliot's biographer Oscar Browning, an elderly man 'tall and slightly bent, his features recalling with a striking veracity the lineaments of the dead'. Isaac had come to pay his last respects to the sister who concluded *The Mill on the Floss* with wishful thinking: 'after the flood [the] two bodies . . . were found in close embrace. . . . In their death they were not divided.'

MARY TYRONE

Eugene O'Neill, *Long Day's Journey into Night* (1956)

Ella O'Neill (1857–1922)

Eugene O'Neill's *Long Day's Journey into Night* was completed in 1941 but not performed until 1956, three years after the dramatist's death. O'Neill had decided on a posthumous production because the play is so intensely autobiographical. The Tyrone family is a group-portrait of the O'Neills with Eugene as Edmund and his alcoholic brother Jamie as Jamie Tyrone. James, O'Neill's father, is in the play (as in life) a man who has known success and celebrity as a Shakespearean actor. The truly tragic presence comes with Mary Cavan Tyrone, Edmund's mother, whose drug addiction haunts all the other characters as she drifts around the house like a ghost. During the drama Mary justifies her pitiful condition by alluding to the difficult birth of Edmund: 'I was so healthy before Edmund was born. You remember, James. There wasn't a nerve in my body. . . . But bearing Edmund was the last straw. I was so sick afterwards, and that ignorant quack of a cheap hotel doctor – All he knew was I was in pain. It was easy for him to stop the pain.'

Ella O'Neill was born Mary Ellen Quinlan in New Haven, Connecticut. At the age of fifteen she was sent to a convent and, like Mary in O'Neill's play, 'wanted to be a nun'. An accomplished pianist, she graduated in 1875 with honours in music; two years later she married James O'Neill, the handsome actor she had admired since first seeing him in her father's house in 1872. After the birth of Eugene in 1888, Ella (as James called her) was in considerable pain; accordingly a doctor friendly with James gave her morphine to comfort her. She quickly became addicted as O'Neill discovered when he came home from school one day in 1900 to find his mother in the act of injecting herself. Mary, in the play, explains the appeal of morphine for the addict: 'It kills the pain. You go back until at last you are happy beyond its reach. Only the past when you were happy is real.'

Adolf Hitler (1889–1945)

Bertolt Brecht's *The Resistible Rise of Arturo Ui* was written in 1941, shortly before the dramatist arrived in America. He had long been fascinated by stories and films about crime in Chicago and saw in the career of a gangster like Al Capone a precedent for the ruthless rise to power of Adolf Hitler. In the play, the burning of a warehouse represents the Reichstag fire and the machine-gun massacre in a garage suggests Hitler's purge of 30 June 1934. Arturo's ambition is to achieve greatness in a criminal context and he sets out to succeed by taking over the greengrocery business in Chicago. By terrorist tactics he increases his authority over his rivals but what he seeks, above all, is an image that will impress the 'little man', the source of demagogic power. Coached by an actor, Arturo adopts pseudo-Shakespearean mannerisms as he postures as a man of honour among thieves. Addressing a group of vegetable dealers he says (in Ralph Manheim's translation) 'For such is man. He'll never put aside/His hardware of his own free will, say/For love of virtue, or to earn the praises/Of certain silver tongues at City Hall./If I don't shoot, the other fellow will.'

Hitler's actual career, up to 1935, is closely paralleled in the play. In 1933 President Hindenburg (Old Dogsborough) appointed Hitler as Chancellor on condition that the East Aid scandal, involving Hindenberg, was suppressed. Once entrusted with political office Hitler astonished his colleagues by his fierce appetite for violence. Nevertheless he also aspired to statesmanship and employed an actor to train him in the art of declamation thus increasing his already considerable gifts as an orator. After the Reichstag fire of February 1933 Hitler unleashed the deadly Night of the Long Knives as a prelude to his reign of terror. Hence, in an epilogue, Brecht warns his audience that 'The world was almost won by such an ape!'

RODERICK USHER
Edgar Allan Poe, *The Fall of the House of Usher* (1839)

Edgar Allan Poe (1809–49)

In *The Fall of the House of Usher* Roderick and his sister Madeline are twins, but are also divided personalities, two sides of the same personality. Both of them fear confinement. Madeline is entombed before she is actually dead. Roderick is sensitive almost to the point of psychosis: 'It was with difficulty that I could bring myself to admit the identity of the wan being before me with the companion of my early boyhood,' the narrator says, of his meeting with Roderick at the house of Usher: 'Yet the character of his face had been at all times remarkable. A cadaverousness of complexion; an eye large, liquid, and luminous . . . lips somewhat thin and very pallid . . . a nose of delicate Hebrew model, but with a breadth of nostril unusual in similar formations; a finely moulded chin, speaking, in its want of prominence, of want of moral energy; hair of a more than web-like softness and tenuity. . . . His action was alternatively vivacious and sullen. His voice varied rapidly from a tremulous indecision . . . to that species of energetic concision – that abrupt, weighty, unhurried and perfectly modulated guttural utterance, which may be observed in the lost drunkard, or the irreclaimable eater of opium.'

A glance at surviving portraits, contemporary photographs or drawings by Ismael Gentz, will show that Poe is describing himself. He struck contemporaries as an oddity. His pale, delicate and intellectual face, with a curling and almost disdainful lip, his invariable black suit, his cadaverous face, strange eyes, curling hair, extensive forehead, his low voice which seemed almost cultivated – it is Roderick Usher exactly. Also Poe had the neurotic qualities he gives to Roderick – he was noticeably tense and moody, and – like his creation – he feared confinement.

JEAN VALJEAN
Victor Hugo, *Les Misérables* (1862)

Pierre-Francois Lacanaire, 'Gaillard'

Les Misérables tells the story of Jean Valjean, who is wrongly
convicted and sentenced to years in the galleys. He attempts to
return to 'normal' life and to build up his life again, but he is
hounded by a tenacious police officer who really destroys his
humanity. Among the most celebrated episodes in the novel is
the tale of the bishop's candlesticks, which Valjean steals after
being offered accommodation there for the night. When he is
apprehended, the authorities find the candlesticks on Valjean's
person. Out of compassion and charity, the bishop tells them
that he had given Valjean the candlesticks as a present.

Victor Hugo based Jean Valjean on the real life assassin, thief
and forger, known as 'Gaillard' to the French authorities.
Théophile Gautier termed him: 'The Manfred of the gutters,
and indeed he assumed a somewhat romantic reputation which
his deeds and lifestyle hardly deserved. He was not even a
brilliantly successful criminal, he spent at least three years in
confinement and was executed at the age of thirty six, but he
was an articulate member of the middle classes with a flair for
public relations and was able to gain a place in the public eye
which brought him to the attention of Victor Hugo. Gaillard
wrote poems and articles about his escapades and expressed an
influential 'philosophy' of crime. Prison, he declared, was the
great university of crime. In attacking the political establishment of the day – the regime of Louis Philippe – he became
the darling of the radical opposition. His *Memoirs* were widely
read and discussed. He became a criminal, he maintained, as a
result of his parents' lack of affection for him. He always
showed an enviable gift for drama and took over the prosecution in his trial as a means of making sure that his accomplices
who had given him away would also go to the scaffold. Among
his fellow inmates in prison he lorded it like an aristocrat. Early
in his career he had public sympathy, and the people were with
him when he was sentenced in 1829 for theft. When he stabbed
an old bachelor and his mother for five hundred francs and
was sentenced to death he no longer commanded such a public
following. But he was flamboyant to the end – arrested in the
provinces he was glad to be sent to Paris to be tried: 'It would
have been very disagreeable to have been executed by a
provincial executioner,' he said.

HONORE GABRIEL VARNEY

Edward Bulwer Lytton, *Lucretia; or The Children of Night*
(1846)

Thomas Griffiths Wainewright (1794–1847)

Gabriel Varney, the son of a French father and English mother, is a characteristic and melodramatic Victorian monster and villain. He is a forger and murderer, who insures his victims for vast sums and then poisons them, claiming the insurance money which he spends lavishly. He is portrayed as a mixture of disarming – almost romantic – charm, and sinister, devilish qualities: 'It is true that he was small for his years; but his frame had a vigour in its light proportions, which came from a premature and almost adolescent symmetry of shape and muscular development. The countenance, however, had much of effeminate beauty; the long hair reached the shoulders, but did not curl; straight, fine, and glossy as a girl's, and, in colour, of the pale auburn, tinged with red, which rarely alters in hue as childhood matures to man; the complexion was dazzlingly clear and fair. Nevertheless, there was something so hard in the lip, so bold, though not open, in the brow, that the girlishness of complexion, and even of outline, could not leave, on the whole, an impression of effeminacy. All the hereditary keenness and intelligence were stamped upon his face at that moment, but the expression also had a large share of . . . irony and malice.' He is eventually convicted and transported for life, which is in fact, a lingering death.

Lytton based the character and much of the narrative on Thomas Wainewright. He researched the story thoroughly, and corresponded with various officials and employees to verify Wainewright's attempts to defraud insurance firms. Wainewright was a painter, art critic and forger. He was educated at Dr Burney's Greenwich Academy and was apprenticed to the artist Thomas Philips. He was sufficiently good to exhibit at the Royal Academy 1821, 1822, 1824 and 1825. He forged powers of attorney so as to gain access to capital he had been left, when he was supposed to enjoy only the interest. He was supposed also to have poisoned victims for their insurance money, but this was never proved. (See JULIUS SLINKTON.)

ANN VERONICA

H. G. Wells, *Ann Veronica* (1909)

Amber Reeves

The heroine of H. G. Wells's novel *Ann Veronica* is an advanced feminist whose fictional behaviour was considered deeply shocking by the Edwardian reading public. Ann Veronica Stanley rejects the domestic tyranny of her father, joins the Fabian Society, is imprisoned as a suffragette, and becomes pregnant after seducing and running off with her biology tutor. Wells describes her lovingly: 'She was slender, and sometimes she seemed tall, and walked and carried herself lightly and joyfully. . . . Her lips came together with an expression between contentment and the faintest shadow of a smile, her manner was one of great reserve, and behind this mask she was wildly discontented and eager for freedom and life.'

Ann Veronica is a portrait of Amber Reeves, a girl twenty years younger than the married author she so admired. Wells got to know Amber through her parents who were well-known figures in the intellectual life of London: Hon William Pember Reeves was to become a Director of the London School of Economics and his wife was head of the Women's Section of the Fabian Society. Amber followed her mother into the Fabian Society and completed her education at Cambridge; she thus attracted Wells by her brains as well as her beauty. In 1908 the two became lovers and Amber was pregnant when she felt obliged to part from Wells. For a while she stayed in a villa, near Paris, provided for her by Wells then she returned home to tell her mother exactly what had happened. Mrs Pember Reeves was, for all her Fabian notions, shocked and disappointed in her daughter. Amber eventually decided to marry a fellow Fabian and gave birth to Wells's baby in December 1909. Nevertheless there was considerable gossip and Wells discussed the affair in letters in one of which he wrote 'I've done nothing I am ashamed of.'

JOHANN ULRICH VOSS

Patrick White, *Voss* (1957)

Ludwig Leichardt (1813–48)

Ulrich Voss, the German explorer, intends to lead an expedition into the Australian hinterland. Before the party leaves they are entertained at the Sydney house of the Bonner family. Ulrich and Laura, Mrs Bonner's niece, find themselves mutually attracted. He sets off with six white companions, including Judd and Palfreyman, an ornithologist. They have two aboriginal guides. The expedition is dogged with bad luck. Their store animals are lost and the party itself is torn with tensions. Judd, with half the group, sets off to return. Palfreyman is killed. Voss and the remainder go on. Voss is murdered and decapitated by Jackie, one of the guides. Judd is presumed to have died also. Towards his end, Voss has believed that Laura has been with him in spirit. Meanwhile, she is taken ill and at the height of fever – the moment of Voss's death – she cries out: 'O God! It is over!' Years later, Laura has embarked on a career as a teacher, when a search party returns with an old man. It is presumed that he is Judd. Although he can have no genuine knowledge of how Voss met his end, Laura accepts his account of how he closed Voss's eyes as he died.

Australia was gradually explored in the 19th century by such pioneers as Blaxland, Lawson, Wentworth, Oxley, Evans, Cunningham, Hume, Hovell, Eyre and Sturt. The mid 1840s was the period of the great inland expeditions of Ludwig Leichardt. He was born in Trebatsch, near Frankfurt-on-Oder, and went to Australia in 1841. In 1844 he set out in search of the overland route from the military station of Port Victoria, on the coast of Arnheim Land, to Moreton Bay. Initially he went along the Dawson and the Mackenzie in Queensland. From there he ascended the source of the Burdekin and he crossed the tableland to the west and reached the Gulf of Carpentaria. He skirted the shores of the Gulf as Roper and crossed Arnheim Land to reach the Alligator River. After a journey of some three thousand miles, completed within a year and three months, he reached Port Victoria. In December 1847 he attempted to cross the continent from east to west. He left the Fitzroy Downs in Queensland. His expedition was never found. His last dispatch was from the Cogoon and was dated 3 April 1848. The journals of his earlier expedition survive.

PHILIP WAKEM
George Eliot, *The Mill on the Floss* (1860)

Francois D'Albert-Durade

Maggie Tulliver, a young woman of poetic and artistic tastes, finds her brother Tom intellectually and spiritually undeveloped, but in Philip Wakem, a deformed son of a local lawyer, a companion who can share her interests. Philip is a shy and sensitive young man, with a humped back, but he is a very clever artist. The two find they are mutually very strongly attracted, though he fears she will not respond to him because he is deformed. He finds her very attractive not only because she is a handsome young woman but because her company is so intellectually rewarding. Maggie's father is very suspicious of Philip Wakem, and these suspicions seem confirmed when his business, Dorlcote mill, goes bankrupt in litigation in which Wakem is the other party. Maggie's brother, Tom (see TOM TULLIVER) discovers the relationship between Maggie and Philip, and they part. She has always felt the relationship tinged with guilt because it had to be kept secret, though she admits she loves him, but feels there is still something lacking in her feelings for him. In a terrible scene, Maggie's father thrashes Philip, and this action brings on Mr Tulliver's death.

Francois D'Albert-Durade was a deformed hunchback artist with whom George Eliot boarded in Geneva in the winter of 1849. She may also have used the character of another artist she met in 1845 at her half-sister's house in Baginton, who confessed his love to her, writing to say she was 'the most fascinating creature he had ever beheld'. She felt that she could not respond to his offer that they should keep in touch as he was a picture-restorer and this profession was not well-paid or very well-esteemed, but she thought him the most interesting young man she had met 'and superior to all the rest of mankind'. The friendship soon cooled.

WALDEN POND
Henry David Thoreau, *Walden* (1854)

Henry David Thoreau's classic *Walden* opens on an assertion: 'When I wrote the following pages ... I lived alone, in the woods, a mile from any neighbour, in a house which I had built myself, on the shore of Walden Pond, in Concord, Massachusetts, and earned my living by the labor of my hands only. I lived there two years and two months.'

Thoreau's beautifully written account of his idyll has been enormously influential and there are many urban dwellers who long to get away from it all and live the life Thoreau claimed to live. Readers of Walden might, however, ponder on the reality. Thoreau did not live alone; not only did he encourage hordes of visitors but he returned almost every day to his family home at Concord to see his mother. Early in his life Mrs Thoreau had taken him to see Walden Pond and it became 'the fabulous landscape of my infant dreams'; in the twenty-two months he spent commuting from Concord to Walden he never lost contact with his beloved mother who lived only a mile away from his hut.

In his book *Stuff of Sleep and Dreams* (1982) Leon Edel suggests a good reason for Thoreau's subterfuge in 1845, when he set up in the woods. He had become persona non grata in Concord on account of an act of accidental vandalism. While out fishing at Fair Haven Bay, Thoreau caught some fish and lit a fire to cook them. The result was a brush fire which spread to the woods around Concord. Before this the people of Concord considered Thoreau as an idler – now they thought of him as a menace to society. So when he retreated to Walden, Thoreau was both protecting himself from the good people and also sending out signals that he was suffering in silence. In his art, however, Thoreau transmuted the matter-of-fact into a myth which many still respond to: 'I went to the woods because I wished to live deliberately, to front only the essential facts of life.'

GLORIA WANDROUS
John O'Hara, *Butterfield 8* (1935)

Starr Faithfull (1911–31)

John O'Hara's *Butterfield 8* describes the squalid culmination of the career of Gloria Wandrous. Since being sexually abused as a child she has gradually disintegrated until she has lost her self-respect. At the beginning of the novel she is in despair: 'It was the kind of despair that she had known perhaps two thousand times before, there being 365 mornings in a calendar year. In general the cause of her despair was remorse, two kinds of it: remorse because she knew that whatever she was going to do next would not be any good either.' Her time is spent drinking in speakeasies and indulging in casual sex. Finally she commits suicide by jumping off an excursion steamer, her body being ripped to shreds by the side-wheel.

O'Hara came across the original story when the newspapers of 9 June 1931 reported that a young woman, Starr Faithfull, had been found washed up on shore at Long Beach, Long Island. She had been at a midnight sailing party on a liner and ignored the order telling visitors to leave the ship. In the somewhat confused circumstances there was a possibility of suicide, or even murder. Starr Faithfull had been a familiar figure in the New York speakeasies where she was known for her stunning good looks and her erratic behaviour. She had received psychiatric treatment for her alcoholism and suicidal depression, disorders possibly determined by a childhood trauma. Apparently Starr had been sexually abused in childhood by a prominent citizen who then paid twenty thousand dollars for treatment to help her over the emotional shock. It did nothing of the kind. As O'Hara noted in his novel 'It would be easy enough to say any one of a lot of things about Gloria, and many things were said. It could be said that she was a person who in various ways – some of them peculiar – had the ability to help other people, but lacked the ability to help herself.'

ADAM WEIR
Robert Louis Stevenson, *Weir of Hermiston* (1896)

Lord Braxfield (1722–99)

Robert Louis Stevenson considered Adam Weir, the Lord Justice-Clerk of *Weir of Hermiston*, to be his most effective character. With his racy use of Scots and his 'hanging face', Weir embodies a grim view of justice and the nature of the man is suitably severe: 'He did not try to be loved, he did not care to be; it is probable the very thought of it was a stranger to his mind. He was an admired lawyer, a highly unpopular judge; and he looked down upon those who were his inferiors in either distinction.'

Stevenson based the character closely on Robert MacQueen, Lord Braxfield, Scotland's most notorious hanging judge who became Justice Clerk in 1788 and so controlled the criminal court. Braxfield was a hard-drinking, blunt Scots-speaking man who obviously enjoyed his work as he administered justice ferociously. He sentenced the revolutionary leader Thomas Muir to transportation for sedition and he told one prisoner that he would be 'nane the waur o' a hangin''. Stevenson was fascinated by Braxfield and told his friends how he intended to use him in his novel: 'Braxfield – Only his name is Hermiston – has a son who is condemned to death; plainly there is a fine, tempting fitness about this.' Stevenson died before completing the story though the description of Braxfield as Hermiston stands as a finely finished verbal portrait: 'my Lord Hermiston occupied the bench in the red robes of criminal jurisdiction, his face framed in the white wig. . . . It was plain he gloried in the exercise of his trained faculties, in the clear sight which pierced at once into the joint of fact, in the rude unvarnished gibes with which he demolished every figment of defence. He took his ease and jested, unbending in that solemn place with some of the freedom of the tavern; and the rag of man with the flannel round his neck was hunted gallowsward with jeers.'

Johann Wolfgang von Goethe (1749–1832)

Werther was one of the most influential works of the early
romantic imagination, and its importance in the development
of European literature is out of all proportion to its literary
merits. The story is a simple one, but its undoubted power does
not lie in its narrative, but in the emotion it evokes. The young
Wilhelm Werther falls in love one spring with his beautiful
cousin Charlotte. She is engaged to Albert. Wilhelm is impetuous and his emotions are headstrong. By contrast, Albert is a
mature and balanced character. In the autumn Werther has to
leave for professional purposes (he is in the diplomatic service)
but he writes to Charlotte at the opening of the new year. He
still loves Charlotte to distraction. He gives up his post and
returns to be near his beloved, even though she is now married
to Albert. He gives up reading Homer in place of Ossian,
which suits his wild moods better. He finds himself particularly
at home in the desolate landscape of November. Charlotte still
wants Werther's friendship, but Albert thinks all traces of the
relationship between them should end. Charlotte is motivated
by pity for Werther's sufferings. She implores him to find
another woman, worthy of his love. But he has resolved to die.
Albert has to leave on business and Werther calls on Charlotte
and shows her some of his new translations of Ossian. His eyes
are full of tears. He borrows some pistols from Albert because
he says he is going on a journey. He then shoots himself,
requesting that he be buried in the clothes he was then wearing
– yellow trousers, a blue coat and boots.

The story is autobiographical and relates Goethe's passionate
affair with Charlotte Buff, daughter of a leading citizen of
Wetzlar, where he was working as a young advocate in the
imperial law courts. He was brought to the very brink of
suicide by the depths of his suffering. In later life he said of this
novel: 'it is a creation which I, like the pelican, fed with the
blood of my own heart. It contains so much from the innermost
recesses of my breast – so much feeling and thought, that it
might easily be spread into a novel of ten such volumes. Besides
... I have only read the book once since its appearance, and
have taken good care not to read it again. . . . I am uncomfortable when I look at it; and I dread lest I should once more
experience the peculiar mental state from which it was produced.'

Charlotte Cradock (died 1744)

Sophia is the beautiful daughter of the drunken and rumbustious Squire Western. Tom Jones falls in love with her, but he is rivalled by the treacherous Blifil who does all that he can to blacken Tom's name. Eventually it is discovered that Tom is really Squire Allworthy's nephew (see SQUIRE ALLWORTHY) and he marries Sophia: 'a middle sized woman; but rather inclining to tall. Her shape was not only exact, but extremely delicate: and the nice proportion of her arms promised the truest symmetry in her limbs. Her hair, which was black, was so luxuriant, that it reached her middle, before she cut it to comply with the modern fashion; and it was now curled so gracefully in her neck, that few could believe it to be her own .... Her eyebrows were full, even, and arched beyond the power of art to imitate. Her black eyes had a lustre in them, which all her softness could not extinguish. Her nose was exactly regular, and her mouth, in which there were two rows of ivory, exactly answered Sir John Suckling's description in those lines – "Her lips were red, and one was thin,/Compar'd to that was next her chin./Some bee had stung it newly." – Her cheeks were of the oval kind; and in her right she had a dimple, which the least smile discovered. Her chin had certainly its share in forming the beauty of her face; but it was difficult to say it was either large or small, though perhaps it was rather of the former kind. Her complexion had rather more of the lily than of the rose, but when exercise or modesty increased her natural colour, nor vermilion could equal it. . . . Her neck was long and finely turned. . . . Here was whiteness which no lilies, ivory, nor alabastor could match. The finest cambric might indeed be supposed from envy to cover that bosom which was much whiter than itself . . . when she smiled, the sweetness of her temper diffused that glory over her countenance which no regularity of features can give.'

This generous portrait is of Charlotte Cradock, whom Fielding loved and married in 1734. He says in *Tom Jones* 'she resembled one whose image never can depart from my breast'.

SHERIDAN WHITESIDE
George S. Kaufman and Moss Hart, *The Man Who Came to Dinner* (play, 1939)

Alexander Woolcott (1887–1943)

Influential critic, reviewer, lecturer and wit Sheridan Whiteside, falls and breaks his hip in a small town in Ohio. The Stanleys, a family of means, offer to accommodate him while he recovers. Although in a wheelchair for most of the play, Whiteside dominates his world, which he turns into an idiosyncratic bedlam – sending telegrams, making telephone calls, issuing orders and ruling the Stanleys himself. He arranges for his secretary to marry the local journalist. The play is packed with sophisticated contemporary references – to H. G. Wells, Jascha Heifetz, the Lunts, Ethel Barrymore, Louella Parsons, Arturo Toscanini, Sacha Guitry, Ginger Rogers etc., as well as actually featuring caricatures of Noel Coward and Gertrude Lawrence. There is general relief when Whiteside eventually recovers. Joy turns to grief as he slips on a piece of ice and breaks his other hip. He is carried back into the Stanley house for a further period of convalescence.

Kaufman and Hart based Whiteside on the journalist and broadcaster, Alexander Woolcott, a renowned wag and egocentric, one of the most influential drama reviewers of his period. He was a make or break critic, who gave free reign to personal prejudices and predelictions, but opposed sham and fully realized the possibilities of personality journalism, wielding tremendous power through his column in the *New York Times*. A member of the Algonquin set (which included Dorothy Parker) Woolcott's wit was deservedly legendary – in person, in telegrams and in the thousands of words he published in various journals including the *New Yorker*. His reviews still read well ('An unfortunate thing occurred at the Maxine Elliott Theatre last night . . .' – 'The score is by Sigmund Romberg, who knows a good tune when he hears one.') He said of himself: 'One day I shall probably talk myself to death. Those who live by the word shall perish by the word.'

VERNON WHITFORD
George Meredith, *The Egoist* (1879)

Sir Leslie Stephen (1832–1904)

To emphasize the triumph of integrity over egoism in *The Egoist* George Meredith builds his novel around two contrasting male characters. Sir Willoughby Patterne parades his wealth and enjoys the exercise of his authority; Vernon Whitford, his cousin, is devoted to his literary work with a disinterestedness that is beyond the Egoist. Throughout the novel Sir Willoughby pursues Clara Middleton because he thinks she will make a suitable Lady Willoughby of Patterne; Clara, however, succumbs to Vernon's quiet charm and chooses him rather than the Egoist. Vernon is seen, by Mrs Mountstuart, as 'a Phoebus Apollo turned fasting friar' – a description, says Meredith, that 'painted the sunken brilliancy of the lean long-walker and scholar at a stroke'.

Vernon is an affectionate portrait of Meredith's friend Sir Leslie Stephen whose critical writing established him as one of the great literary Victorians. He wrote biographies (of Johnson, Pope, Swift, George Eliot and Hobbes), helped found the *Pall Mall Gazette*, edited the *Cornhill* for eleven years with great distinction, and did outstanding editorial work on the *Dictionary of National Biography*. As befits his arrogant manner, Sir Willoughby treats Vernon as a rose in his lapel for he considers it prestigious as well as useful to have such a scholar to hand: 'Now Vernon was useful to his cousin; he was the accomplished secretary of a man who governed his estate shrewdly and diligently. . . . Furthermore, [Sir Willoughby] liked his cousin to date his own controversial writings, on classical subjects, from Patterne Hall. It caused his house to shine in a foreign field; proved the service of scholarship by giving it a flavour of bookish aristocracy that, though not so well worth having, and indeed in itself contemptible, is above the material and titular; one cannot quite say how. . . . Sir Willoughby could create an abject silence at a county dinner-table by an allusion to Vernon "at work at home upon his Etruscans or his Dorians".'

DICK WHITTINGTON

Traditional British pantomime hero.

Richard Whittington (died 1423)

The earliest version of the Dick Whittington story dates from a stage play and ballads licensed for the press in 1605. The stories tell of a runaway apprentice from Gloucestershire who comes to London to seek his fortune. He finds shelter in the household of the rich alderman, Fitzwarren. Fitzwarren allows his staff to invest in overseas ventures. All Dick has to send is his cat. Dick runs away because he is badly treated by the other servants. Resting at Highgate Hill he hears a voice in the sound of the bells: 'Turn again Whittington, thrice Mayor of London.' He returns to find his cat has made a fortune. It was bought by the King of Barbary, who was plagued by rats and mice. Dick marries Fitzwarren's daughter, Alice, and does in fact become Lord Mayor three times.

The real Dick Whittington was born in Pauntley, Gloucestershire. He became a mercer in London, later alderman and three times Lord Mayor – 1397–98, 1406–07 and 1419–20. He actually married Alice Fitzwarren, who was the daughter of Ivo Fitzwarren, and through this marriage acquired substantial property in the south-west counties. Richard Whittington was a substantial benefactor to the city of London, and advanced loans to Richard II, Henry IV and Henry V, subsidizing his Agincourt campaign. He left legacies towards rebuilding Newgate prison and founding almshouses. The true life history of Richard Whittington soon merged into the stuff of legend and myth – the process can be seen in John Stow's *Annals, or A General Chronicle of England* (1580) and in Richard Johnson's *Crown Garland of Roses* (1612) in which the picturesque episode of the sound of Bow Bells makes its first appearance in the narrative.

Sir Robert Walpole (1676–1745)

Henry Fielding uses the story of the real life English criminal, Jonathan Wild, to explore the nature of 'greatness' in society. Wild ran a gang of thieves and received stolen goods. He betrayed the members of his gang to the authorities if they would not obey him, and rewarded those who did what they were told, and kept their mouths shut. The real Wild was hanged at Tyburn in 1725. In Fielding's version of the story Wild is baptized by Titus Oates, the fabricator of the 'Popish Plot' and develops into a consummate rogue. He learns to tread the path of crime while at school, and becomes first a pickpocket, under the leadership of Mr Snap, who keeps a sponging house. He then gradually develops a business of his own, running a large gang, contriving crimes, always taking the biggest share of the booty himself, and handing over unreliable members to the law. Snap's daughter, Letitia, becomes his wife. His main policy is to bring an old school friend of his, Heartfree, to ruin. Heartfree's jewellers business goes bankrupt and he nearly succeeds in getting Heartfree condemned for the murder of Mrs Heartfree.

This is a political satire on the Whig politician and statesman, Sir Robert Walpole, who rose to supreme power, and maintained his control of the political system by bribery, corruption and the impeachment of his enemies. He is referred to as 'Bob Booty' in John gay's *Beggar's Opera*, but the idea of a career politician seen in terms of a master criminal gets full treatment in *Jonathan Wild*. Fielding had little cause to love Walpole; his Licensing Act of 1737 put an end to Fielding's career as a dramatist. As a young MP Walpole had been imprisoned for alleged corruption, but was in the ascendancy after the South Sea Bubble. He staved off threats to his power from Carteret, Bolingbroke, Pulteney. He resigned the premiership in 1742 and a committee investigating his affairs estimated at least £60,000 was spent in buying the press, as well as huge sums bribing MPs. He also used preferment.

Edgar Allan Poe (1809–49)

William Wilson is one of the finest examples of the story of the Doppelgänger. Wilson is a degenerate, spendthrift and dissolute young man who drifts through school, college and into a life of gambling and irresponsibility. Wherever he goes he is accompanied by his double; he talks to him continuously, in the manner of his conscience. At the climax he kills the double, and sees in a mirror that he has killed himself: 'mine own image, but with features all pale and dabbled in blood, advanced to meet me with a feeble and tottering gait'. Poe is portraying himself. He gave Wilson the same birthday and he sets his schooling in the institution in Stoke Newington where he himself had been educated. The headmaster was the Revd John Bransby, and Poe uses the same name in *William Wilson*. He describes the school accurately: 'a large, rambling, Elizabethan house, in a misty-looking village of England'. Wilson's character and career are presented as a kind of vicious parody of Poe's: 'a cause of serious disquietude to my friends, and of a positive injury to myself . . . addicted to the wildest caprices . . . a prey to the most ungovernable passion'. This is followed by a period of 'thoughtless folly' and 'miserable profligacy' at Eton, and to a catalogue of vices at Oxford. Like Poe himself, Wilson develops into a compulsive gambler.

The account of Wilson's career at Oxford is a perverted version of Poe's at the University of Virginia, where he caroused, gambled and accumulated debts of $2,500 and left after a year in residence. Poe also talked to himself, and showed signs of derangement similar to Wilson's. Poe's literary executor, Rufus Griswold, records that 'he walked the streets, in madness or melancholy, with lips moving in indistinct curses, or with eyes upturned in passionate prayers . . . and at night, with drenched garments and arms wildly beating the wind and rain, he would speak as if to spirits'. The engraver, John Sartain, recorded Poe's bizarre behaviour and accounts of his delusions – two men in a train were plotting to murder him – he had been put in the cells where the attendants had tried to frighten him to death – his mother-in-law had been brought in and they had cut her legs off a piece at a time, 'her feet at the ankles, then her legs up to the knees, her thighs at the hips, and so on'.

LORD PETER WIMSEY

Dorothy L. Sayers, *Whose Body?* (1923), *Clouds of Witness* (1927), *Unnatural Death* (1928), *The Unpleasantness at the Bellona Club* (1928), *Lord Peter Views the Body* (1929), *The Documents in the Case* (1930), *Strong Poison* (1930), *The Five Red Herrings* (1931), *Have his Carcase* (1932), *Murder must Advertise* (1933), *Hangman's Holiday* (1933), *The Nine Tailors* (1934), *Gaudy Night* (1934), *Busman's Honeymoon* (1937), *In the Teeth of the Evidence* (1940), *Striding Folly* (1973)

Eric Whelpton

Like his predecessor Sherlock Holmes, Lord Peter Wimsey combines a talent for detection with considerable cultural accomplishments. In *Whose Body?*, the first Wimsey mystery, he sends his man Bunter to a rare-book sale and tells him 'Don't lose time – I don't want to miss the Folio Dante nor the de Voragine.'

At the time that Dorothy L. Sayers created Lord Peter she was deeply in love with Eric Whelpton, a friend whose good looks and war-weariness greatly appealed to her. After the First World War, Whelpton took up a post near Paris teaching English to the French nobility; Dorothy went along as his secretary. He never returned Dorothy's passion so she consoled herself by exchanging mock-scholarly notes on popular detective fiction with her fellow enthusiast Muriel Jaeger. This correspondence led to the creation of Lord Peter Wimsey who assumed some of Whelpton's characteristics such as a flair for languages and a taste for the good life. In his book *The Making of a European* (1974) Whelpton writes 'In spite of my close association with Dorothy Sayers, I have never succeeded in finishing any of her books, though some of her friends have declared that I am the original of Lord Peter Wimsey, a suggestion that has also been made in the Sunday Press.'

Dorothy L. Sayers married, in 1926, Oswald Arthur 'Mac' Fleming and Whelpton suggested that he 'also contributed to the creation of Lord Peter'. However, the detective came complete in 1923 and hardly changed in a dozen novels though his height increased from five feet nine, in the early books, to six feet in his final full-length adventure *Busman's Honeymoon*.

WORLDLY WISEMAN
John Bunyan, *The Pilgrim's Progress* (1678)

Paul Cobb

On the restoration of Charles II in 1660 the authorities decreed
that unlicensed preachers must not address their congregations.
Well aware of this ruling John Bunyan, the Puritan preacher,
held a meeting on 12 November 1660 and was duly arrested
and held in Bedford jail. Paul Cobb, the Clerk to the Justices
of Bedford, visited Bunyan and advised him to submit to the
authority of the Church (of England) and State or suffer the
consequences of transportation 'or else worse than that'. Bunyan was obliged to listen to Cobb's pragmatic advice: 'Well,
neighbour Bunyan. . . . You may do much good if you continue still in the land: But alas, what benefit will it be to your
friends, or what good can you do to them, if you should be
sent away beyond the seas into Spain, or Constantinople, or
some other part of the world? Pray be ruled.'

After the coronation of Charles II, Bunyan hoped to be
included in the general amnesty but Cobb personally prevented Bunyan from appearing in court. In his second period
of imprisonment, in 1675, Bunyan began to write *The Pilgrim's
Progress* and included a portrait of Cobb as Worldy Wiseman
who 'dwelt in the Town of Carnal Policy, a very great Town,
and also hard by from whence Christian came'. Wordly
Wiseman attempts to seduce Christian from the true path and
to accept established authority instead. Evangelist explains to
Christian: 'The man that met thee is one Worldly Wiseman,
and rightly is he so called: partly because he savoureth only
the doctrine of this world (therefore he always goes to the
Town of Morality to church); and partly because he loveth
that doctrine best, for it saveth him from the Cross. And
because he is of this carnal temper, therefore he seeketh to
prevent my ways, though right.'

TOM WRENCH

Arthur Wing Pinero, *Trelawny of the 'Wells'* (1898)

Thomas Robertson (1829–71)

Trelawny of the 'Wells' is without doubt among the finest plays about the theatre ever written. The theme of the play is the change in theatrical taste in mid-Victorian drama, towards a more naturalist kind of theatrical experience. This revolution in dramatic style was to a considerable extent pioneered by Thomas Robertson, who appears in Pinero's play in the character of Tom Wrench.

As the play opens Rose Trelawny, a successful actress, is preparing to leave the theatrical company as she is to marry Arthur Gower and move into society. Amid the sad farewells and general banter of various members of the company as they wish Rose all the best of happiness, Tom's theories of drama are discussed – but it seems what he wants to present is too ordinary and everyday to pass as 'theatre'. In the second act Rose's old companions call at her new address in the West End. They have been celebrating another marriage in the company, and are out on the town – Rose is tempted to give up her forthcoming marriage into the Gower family and return to tread the boards: 'I've seen enough of your life – my dear boy – to know that I'm no wife for you,' she tells Arthur. But Rose has been changed by her experience, she can no longer put on the grand manner but is subdued. In fact, the times are changing and are ready for Tom Wrench's 'new' kind of drama. Arthur Gower joins the company which, backed by capital put up in part by Gower's family, successfully mounts drama with the new style of acting. In important respects it is the case that Robertson really paved the way for Bernard Shaw.

Robertson was born into a theatrical family, and was at one time prompter at the Olympic under the management of Charles Mathews (a comic actor much admired by Dickens). He wrote successful comedies and farces, and *David Garrick*, which held the stage for many years. It was *Society* staged at the Prince of Wales in 1865 which really made his name and London flocked to see the new 'cup-and-saucer' comedy – no wit, no sparkle, no exaggeration – an attempt to portray commonplace life. *Caste* (1866), *Play* (1868), *School* (1869) and *MP* (1870) were his most famous plays.

Richard Tarlton (died 1588)

In Act V, Scene 1 of *Hamlet*, the Prince of Denmark takes the skull cast up by the gravedigger and says: 'Let me see. Alas, poor Yorick! I knew him, Horatio: a fellow of infinite jest, of most excellent fancy; he hath borne me on his back a thousand times.... Here hung those lips that I have kiss'd I know not how oft. Where be your gibes now, your gambols, your songs, your flashes of merriment that were wont to set the table on a roar? Not one now to mock your own grinning.'

Tradition has it that these are references to the celebrated English comic actor and clown Richard Tarlton, who was 'discovered' by the Earl of Leicester and brought to court. He is described as having a squint and a flat nose. In 1583 he had been instituted as one of Queen Elizabeth's twelve players, and on one occasion is reputed to have pointed at Sir Walter Raleigh and said: 'See – the Knave commands the Queen!' and to have made sundry gibes at the power of the Earl of Leicester. He was renowned for his abilities as an ad-libbing comedian, improvising doggerel verses ('Tarltonising') and his skill at dancing jigs and playing the pipe and tabor.

Various biographical data appeared after his death, of varying reliability, and little is known about his early life, but many examples of his material survive, including *Tarlton's Jests*, the earliest editions of which date from circa 1600. He is supposed to have doubled the roles of the clown and the judge in *The Famous Victories of Henry V* and to have taken the part of Pedringano in Kyd's *Spanish Tragedy*. His great gift as a performer seems to have been in impromptu cut and thrust and in 'playing' an audience. This seems to be behind Hamlet's advice to the players in Act III, Scene 2: 'And let those that play your clowns speak no more than is set down for them; for there be of them that will themselves laugh, to set on some quantity of barren spectators to laugh too.' Thomas Heywood, the dramatist and actor, wrote of him in his *Apology for Actors* (1612): 'I must needs remember Tarlton, in his time gracious with the Queen his sovereign and in the people's general applause, whom succeeded Will Kemp, as well in the favour of Her Majesty as in the good thoughts of the general audience.'

ZULEIKA
Lord Byron, *The Bride of Abydos* (1813)

Augusta Leigh (born 1783)

The Bride of Abydos is subtitled 'A Turkish Tale' and is the story of the love between Zuleika, daughter of the Pasha Giaffir, and her cousin, Selim. Zuleika is presented as the perfection of Eastern beauty: 'So bright the tear in Beauty's eyes,/Love half regrets to kiss it dry;/So sweet the blush of Bashfulness,/Even Pity scarce can wish it less!' But it is her father's wish that she marry the rich boy of Karasman. She has never even seen him. In her distress at hearing this from her father's lips, she confesses her grief to her beloved brother, Selim. But Selim now tells her that he is not her brother, but her cousin, the son of Zuleika's uncle, who has been killed by the Pasha Giaffir. He also tells Zuleika that he is a pirate chief in disguise and asks her to run away with him. The Pasha appears and Selim is killed. Zuleika dies of grief: 'though deep – though fatal – was thy first!/Thrice happy ne'er to feel nor fear the force/Of absence, shame, pride, hate, revenge, remorse.'

The Bride of Abydos really presents the passionate and illicit love of Byron for his half-sister, Augusta. In the first draft of the poem Selim and Zuleika were actually brother and sister. Incest was a theme which had always fascinated Byron. The relationship with Augusta took place in the summer of 1813. Her husband, Colonel Leigh, was absent during the racing season and Byron and Augusta were constantly in each other's company. Byron confessed his passion in a veiled manner to Lady Melbourne. He wrote to a friend: 'I am at this moment in a far more serious, and entirely new, scrape than any of the last twelve months, and that is saying a great deal.' (letter dated 22 August 1813). He revealed the matter to Lady Melbourne. Nine months later Augusta gave birth to a daughter. He wrote to Lady Melbourne in November: 'For the last three days I have been quite shut up, my mind has been from *late* and *later* events in such a state ... that as usual I have been obliged to empty it in rhyme, and am in the heart of another Eastern tale.' He is referring to *The Bride of Abydos*. (See also ASTARTE.)

Authors, titles (in italics) and true characters (in bold) are listed below.
Fictional characters appear throughout the text in alphabetical order.

Longman Group Limited,
Longman House, Burnt Mill, Harlow,
Essex CM20 2JE, England
and Associated Companies throughout the world.

© Alan Bold and Robert Giddings 1984
All rights reserved; no part of this publication
may be reproduced, stored in a retrieval system,
or transmitted in any form or by any means, electronic,
mechanical, photocopying, recording, or otherwise,
without the prior written permission of the Publishers.

First published 1984

British Library Cataloguing in Publication Data

Bold, Alan
    True characters: real people in fiction:—(Longman pocket
    companion series)
    1. Characters and characteristics in literature
    I. Title   II. Giddings, Robert
    823'.8'0927   PR858.C47

    ISBN 0–582–55687–2

Set in 8/10 pt. Bembo

Typeset by CCC, printed and bound in Great Britain by William
Clowes Limited, Beccles and London